Letting Go of the Words

The Morgan Kaufmann Series in Interactive Technologies

Series Editors:
- Stuart Card, PARC
- Jonathan Grudin, Microsoft
- Jakob Nielsen, Nielsen Norman Group

Letting Go of the Words

Writing Web Content that Works

Janice (Ginny) Redish

AMSTERDAM • BOSTON • HEIDELBERG • LONDON
NEW YORK • OXFORD • PARIS • SAN DIEGO
SAN FRANCISCO • SINGAPORE • SYDNEY • TOKYO
Morgan Kaufmann Publishers is an imprint of Elsevier

ELSEVIER

MORGAN KAUFMANN PUBLISHERS

Publisher	Diane D. Cerra
Publishing Services Manager	George Morrison
Project Manager	Marilyn E. Rash
Assistant Editor	Asma Palmeiro
Cover Design	Yvo Riezebos Design
Composition/Production	Graphic World Inc.
Interior and Cover Printer	Hing Yip Printing Co., Ltd.

Morgan Kaufmann Publishers is an imprint of Elsevier.
500 Sansome Street, Suite 400, San Francisco, CA 94111

This book is printed on acid-free paper.

Library of Congress Cataloging-in-Publication Data

Redish, Janice. Letting go of the words : writing Web content that works / Janice (Ginny) Redish.—1st ed.
  p. cm.—(The Morgan Kaufmann series in interactive technologies)
  Includes bibliographical references and index.
  ISBN-13: 978-0-12-369486-7
  ISBN-10: 0-12-369486-8
  1. Web site development. 2. Web sites—Design. I. Title.
TK5105.888.R427 2007
006.7—dc22
2007012868

For information on all Morgan Kaufmann publications, visit our Web site at *www.mkp.com* or *www.books.elsevier.com*

Printed in Canada

07 08 09 10 11   10 9 8 7 6 5 4 3 2

For Edward F. Redish,
who has always been called "Joe,"
with love and deep appreciation

Contents

10 Breaking Up Your Text with Headings   235

Interlude: Legal Information Can Be Understandable, Too   263

13 Getting from Draft to Final Web Pages   329

Interlude: Creating an Organic Style Guide   345

Foreword

I have to admit that when Ginny Redish first mentioned that she was thinking of doing a book about writing for the web, my first reaction was a sense of extreme personal relief.

For years, I'd really wanted to read a great book about writing for the web, and for years, one hadn't appeared. There were some *very good* books about it, but not the book I was waiting for: the one that explained how writing for the web is *really* different, and why, and exactly what to do about it.

This missing book was starting to feel like one of those puzzling gaps in the fabric of the universe, like the fact that you never see any baby pigeons.[1] And it was beginning to look like the only way I was ever going to get to read it was to write it myself. Which I *really* did not want to do, being by nature averse to both hard work and writing – and fond of my wife and being married to her.[2]

Knowing Ginny, I knew immediately that she would write the book I wanted to read, hence my relief.

I was also very happy to hear that she was taking it on, because I knew that a lot of people besides me really needed this book. After all,

- Most of the web is about words. The pictures, video, and animation are great, but the words do almost all of the heavy lifting.
- Very few of the millions of sites out there can afford a full-time writer. As a result, most of the people (like you, perhaps) who have to write all those words aren't professional writers. They (you) need some help.

---

[1]While Googling to try to find out whether Holden Caulfield was really the first to raise the "Where are all the baby pigeons?" question, I came across a terrific answer: What you see *are* the babies. The adults are 12 feet tall and only come out at night.

[2]Years ago, I wrote a tiny 4½-page chapter about writing for the web in *Don't Make Me Think!* and it took me, literally, three solid weeks of 10-hour days. No kidding.

- And even for most professional writers, writing for the web is very different from the writing they're used to doing. They could use some expert help, too.

In retrospect, I shouldn't have been puzzled that no one had written this book sooner, since it requires a sort of "perfect storm":

- **Someone who really knows her stuff.** No one is more qualified than Ginny to do this book. As the saying goes, "She's forgotten more about writing and reading than most people will ever know." And she has a wonderful generosity of spirit that drives her to share freely what she knows, rather than save it for her clients or make it into a proprietary "method."

- **Someone who can communicate what she knows.** I've always gone out of my way to read everything that Ginny writes or to hear her speak whenever I can, because I know I'll always learn something important and useful. She gets to the heart of things and explains them in a way that makes her readers and audiences feel smarter.

- **Someone who's willing to give up a year of her life.** No matter what anyone tells you, it takes a year out of your life to write a book like this. Not just a normal calendar year, either, but a year rudely sucked out of your life span, rather like the torture device in *The Princess Bride*.[3] And the truth is, unless you're *very* lucky (like, lottery-ticket lucky), you'll end up earning pennies an hour for the lost year in the long run.

Having this book – at long last – in my hands reminds me of the way Calvin Trillin once described a miracle-fabric parka his wife had given him that weighed nothing yet allowed him to stand comfortably in the freezing cold for hours: "I don't know how much it cost, because it was a gift. But I have to think . . . about a million dollars."

If you have to do any writing for the web, the advice Ginny is giving here is, as they say in the commercials, priceless. In the years ahead, I'm certain it's going to make the web a much better place to be.

Steve Krug
Brookline, Massachusetts

---

[3]Come to think of it, a *lot* like the torture device in *The Princess Bride*. Especially for your loved ones, who over the years may have grown used to seeing you and talking to you and having you take out the trash occasionally.

Acknowledgments

With gratitude to all who helped me bring this book to you:

- Steve Krug for writing the Foreword
- Elaine Brofford for finding many of the wonderful examples in the book
- Carol Barnum, Tom Brinck, Caroline Jarrett, Jeff Johnson, Steve Krug, Gina Pearson, and Whitney Quesenbery for reviewing drafts and offering excellent suggestions
- Ronnie Lipton for reading a late draft and helping me to let go of some of my words

- Tom Brinck for the great quote in Chapter 13 and for sharing several other stories and examples
- Catherine Courage and her colleagues at Salesforce.com for intranet screens
- Caroline Jarrett, Whitney Quesenbery, and Ian Roddis for sharing stories and screens from work on The Open University's web site
- Caroline Jarrett, again, for sharing the case study of CompareInterestRates.com
- Beth Mazur of AARP for arranging permission to use the personas of Matthew and Edith – and Amy Lee, formerly of AARP, for sharing the personas for a project we did together
- Jakob Nielsen for the eye-tracking pictures that you'll find in Chapters 6 and 10
- Jared Spool for the graph from his research on ideal link length – and for other research
- Marie Tahir of Intuit for her picture of working with a persona

- Diane Cerra, Publishing Director at Elsevier/Morgan Kaufmann, for believing in the book and encouraging me throughout the process
- Asma Palmeiro, Diane's assistant, for helping in so many ways from acquiring pictures to keeping track of the files

- Suzanne Kastner and her team at Graphic World for careful copy editing and production

- Marilyn Rash and her team at Elsevier for design and production coordination

- All my clients, colleagues, and workshop participants for helping me hone my key messages so that I can share them with you clearly and concisely

- Edward (Joe) Redish for always being there for me

Content!
Content!
Content!

Yesterday, while on the web, I

- downloaded a file
- ordered a book
- compared prices on a new camera I'm thinking of buying
- read a few of my favorite blogs
- checked the Wikipedia entry for *usability*
- looked for information on a health topic for my elderly aunt

 What did you do on the web yesterday? Were you just browsing around without any goal or were you looking for something specific?

Most people say "something specific." They want to send a baby gift or arrange a trip. They need to reorder their favorite specialty food or download a software upgrade. They have a question about company policy or want to check the balance in their vacation account. They have a problem with one of their gadgets and think they might find help for the problem online. Or they want to see what bloggers are saying about the latest political turmoil. They have a goal in mind when they go the web.

People come to web sites for the content

People come to web sites for the content that they think (or hope) is there. They want information that

1

- answers a question or helps them complete a task
- is easy to find and easy to understand
- is accurate, up to date, and credible

Information = content. In this book, I'm going to use both words – "information" and "content" – to talk about the words and pictures that you and your team put on your web site.

In a survey of business professionals, 95 percent said "that it is very or extremely important that the information they need to do their jobs be accessible, up-to-date, and easy to find on the web." www.enterpulse.com/ news-051502.html#

Web users skim and scan

 Last time you were on the web, how much did you want to read? How quickly did you want to get past the home page of the site you went to?

 Did you search? How much of the search results page did you read? Did you navigate? How much did you want to read on the pathway (menu) pages you had to go through to get to the information you were looking for?

 What did you do when you got to the page where you thought the information was? Did you start to read right away? Or did you first skim and scan?

Most people skim and scan a lot on the web. They hurry through all the navigation, wanting to get to the page that has what they came for. Even on the final (destination, information) pages, most web users skim and scan before they read.

Most web users are very busy people who want to read only as much as they need to satisfy the goal that brought them to the web.

For a study showing that most people scan web pages, see Morkes and Nielsen, 1998, and Nielsen, 2000.

In another study, people spent an average of 27 seconds on each web page (Nielsen and Loranger, 2006).

Web users read, but . . .

Do people ever read on the web? Yes, of course, they do. They read links, short descriptions, and search results – but they want to read those very quickly. They read news. They read blogs. They read on topics they are interested in.

Note, however, how much of this reading is "functional." In this book, I'm not talking about novels and poetry on the web. I'm talking about information sites, e-commerce sites, blogs that are trying to be informative, and information parts of web applications and e-learning programs.

People don't come to the web to linger over the words. Most uses of the web are for gathering information or doing tasks, not for the pleasure of reading. If your busy web users lose interest or don't find the information relevant, they'll stop reading. If they can't find what they need quickly enough, they'll leave your site and go elsewhere.

And if people don't find your site useful, they are not likely to come back. The Enterpulse study in the margin note on page 2 found that "66% [of the professionals in the study] rarely – if ever – return to a site once they've had a bad experience."

In the study reported by Nielsen and Loranger, web users spent, on average, less than 2 minutes before deciding to abandon a site.

They don't read more because . . .

I've got a client on the phone. I need the policy on international travel!

Just help me fix the printer jam!

What's the score in the World Cup game going on right now?

- They are too busy.
- What they find is not relevant to what they need.
- They are trying to answer a question. They want to get right to the answer and read only what they need to answer the question.
- They are trying to do a task. They want to read only what is necessary to do the task.

- They are bombarded with information and sinking under information overload.
- As Nielsen and Loranger (2006, 22) say, "If people carefully studied everything they came across online, they would never get to log off and have a life."

What makes writing for the web work well?

Good web writing

- is like a conversation
- answers people's questions
- lets people grab and go

Good web writing is like a conversation

Think of your web content as your part of a conversation – not a rambling dialogue but a focused conversation started by a very busy person.

www.tfl.gov.uk

 How often does someone come to your web site to ask a question: How do I . . . ? Where do I find out about . . . ? May I . . . . ?

Caroline Jarrett's three-layer model of forms as relationship, conversation, appearance is as relevant to web sites as it is to forms. See www.formsthatwork.com.

In many cases, web sites are replacing phones. In many cases, the point of web content is for people to get information for themselves from your web site rather than calling.

When site visitors come with questions, you have to provide answers. When site visitors come to do a task, you have to help them through the task. But, because you aren't there in person to lead them to the right place, give them the answer, or walk them through the steps, you have to build your site to do that in your place. You have to build your side of the conversation into the site.

Good web writing answers people's questions

As we'll see in later chapters, if you think of the web as conversation, you'll realize that much of your content is meant to answer the questions that people come with. You do not want an entire site to be in a section called frequently asked questions. You do want to think about what people come wanting to know and then about how to give them that information as concisely and clearly as possible.

Good web writing lets people "grab and go"

On the web, breaking information into pieces for different users, different topics, different questions, and different needs helps web users to *grab* just what they need and *go* on to look up their next question, do their next task, make a decision, get back to work, or do whatever comes next for them. In this book, we'll look at several ways to write so that busy web users can grab and go. Figures 1-1 and 1-2 show you just one example of how we can transform traditional writing into good web writing.

NEW AIRPORTS [top]

Proponents wishing to build a new airport must file a <u>Notice of Landing Area Proposal</u> (FAA Form 7480-1), a Landing Area Sketch, and location plotted on a copied portion of a 7-1/2 minute USGS Quadrangle Map (usually available at your county USDA Soil Conservation Service). The information must be submitted at least 90 days in advance of the day that work is to begin. Heliport proponents must submit the Notice of Landing Area Proposal (FAA Form 7480-1), a 7-1/2 minute quad map, and a sketch or plan showing the relationship of the helipad to hospital buildings, parking areas, and surrounding structures. The FAA will conduct an aeronautical study and issue a determination to the proponent. A determination does not

Figure 1-1 Paragraph style makes it very difficult to quickly grab information.   www.faa.gov

---

Building a new airport or heliport

What must I submit?

Airport	• <u>Notice of Landing Area Proposal</u>
	  FAA Form 7480-1
	
	• Landing Area Sketch
	• location plotted on a copied portion of a $7^1/2$ minute USGS
	  Quadrangle Map

Heliport	• <u>Notice of Landing Area Proposal</u>
	  FAA Form 7480-1
	
	• sketch or plan showing the relationship
	  of the helipad to hospital buildings, parking areas, and
	  surrounding structures
	
	• location plotted on a copied portion of a $7^1/2$ minute USGS
	  Quadrangle Map

When must I submit these documents?

At least **90 days** before the day that work is to begin.

Figure 1-2 My suggested revision makes it easy for different users to quickly grab the information that they need.

Introducing *Letting Go of the Words*

My goal in this book is to help you provide your site visitors with high-quality content that is easy to find and easy to understand. *Letting Go of the Words* is about planning, selecting, organizing, writing, illustrating, reviewing, and testing content that meets people's needs – that gives them a successful and satisfying web experience.

Let's talk a bit about what this book is and what it is not, as well as about how you might work with *Letting Go of the Words*.

It's about writing and design, not technology

Letting Go of the Words is about strategy and tactics, not about tools. I'll help you think about the people who come to your web site and help you write so that they have a successful web experience and you have a successful web site. Technology changes too fast to be a major part of the book – and the principles of good writing for the web transcend the technology you use.

It's full of examples

I know you want examples, so I've included lots of screen shots. (It's smart to want examples; it's easier to understand a point if you can see it as well as read about it.)

In many cases, I've also shown how I might revise the web page. In consulting projects, of course, I work closely with the subject matter experts to be sure that the final writing is accurate and consistent with the web site's personality and style. Here, I've shown what I *might* do because I have not worked with every web site that I show in the book.

Also, web sites change. In a few cases, the site changed while I was writing the book and I've included two shots to make a point about the change. Many more of the sites in this book may have changed by the time you go to look at them. That does not invalidate what I am showing. Even old examples can make excellent learning opportunities. If you see ways to improve the web writing on your site from any of the examples in the book, the examples will have done their job.

It's based in a user-centered design process

User-centered design is a process for creating products that work well for their users. When you practice user-centered design, you focus on people: their goals, their needs, their ways of working, and their environments. User-centered design means that you are using technology to help people achieve their goals in ways that work for them.

The concepts and processes of user-centered design flow through this book. My goal is to help you develop a usable and useful web site *for your audiences.* When you talk to others, you may hear terms like "reader-focused writing," "usability," and "plain language." To me, those are all names for what we are striving for. They are all part of the same idea; they are all aspects of user-centered design.

You can start the process in several places

If you are revising an existing web site, you might want to start by finding out how well it works for the people whom you want to use it. The best technique for finding out how well a site works is usability testing: watching and listening while representative users try to find specific information or accomplish specific tasks with the web site.

You should not wait until the end of a project to do usability testing. In fact, usability testing is a great way to *start* your web project. Test early; test often; test on a small-scale, iteratively.

You can jump around in the book

A book has to be linear, but you don't have to use it that way. The path I've set up through the book is one logical way to move: from users to scenarios to home pages to pathway pages to destination pages – and then within destination pages through overall design, writing, lists and tables, headings, illustrations, and links – ending with getting from first draft to final web page.

But that may not be the most logical path for you or for your project. Feel free to jump around in the book. Read it once through quickly now and then come back to it again when you have a specific question or need.

You can join our web community

I hope that you will learn from *Letting Go of the Words* and that it will answer most of your questions. I would also like to continue the conversation that I'm starting in this book. Join us on the web site at www.redish.net/writingfortheweb to ask a question, voice an opinion, get information about usability testing and other topics, and share your examples.

I'm putting lots of information about usability testing on the book's web site at www.redish.net/writingfortheweb.

Other good sources are www.usability.gov and the books by Barnum, 2002; Dumas and Redish, 1999; and Rubin, 1994.

SUMMARIZING CHAPTER 1

Here are key messages from Chapter 1:

- People come to web sites to satisfy goals, to do tasks, to get answers to questions.

- They come for information, for the content.

- They don't read much, especially before they get to the page that has the information they want.

- Even on information pages, they skim and scan before they start to read.

- They want to read only enough to meet their needs.

- Think of the web as a conversation started by a busy web user.

- Answer people's questions – throughout your web content, not only in sections called frequently asked questions.

- Write so that busy people can *grab* the information they need and *go* on to whatever they need to do next.

- Start with a usability test. Test early; test often; test on a small-scale, iteratively.

People!
People!
People!

2

To create a web site that communicates well, you must think about the people you are communicating with. Understanding your audiences and what they need is critical to deciding what to write, how much to write, the vocabulary to use, and how to organize the content on your web site.

We all interpret as we read

People aren't just passive receptacles into which writers can pour information. We are all constantly interpreting what we see on the screen in light of our own experiences and expectations. Even when we think that we share the same language, it isn't entirely the same. We may not know the same words. We may have different meanings for the same words.

All of us interpret what we read in light of our own knowledge and experiences. (In case you don't live in London: an Oyster card is a prepaid travel card for public transportation.)

Successful writers focus on their audiences

Writing successful web content doesn't start with typing words. It starts with finding out about your audiences and their needs.

- Who will (or should) come to your content? What about them should you keep in mind when writing your web content?
- Why do they come? What are their questions, their tasks, their stories, their scenarios?

Understanding your audiences will help you write the content they need in the words and the way they need it.

Understanding why your web users come will help you select and organize the content so that it best meets both your goals and theirs.

Seven steps to understanding your audiences

The rest of this chapter gives you seven steps with lots of tips for getting and using information about your web users and why they come to your site:

1. List your major audiences.
2. Gather information about your audiences.
3. List major characteristics for each audience.
4. Gather your audiences' questions, tasks, and stories.
5. Use your information to create personas.
6. Include the persona's goals and tasks.
7. Use your information to write scenarios for your site.

1. List your major audiences

One way to list your major audiences is to ask: "How do people identify themselves with regard to my web content?" For example:

- patients, health care professionals, researchers
- parents, teachers, students
- passengers, pilots, mechanics, airport operators

Another way is to ask: "What about my site visitors will help me know what content the web site needs and how to write that content?" This may lead to listing your audiences as

- experienced travelers, occasional travelers
- local residents, tourists coming to town
- lookers, bookers
- shoppers, browsers

Notice that when I list these user groups, I'm always referring to people – to human beings. Don't get caught up in naming departments, institutions, or buildings as users of your site.

Don't say that you are writing for "Finance." "Finance" may be a department with many people who have different jobs, different knowledge, and different needs from your web site.

Don't say you are writing for "banks." The bank is a building and buildings don't use web sites. Are you writing for bank executives? branch managers? tellers? customers of the bank? Those are all different audiences and the differences may be important. They may be looking for different content on the site. They may know or not know specific vocabulary that you want to use.

2. Gather information about your audiences

You can start to understand your audiences by thinking about them. But that's not enough. To really understand who they are, why they come, what they need, and how to write web content for them, you have to know them and their realities.

If you write your web content only on what you *think* your audiences are like, you will be writing from *assumptions*. If your assumptions are wrong, your content won't work.

Here are several suggestions for finding out about your audiences. Try to do them all; the ones at the end – actually watching, listening to, and talking with your web users and potential users of your site – are the most useful of all.

- **Think about your mission.** Whom are you supposed to serve? What are you supposed to help them accomplish?

- **Read the emails that come through your Contact Us and other feedback links.** Who is writing? What are they asking?

- **Talk to Marketing.** Whom are they targeting as web users?

- **Talk to Customer Service.** Who is calling with questions? What are those questions?

- **Get people who come to the site to fill out a short questionnaire.** Ask people a few questions about themselves, why they came to the site, and whether they were successful in finding what they came for.

- **Watch and listen to people.**
  - If your web site mirrors a brick-and-mortar business (e-commerce, banking and other financial institutions, travel, and so on), spend time in the physical location observing and listening to customers.
  - If yours is a government site, realize that government agencies often have "brick-and-mortar" equivalents. Spend time in a local office of the agency watching and listening for whatever is relevant to your web content. This might mean watching as people come to renew their driver's license or get a permit or sign up for benefits or ask for tax forms.
  - If you are creating an intranet, spend time observing and listening to employees from different areas and in different jobs.

- **Interview people who use or might use your web site.** Use these techniques:
  - contextual interviewing (where you watch and listen as people do their own work)
  - critical incident interviewing (where you ask people to tell you about specific times that they used the site; sometimes, you can also have them show you what they did)

- **Do usability testing of the current content.** Watch and listen to usability test participants work with your web site. Also ask them about themselves, their needs, and their ways of using content.

For information on many techniques for understanding your web users, see Courage and Baxter, 2004.

Designing a good survey is not trivial. A good book on survey design is Dillman, 2007.

For ideas on watching, listening to, and talking with people at their work, see Hackos and Redish, 1998.

For information on contextual interviewing, see Holtzblatt, Wendell, and Wood, 2005.

For information on the critical incident technique, see the Wikipedia article on that topic.

3. List major characteristics for each audience

As you find out about the people who come (or should come) to your web site, list relevant characteristics for each of your user groups. Here are some categories to cover:

- key phrases or quotes
- experience, expertise

- emotions
- values
- technology
- social and cultural environments
- demographics (age, ability, and so on)

Key phrases or quotes

If you asked your web users what they want you to keep in mind about them as you write to them, what would they say?

Experience, expertise

Consider your site visitors' experience and expertise in both the subject matter and in using the web. You may have differences here for different user groups. (You may also have a range of experience or expertise within a user group; note that, too.)

For example, for a travel site:

Experienced travelers	Probably familiar with other travel sites; probably know how e-tickets work; may know airport codes of places they travel to frequently; want fast ways of working – probably need little explanation at each step
Occasional travelers	May not be familiar with travel sites; may not know how e-tickets work; probably do not know airport codes; may need explanations at each step

For example, for a health information site:

Researchers and health care professionals	Probably know the medical terminology
Patients	May not know the medical terminology • Some may want to get the information without ever learning the terminology • Some may want to learn the terminology to talk to the doctor

Emotions

In some situations, people's emotions are important user characteristics. Your users might be

- fun-loving
- passionate
- intrigued
- curious
- impatient
- angry
- deadline-driven

- nervous
- anxious
- frustrated
- skeptical
- stressed
- pressured

 In Chapter 6, we'll consider writing for injured workers who are checking on their worker's compensation claims. What would you say about their emotional state? Did you say: Anxious, nervous, skeptical about whether the agency really wants to help them?

 If reporters are one of your audiences, what would you put down for them? Did you say: Deadline-driven, impatient?

 What about people seeking help with a product problem (like a paper jam in the printer)? Did you say: Angry, frustrated, anxious?

If the web site focuses so strongly on marketing messages that information about customer service is hard to find, will that only frustrate these web users more? If your content about the problem is in convoluted, technical language, will that only make them angrier? And what will they do if the web content doesn't help? Call up – and cost the company more money? Write a scathing review on a "what should I buy" web site? Buy someone else's product next time?

Web content for people who are angry, frustrated, anxious, or stressed has to be particularly clear and simple.

Values

Knowing what matters to your site visitors may help you decide what content to include and what to focus on or emphasize in the content. Knowing their values may help you understand why they don't want to read much, why letting go of the words and writing in clear, conversational style matches their needs.

Technology

What resolutions are your site visitors working at? What speeds are they connecting with? How steady is their connection? Do they pay for every minute they are on? Are some people getting your web content on small screens – on personal digital assistants (PDAs)? on cell phones? You'll want to know that as you make decisions about your web content.

Despite the tremendous growth of broadband, it is not universal. In many places, people pay for each minute of connection – they don't have unlimited access for a monthly charge. Many users are still on slow connections and slow computers, including many home users, older adults, and even users in large companies and in organizations that can't afford to update their computers regularly.

Technology changes so rapidly that any statistics I put into the book would be quickly out of date. So instead of numbers, here are some web sites you can check to track the growth of broadband and other technology issues:

- www.clickz.com/stats/
- www.oecd.org (and search for broadband statistics)
- www.upsdell.com/BrowserNews/stat_trends.htm

Social and cultural environments

You should also understand where and when people come to your web content.

- Are they likely to be alone or with someone else?
- Are they likely to be in an office cubicle or at home or at the public library?
- Are they going to be doing research on a site like yours for a long time each day?
- Are they likely to be interrupted as they work with your information?
- Are they answering questions for someone else, so they might have someone on the phone waiting for the answer while they try to get that answer from your web content?

All of these characteristics might be important for you to consider as you decide what to say and how to say it.

Demographics

Age may matter for your site. If you are writing content for a particular age group – for example, for young children or for teens – that will likely affect your writing style as well as the design of your site.

For more on older adults and the web, see articles at www.aarp.org/olderwiserwired.

But age isn't all there is to demographics. In fact, recent studies of older adults have shown how diverse the audience of 50+ or even 65+ is. Even within the older adult audience, you have to think about differences in computer and web expertise (aptitude), in feelings about the web (attitude), and in ability (vision and other problems).

Vision and other problems are not limited to older adults. In the United States, all federal government web sites and any site paid for with federal government money must be accessible to all. Many other countries also require attention to making web sites work for everyone.

For a list of accessibility requirements in different countries, see www.w3.org/WAI/Policy/.

4. Gather your audiences' questions, tasks, and stories

From all your sources, gather lists of the questions that people expect the web site to answer, the tasks they need the web site to support, and the stories they tell about their experiences with your web site, with other web sites, and in relevant non-web situations.

As you gather their questions, tasks, and stories, don't translate! Keep the users' words. One of the most important parts of gathering information from your audiences is understanding the words they use to describe what they want and need. Then you'll have their vocabulary to use in your web content.

5. Use your information to create personas

If you've done the first four steps in this chapter, you have a lot of facts about the people who will or should come to your web site. But it may be hard to imagine real people in the facts you've gathered. Do the facts seem dry? Do they lack "human interest" – a real sense of the *people* your web content is for?

Alan Cooper popularized personas in design. Cooper's books are listed in the bibliography.

A great way to bring your web users "alive" for yourself and your team is to create personas.

For more on personas, see Pruitt and Adlin, *The Persona Lifecycle*, 2006.

A persona is an individual with a name, a picture, and specific demographic and other characteristics. A persona is not a specific real person; a persona is a composite of characteristics of many real people.

A persona brings together in one example the facts you've gathered from thinking about or, even better, watching and listening to the people who come to your web content. Your personas don't have to be fancy. You don't need to spend lots of time and money creating elaborate presentations. You do need to be true to the data you have to make sure the personas represent your web users – not you.

Figures 2-1 and 2-2 introduce you to Matthew and to Edith, two of eight personas that AARP focuses on in planning and writing their web site.

"The web is a tool to get things done. Fast."

"If it doesn't work right, I move on. I don't have time to figure it out."

Typical web tasks:

- read news
- check sports sites
- arrange travel
- buy things for their weekend house in Connecticut
- check out health information after seeing the doctor

When it's time to renew his AARP membership, he'll try it online this year and save himself the paperwork – if it's easy to do.

Matthew

- 54 years old
- attorney
- lives in New York City
- married
- wife works full time
- no children

Matthew and his wife work full time. They make six-figure incomes, and they put in the hours that requires.

They don't have kids, but they enjoy having nieces and nephews come to visit – sometimes for as much as a week on school breaks.

Matthew uses email but doesn't get on the web much at work. His web use is mostly personal, at home. That doesn't mean he has time to waste. He's impatient at home, too. Time is very precious for Matthew and his wife.

Matthew is still feeling fine, although his doctor says he needs to exercise more.

He wears contacts; his eyes aren't what they were when he was younger. He hates web sites with tiny print; they make him feel old.

Figure 2-1 Matthew represents the younger, still working part of AARP's audience. AARP is a membership organization that every American is invited to join at the age of 50. Used with permission.   www.aarp.org

What information goes into a persona?

Use all the categories of information you gathered:

- key phrases or quotes
- experience, expertise
- emotions
- values
- technology
- social and cultural environments
- demographics (age, ability, and so on)

"I love getting pictures of the grandkids in email, but I don't understand how the kids make that happen."

"My son, Jerry, showed me how to print out the pictures. I always follow just what he said to do."

Typical web tasks:

- email
- find health information for herself and Doug and sometimes for friends
- get information for travel – she hasn't yet actually bought online, even though the kids do it all the time and say it's very safe

Edith didn't even know there was an AARP web site until she saw something about it in the AARP magazine. The magazine said there was more travel information on the web site, and Edith likes to plan trips that include visiting grandchildren and also doing some sightseeing.

Edith

- 73 years old
- retired restaurant owner
- now lives in Miami
- married almost 50 years to Doug
- limited income
- four children, ten grandchildren

Edith and Doug get by on Social Security and what they got when they sold the restaurant.

They put down a lot of cash for their small retirement house to keep the payments low.

Edith and Doug are enjoying retirement. They like the slow pace (especially after all those hectic years in the restaurant). They like the sunshine and the social life.

Edith is a cautious web user.

She checks her email regularly because the children are so busy that they don't come to visit or call as often as she would like – but they do send email.

Edith uses hearing aids and glasses. She took off the glasses for the picture, but she needs them to read or look at the computer. She has slight arthritis in her hands, so sometimes using the mouse is a problem.

Figure 2-2 Edith represents the older (but not oldest), retired part of AARP's audience. AARP members range from 50 to 100+. Used with permission.   www.aarp.org

You may want to put the information in a different order. We usually start with demographics so that the persona has a specific age, family status, education, job, interests, income level, and so forth.

Also, we add

- picture
- name

The picture and name are critical parts of a persona description. They make a user profile into a persona.

You know you have a good picture and a good name when they resonate with your web team. And that really happens: I was helping a team develop personas for a particular user group. They had all met with several people in the user group, although I had not. I had brought about 20 pictures with me of people of different gender, age, ethnicity, emotion in their faces, and so on. As soon as I spread out the pictures, they pounced on one. "That's her!" they said. And they knew her "name," too.

Be sure to select a name and picture that make the team respect the persona. Funny or cute names are signs of disrespect. You must have good conversations with your personas to write web content that will make good conversations with your actual web users.

You can buy or license stock photography, but many teams find that casual, personal photos are better than photos of models. Don't use a picture of someone the team knows. They'll find it too hard to talk about "Jack" if they know it's really a picture of Lisa's brother Mike. But photos of friends or family that the team doesn't know often work well. Just be sure to have the person's permission to use the photo.

How do personas work with a web team?

Personas become members of your web team. Figure 2-3 shows how one team keeps their persona in clear view as they work. They can turn to her and "ask" her what path she would take to get to information or how she would do a task in what they are developing.

Instead of talking generically about "users" for your web content, you start talking about your personas by name.

- Will Matthew be able to find this information about his insurance policy?
- What will Edith do if she has a question about her problems with her eyesight?

Figure 2-3 Marie Tahir (in the red blouse) and her colleagues at Intuit have Lindsay with them as they plan and develop their product. Used with permission.

- What questions will Kristin ask about this topic?
- When Sanjay comes to this web site, will he search or navigate? What search terms will he use to get to the content I am writing?

Here are some ways that personas have become members of web teams:

- They come to team meetings as life-size cardboard cutouts.
- Their pictures and information hang on the wall in the team's work space.
- Their pictures and information are printed on place mats or mouse pads so that they are on the table at meetings and in team members' work spaces.
- Emails from them and about them circulate in the team.

"Users" yes or no? – a note on vocabulary

Pruitt and Adlin, in their book on personas, strongly advocate removing "user" from your vocabulary. They say not to talk generically about "users" – rather always focus on your specific personas by name. That's a great idea for a specific web site or specific web content.

In this book, however, I need more generic words. You – my audience – are so diverse (I hope) that you are dealing with many different types of web content for many different types of people. The personas for your web content differ from the personas for other people's web content. What generic words should I use?

You'll notice that I am using "people," "web users," "site visitors," and "audience." I hope that all of those words work well for you.

Shortening "web users" to "users" bothers some people, so I avoid doing that most of the time. However, I prefer "user" to "reader" for most discussions of web content because people do not come to web sites for the pleasure of reading. They come to gather information. They "use" web sites; they "use" web content.

"User" emphasizes that people come with goals, with tasks, with questions. "User" helps us focus on the functional nature of web content and the need to help people skim, scan, and grab and go. "User" is not a pejorative word; it's an accurate description of people interacting with web content. I hope that when you see the word "user" in this book, you'll read it with the friendly meaning: "person coming to my web site to ask a question, do a task, or see what I have to say."

6. Include the persona's goals and tasks

The persona's major goals and tasks for your site are an important part of your persona description. Figure 2-4 gives you an example for one of five personas developed by a web team that researches and reports on issues in agriculture and food production.

7. Use your information to write scenarios for your site

Scenarios are short stories that give you a good sense of the people who come to your site, what their lives are like, and what they want to do at your web site. Scenarios give life to goals and tasks in the same way that personas give life to lots of data about your web users.

To understand how useful story-telling (scenarios) can be in developing useful and usable web sites, read Whitney Quesenbery's chapter in the Pruitt and Adlin book.

Information goals

- Looks for market analysis and topics dealing with company's market segment

- Wants summaries, trends, and value-added analysis rather than raw data

- Keeps abreast of current legislation and regulations

- Seeks comparative information on what other companies are doing

- Seeks information that is timely and credible

Figure 2-4 The goals section of a persona — Curtis, Vice President in charge of buying products for a major grocery chain

Scenarios tell you the conversations people want to start

People's stories are the beginnings of their conversations with you. Scenarios can be as short as the two sentences in the thought bubbles below or as long as the stories about Mark and Mariella on the next pages.

I'm traveling from the U. S. to India next month. Do I need a visa?

My niece will be two years old next week. I'm looking for a cute dress to send to her.

Scenarios can be very short.

If you have developed one or more major personas for your site, you should have several scenarios for each of them.

- These may elaborate the goals and tasks that you have on your persona posters into fuller stories that make the persona's use of your site even more realistic to the team.
- You may want to add scenarios for more goals and tasks than you fit onto your original persona poster.

Scenarios help you understand all types of users

You may also want to have scenarios for a few secondary personas. For example, if your main personas are frequent shoppers and casual shoppers but you also have investors and newspaper people coming to the site, you may want to do "mini-personas" for them along with their scenarios.

 Do the mini-personas with scenarios in Figures 2-5 and 2-6 give you a sense of these people and their lives? Would they be helpful to you in creating web sites for people like them?

 Mark Williams is a sales coordinator for one of the divisions of FGH Corporation. His job, like that of most of his friends, includes many different responsibilities. He often feels as if he's juggling tasks all day long.

Today he's trying to put together some projections that his boss wants "immediately." But Mark also has to deal with questions that his staff can't handle on their own, and that often involves looking up policies on the company's intranet.

The telephone just interrupted Mark's work on the projections for his boss. It's Anu Pati out in the field negotiating a deal with a client. Anu needs to know whether company policy allows her to offer volume discounts to this client and what those discounts can be.

Mark needs to find the right policy quickly both to keep Anu and her potential client happy and because he wants to get back to the job for the boss. He also hopes the policy is clearly stated so that he and Anu are both confident they are giving the client correct information.

Figure 2-5 A scenario for developing an intranet site.

Don and Mariella Garcia just had their second baby, so they need a bigger car. Don's construction work is going well, but Mariella is staying home for a while, so they're worried about money. They're going to need a loan to buy the new car, and they want a good deal.

Mariella knows about computers and the web from the job she was doing before she got married. But she can only go look on the web in spurts – when the children are napping or late at night when Don can look with her. And then they are both very tired.

They're not financial experts; they don't know all the banking terms that some of these sites use. They're trying to find a site with good loans that talks to them with words they understand.

Figure 2-6 A scenario for developing a bank or credit union site.

Everything on your web site should fulfill a scenario

Everything on your web site should relate to at least one scenario that a real user might have for coming to the web site. (You do not need to have actually written the scenario for every piece of content, but there should be a plausible one that you could write.)

If no one needs or wants the information – if there is no plausible scenario for the content – why have it on the web site? It's only taking up server space and perhaps showing up in search results where it distracts people from what they really need.

Scenarios can help you write good web content

If your scenarios are based on watching, listening, and talking with people, they can help you

- focus on what is important to your site visitors
- write with their words
- realize how goal-oriented most web users are

As you plan your web content, always ask: Who will use it? What should I keep in mind about them? What story (scenario) will bring them to this web content?

SUMMARIZING CHAPTER 2

Here are key messages from Chapter 2:

- We all interpret as we read.

- Successful writers focus on their audiences.

- List your major audiences.

- Gather information about your audiences from several sources.

- If you develop the web site only by *thinking* about your audiences, you are working from your *assumptions.* If your assumptions are wrong, your content won't work.

- List major characteristics for each audience, including
  - key phrases or quotes
  - experience, expertise
  - emotions
  - values
  - technology
  - social and cultural environments
  - demographics

- Gather your audiences' questions, tasks, and stories.

- Use your information to create personas.

- Include the persona's goals and tasks.

- Use your information to write scenarios for your site.
  - Scenarios tell you the conversations people want to start.
  - Everything on your web site should fulfill a scenario.
  - Scenarios can help you write good web content.

Starting Well: Home Pages

3

Both you – and all those people whom you thought about, visited, observed, listened to, and created personas and scenarios for – want your web site to succeed.

To have a successful experience on a web site, people have to

- find what they need
- understand what they find
- act appropriately on that understanding

And they have to be able to do all that in the time and effort that they think it is worth.

Most of this book is about "understand what they find." It's mostly about writing destination (information) pages beyond the home page and beyond the pathway (menu, gallery) pages that people may have to go through on their way to what they want.

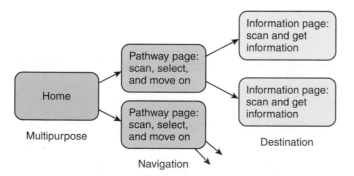

Information-rich web sites set up pathways to the information through the home page and one or more layers of pathway (menu) pages.

Although we'll concentrate later in the book on information pages, all web pages have content. Home pages have content. Pathway pages have content.

Letting go of the words is especially important on home pages and pathway pages. So before we get to writing information pages further down in your site, let's briefly explore home pages in this chapter and pathway pages in the next chapter.

Home pages – the 10-minute mini-tour

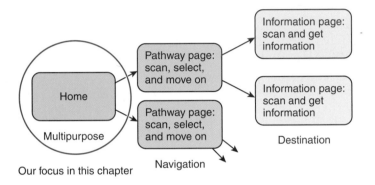

Most people read very little on the home page. They want to grab the information they need and move on because what they need from the site is almost always beyond the home page. Home pages can be content-rich, but they must not be wordy.

In the rest of this chapter, we'll discuss five major functions of home pages:

- identifying the site, establishing the brand
- setting the tone and personality of the site
- helping people get a sense of what the site is all about
- letting people start key tasks immediately
- sending each person on the right way, effectively and efficiently

We'll see how to accomplish all that without asking people to read much.

We'll end the chapter with a brief case study of revising the home page of a portal site, as well as a short section on how important it is to plan

Many of your site visitors may be bypassing your home page and pathway pages by coming to specific information pages in your site through a search engine like Google.

Nonetheless, you must still set up your site for those who do start at your home page – or who get to your home page after looking at the information page the search engine sent them to.

For an analysis of many home pages, see Nielsen and Tahir, *Homepage Usability, 50 Websites Deconstructed,* 2001.

your site from your information topics *up* to the home page – not only from the home page *down* to the information topics.

Identifying the site, establishing the brand

Your site's logo, name, and tag line identify it. Don't use a paragraph to explain the site. Don't put paragraph-long mission statements on the home page. Most people won't read them.

Instead, encapsulate your company's or organization's mission in a memorable tag line – a short phrase that tells people how to think about the site.

Consider Figure 3-1, the top of the Aspen Square Hotel's home page. The identifying information here works well with very few words, as long as people coming to this site know what a condominium hotel is and recognize Aspen as the famous resort in Colorado.

For more on tag lines and other aspects of home pages, pathway pages, and navigation, see Krug, *Don't Make Me Think!* 2005.

Figure 3-1 Even if you have never heard of the Aspen Square Hotel, you probably immediately understand what it is and where it is from the logo/name and tag line.   www.aspensquarehotel.com

Setting the tone and personality of the site

Remember that your web site is part of a conversation. You set the tone for your side of the conversation by sharing the web site's personality with your site visitors. Indeed, different web sites have different person-alities – expressed in the site's visual style, colors, graphics, typography, writing style, and words.

A few years ago, the U. S. Internal Revenue Service (IRS, the tax collec-tors) had a home page that looked like a tabloid newspaper (Figure 3-2).

For an interesting paper on web sites having personalities, see Coney and Steehouder, 2000.

Figure 3-2 The web site of the U. S. Internal Revenue Service in 2001.

What impression does the IRS home page give you of the agency? What adjectives would you use to describe this page? Do those adjectives match your expectations for the IRS web site? What personality should the IRS web site have?

Figure 3-3 is the 2005 IRS home page. It may not be exciting, but it is much more appropriate. The rest of the pages in the site are in compatible templates with the same visual style so that they meet the expectations this home page sets.

Figure 3-3 The web site of the U. S. Internal Revenue Service in 2005.   www.irs.gov

Deciding on the personality that you want your site to project is part of developing your "brand." Both commercial companies and government agencies need to consider their "corporate image," their brand. Branding and marketing specialists can help you decide on an appropriate brand.

Who decides on the site's personality?

If you own the site (it's your blog; it's your company), you decide on the tone and personality you want your site to have. However, if you are part of a larger organization, it's not your decision alone. In fact, another division of the organization (for example, marketing or corporate communications) may dictate aspects of the site's brand – colors, templates, and writing style.

Don't arbitrarily reject those decisions; there's value to your site visitors in finding a consistency in personality and style across subsites within a larger site. Always connect your site to the home page (and other parts) of the larger site so that people who come into the organization's site through your part get the value of your belonging to that larger organization.

If you want to influence the tone and personality the organization is using on the site, get involved. Communicate up the chain and across groups. Become part of the web site task force (if your organization has one).

As you think about the site's tone and personality, think broadly about all of the organization's audiences, not just the specific audiences for your part of the site. A web site is the whole organization's face to the world.

Branding specialists often start by asking for the adjectives you want people to use when referring to your site.

 What adjectives come to mind when looking at the Crayola page in Figure 3-4? Do those adjectives seem appropriate for the audiences and scenarios of the site? What about the Car Talk page in Figure 3-5?

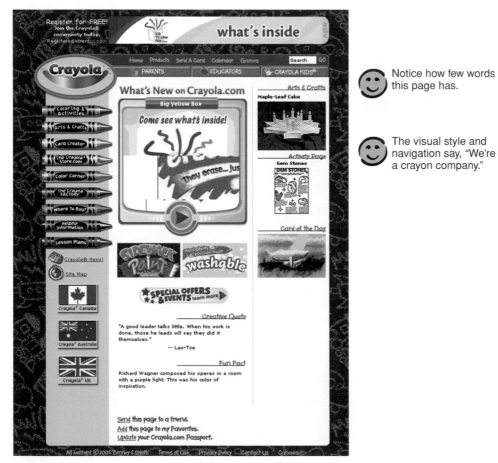

Notice how few words this page has.

The visual style and navigation say, "We're a crayon company."

Figure 3-4 Crayola sells crayons and art supplies. The visual style seems appropriate for the audience of children, parents, and teachers.   www.crayola.com

Notice the irreverent section names.

The graphics and writing style match the site's personality.

Figure 3-5 This site matches the irreverent tone of the popular U. S. call-in radio show on which it is based. Other companies would not help their image by labeling their e-commerce section "Shameless Commerce."   www.cartalk.com

Notice how you can set the tone and personality with very few words. Even if you want to say "we're a friendly site; we're glad you're here," you should do it without a paragraph of text because most people won't read the paragraph.

Helping people get a sense of what the site is all about

Many people coming to your site for the first time want to know:

- Whose site is this? (Did I get where I thought I was going?)

- Who are these people? (if I don't already know that)

- What is this site all about? (What do they have? What can I do here?)

But they want to grab that information quickly because they also want to know:

- How do I keep going on the question or task that brought me here?

Return visitors often just do a quick check to be sure they are on the right site and, perhaps, to see if there's anything new and exciting before they plunge further into the site.

Both too little and too much can keep people from understanding what the site offers.

A useful home page makes it instantly clear what the site is about

Look at Figure 3-6, the 2005 home page of SBC. Is it instantly clear what their business is?

Web sites must serve both those who already know the company and those who do not. Managers and staff inside a company are often so familiar with the company's history and business that they forget that other people are not. If a web site is going to help a company market itself successfully, it must speak to people who do not yet know the company.

Figure 3-6 The 2005 web site of SBC had too little information for people who did not already know what SBC did, making it difficult for them to find out at a glance.

SBC merged with AT&T in late 2005. As you can see in Figure 3-7, the new site does a much better job of showing at a glance what businesses the company is in and what it offers.

Figure 3-7 The 2006 web site of SBC/AT&T does a much better job of telling people at a glance what the company and site are all about.   www.att.sbc.com

A useful home page is mostly links and short descriptions

A useful home page for both new and returning site visitors is almost all links with just a few brief descriptions to help people very quickly understand what the site is all about and to know which link to choose to move on.

Look at Figure 3-8, which shows more of the Aspen Square home page.

 Where do your eyes go? Did you look at the pictures first and scan the picture captions? How much of the text did you read?

ASPEN SQUARE
Condominium Hotel

*the Condominium Hotel
in the Heart of Aspen*

Click Here
**Book
Online**

1-800-470-0530
1-970-925-1000

**Daily News | Live Web Cam | Calendar | Aspen Links | Transportation
Summer Information | Winter Information | Snow Report | Weather**

Book Online

Accommodations

Rates

Specials

Groups

Newsletter

Contact Us

Media Center

**Aspen Square's
Olympic Racer!!**

*Hospitality first...
and a great place to stay!*

***All Units Now Feature Air-Conditioning
and FREE High-Speed Internet Access***

Aspen, Colorado's Summer Season is here, and the time is right to make plans to visit the Aspen Square Hotel and see what the warm weather months are all about in Aspen! There is so much to do and see in Aspen when the winter snows disappear. Summer Information is right here! Get more timely Aspen news: Check out our Daily News, the Live Web Cam, our Aspen Lodging Specials and the latest Weather and activity information.

For Aspen accommodations, look no further for lodging at Aspen Colorado's most convenient condominium hotel, offering nightly condo rentals for lodging. Aspen Square Hotel is located right in the heart of this renowned mountain resort, just steps from the many outstanding Colorado restaurants, unique shops and art galleries. Even the Aspen Silver Queen Gondola is right across the street at the base of Aspen Mountain!

Lodging at The Aspen Square Hotel features cozy fireplace studio suites as well as one and two-bedroom condos for nightly rentals. Each condominium has a fully equipped kitchen, wood-burning fireplace, comfortable living room and private balcony. Lodging amenities include full-service concierge services, heated pool and hot tub, health club facilities,

Aspen Square Hotel is a full service condominium hotel with superior lodging.

Relax in our hotel lobby after a great day!

Figure 3-8 More of the home page of the hotel site we saw in Figure 3-1. The page uses long paragraphs of text.
www.aspensquarehotel.com

Many people scan. For them, the page might look like Figure 3-9.

People might actually take away more information from this page if it looked like Figure 3-10.

ASPEN SQUARE
Condominium Hotel

the Condominium Hotel in the Heart of Aspen

Click Here
Book Online

1-800-470-0530
1-970-925-1000

Daily News | Live Web Cam | Calendar | Aspen Links | Transportation
Summer Information | Winter Information | Snow Report | Weather

Book Online

Accommodations

Rates

Specials

Groups

Newsletter

Contact Us

Media Center

Aspen Square's
Olympic Racer!!

Hospitality first...
and a great place to stay!

All Units Now Feature Air-Conditioning
and FREE High-Speed Internet Access

Aspen, Colorado's Summer Season is here, and the time is right to make plans to visit the Aspen Square Hotel and see what the warm weather months are all about in Aspen! There is so much to do and see in Aspen when the winter snows disappear. Summer Information is right here! Get more timely Aspen news: Check out our Daily News, the Live Web Cam, our Aspen Lodging Specials and the latest Weather and activity information.

For Aspen accommodations, look no further for lodging at Aspen Colorado's most convenient condominium hotel, offering nightly condo rentals for lodging. Aspen Square Hotel is located right in the heart of this renowned mountain resort, just steps from the many outstanding Colorado restaurants, unique shops and art galleries. Even the Aspen Silver Queen Gondola is right across the street at the base of Aspen Mountain!

Lodging at The Aspen Square Hotel features cozy fireplace studio suites as well as one and two-bedroom condos for nightly rentals. Each condominium has a fully equipped kitchen, wood-burning fireplace, comfortable living room and private balcony. Lodging amenities include full-service concierge services, heated pool and hot tub, health club facilities,

Aspen Square Hotel is a full service condominium hotel
with superior lodging.

Relax in our hotel lobby after a great day!

Figure 3-9 What many people see on a site like this. Their eyes go to the pictures and the links, but they don't read the text.

Figure 3-10 What I might suggest for the Aspen Square site, to make the links stand out and to use many fewer words.

Letting people start key tasks immediately

When people come to a web site to do a task, they usually want to start that task right away. Many tasks involve forms, and it's been interesting to watch over the years as more and more forms come to the front of sites. If people need a form, putting the form on the home page is a good strategy.

Put forms people want right away on the home page

For example, on travel sites what people most want to do is set up travel. That's why most travel sites let people start a reservation right from the home page. Figure 3-11, the Scandinavian Airlines site, is an example.

Make sure the forms are high on the page

If you have forms on the home page, make sure they are easy to find – high enough on the home page to be seen immediately. The large pictures that many sites have on their web pages push critical tasks and critical information far down on the page. These large pictures hinder people from finding the critical information or critical field quickly and easily. See the FedEx example in Figure 3-12.

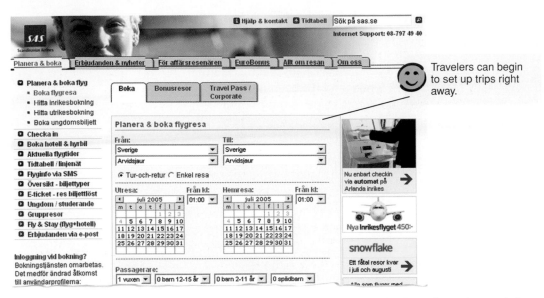

Figure 3-11 Like most travel sites, SAS lets travelers describe their plans immediately. Users of any other travel site are likely to know what to do here even if they don't speak Swedish.   *www.sas.se*

Don't assume full screens at high resolution

Some web users still have small screens or work at low resolution. Those of us who work on large screens at high resolution – and I'm looking at what I'm typing on a 24-inch monitor at a screen resolution of 1900 × 1200 – tend to forget that most of the people who use what we develop aren't working in that environment. Most of your site visitors are probably working at 1024 × 768; but a sizable minority are still using 800 × 600 screens. (Summer 2006: About 20 percent of web users are still at 800 × 600.)

For up-to-date information on screen resolutions most people are using, see the web sites I listed in Chapter 2, page 18.

Furthermore, even sophisticated business people and research scientists don't all work with small type on large screens. In a field study with employees of a large health information group in which everyone had monitors that could display at least 1024 × 768, the client and I were surprised to see that many employees had changed their displays to lower resolutions or large type. They were seeing much less on the screen at one time than we had assumed.

Many expert web users open multiple windows and let those windows share screen space. They don't maximize the windows; they see only part of your web page at one time.

These realities are all good reasons not to use most of the upper part of a web page for a large picture that serves only for emotional appeal. Use the space instead for the most important forms or information that people come to your site to get.

Home pages must balance branding and work. Does this favor branding so much that it makes the place to start working hard to find?

Most of the form for tracking shipments is not visible at 800 × 600 – or to people who don't open the window all the way.

Figure 3-12 People would find it easier to get immediately to the box for tracking shipments if it were higher on the page.

www.fedex.com

Put Search near the top – where site visitors expect it

Always put the Search box near the top of the page. If your site has search capability (and any large site should), a Search box (not just a link to another page) should be in the same place on every page of the site.

People have come to expect that the Search box will be either at the top right or at the left at the top of the left navigation column. Those are both good places.

A long home page with the Search box at the bottom is not a good idea if the site will draw visitors who have small monitors, use low resolution, or don't maximize each window. If the Search box is below the fold, many people will assume the site does not have search capability. They won't scroll down to look for it.

Blind web users who like to search also want to find the Search box very close to the top of the web page. Screen-readers start to read from the top of the page. If the Search box is before other content, blind web users get to what they need quickly.

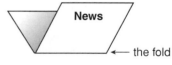

← the fold

"Above the fold" for a web page is whatever the site visitor sees when the page first opens – at whatever resolution or window size that person is using.

Information that is "below the fold" becomes visible only if the web user scrolls down the web page.

The phrase "above the fold" comes from print newspapers, where you see only what is above the fold when the paper is delivered to your doorstep or is being sold in a vending machine.

Newspaper editors know they must put the most important and interesting information above the fold to attract people's attention.

Don't make people fill out forms they don't want

Starting people on forms they want on the home page is good. However, forcing people to fill out forms that they don't want – or before they are ready to give you the information – is likely to be counterproductive.

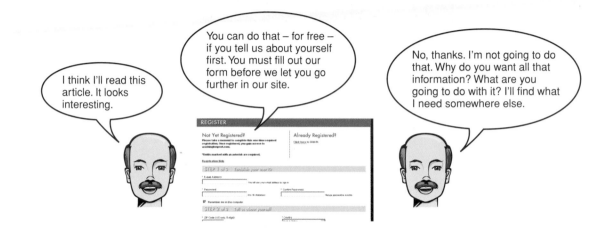

Think carefully about the benefits and perils of asking for information when people are not ready to give it to you. If you ask too early, or you ask for too much, or you ask for information that people have to struggle to get for you, you risk losing more than you might gain. Consider the trade-offs. If you are asking people to register so that you can market to them later, do you lose more than you gain by having people leave early? If people put in fake information just to get past your form, does that end up being a costly pain to you?

Sending each person on the right way, effectively and efficiently

Most people want to move off the home page quickly. Even most first-time visitors spend almost no time getting a sense of the site; they immediately try to find the link they need to move on.

Chapter 12 is all about writing meaningful links. If that's important for you right now, feel free to go there and then come back to the rest of this chapter. Here I'm going to focus on two critical guidelines about writing links to help people get started down a good path from the home page:

- Use your site visitors' words.
- Don't make people wonder which link to click on.

In the study reported by Nielsen and Loranger, average time on the home page was 25 to 35 seconds! People want to get on with the task that brought them to the site.

Use your site visitors' words

When people come to your web site to start a conversation with you, they have a topic or question in mind. They are looking for the words they have in their minds – words that give them confidence that if they click there, they'll get closer to the information they are seeking.

To make connections between what your site visitors want and the content you have, you must use their words – not cute, made-up names that they do not know. Cute doesn't work if it doesn't help your site visitors know where to click.

Use all the sources of information about your web users that we discussed in Chapter 2 to get their words.

Don't make people wonder which link to click on

Site visitors want to think about their topic, their need – not about how you've put together your site. If people don't feel confident that you are helping them get to what they need, they might not feel confident that your information is credible or that you are a good firm to do business with.

The web site in Figure 3-13 might make people who come to it unsure about going further. Lots of other sites offer car loans and ways to invest money. Busy web users might just go elsewhere rather than try to figure out what's where on this site.

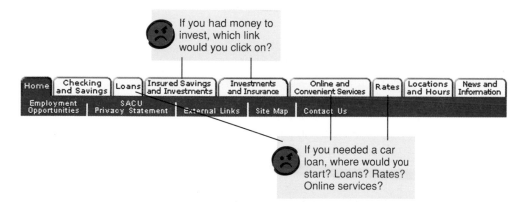

Figure 3-13 Web users don't want to have to figure out where you've put the information they need. They want to feel comfortable and confident as they move through your site.

Putting it all together: A case study

Let's see how our five points play out in a specific case. This case study is of revising the portal site to all the information in all the agencies that make up the U. S. Department of Health and Human Services.

Case Study 3-1	Revising the home page of a portal

With 12 major agencies, more than 300 programs, more than 65,000 employees, and an annual budget of more than $500 billion, the U. S. Department of Health and Human Services (HHS) is larger than many major worldwide corporations. Its agencies include the Centers for Disease Control and Prevention, the Centers for Medicaid and Medicare Services, the Food and Drug Administration, and the National Institutes of Health – sources of information on health and safety for people all over the world and on medical benefits for elderly and poor Americans.

Each HHS agency has web sites (and subsites and subsites of those subsites). The main page at www.hhs.gov has to serve as a portal to all the topics on all those agency sites – as well as give visitors the "big picture" of what HHS does.

A team of HHS subject matter experts, web designers, and usability specialists – with my help as an external usability consultant – revised the site in 2002. One of our first steps was to do a usability test of the existing site, both to get baseline data against which we could later compare a revised site and to identify problems to address in revising the site.

Here is the old HHS home page and what we learned from watching and listening as people tried to use it:

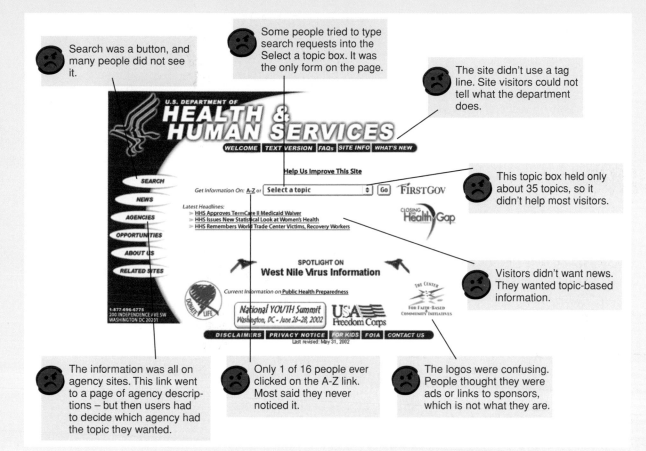

Search was a button, and many people did not see it.

Some people tried to type search requests into the Select a topic box. It was the only form on the page.

The site didn't use a tag line. Site visitors could not tell what the department does.

This topic box held only about 35 topics, so it didn't help most visitors.

Visitors didn't want news. They wanted topic-based information.

The information was all on agency sites. This link went to a page of agency descriptions – but then users had to decide which agency had the topic they wanted.

Only 1 of 16 people ever clicked on the A-Z link. Most said they never noticed it.

The logos were confusing. People thought they were ads or links to sponsors, which is not what they are.

How did the site do on our five functions?

The site failed on all five of the functions we discussed in this chapter:

- **Identifying the site, establishing the brand:** People could name the department from the top of the page, but they had no sense of "brand." They didn't know what topics or agencies were part of HHS.

- **Setting the tone and personality of the site:** The news in the center of the home page made people feel that the site was there to disseminate news, not to help them with information – not the tone or personality the site's owners wanted to project.

- **Helping people get a sense of what the site is all about:** With so little real information on the home page, people could not get a sense of what they would find through the site.

- **Letting people start key tasks immediately:** Most people come to this site to search or to try to find a good path to specific information. Even starting a search proved impossible for most visitors.

- **Sending each person on the right way, effectively and efficiently:** In many situations, our usability test participants gave up after trying to find a way off the home page toward what they were looking for.

What lessons did we learn?

Here are a few of our take-aways that you might find relevant for your site:

- **Unless news stories are your main product, don't make news the central focus of your home page.** People are much more interested in your products and services than in who was just appointed to your staff or what speech your vice president gave last week.

- **Someone has to be in charge to keep the home page (and the rest of the site) focused on your users' needs and your business goals.** Many groups compete for space on the home page for their pet project. Unless someone with authority and a focus on the users' interests is in charge, you may end up with tidbits scattered around the page like the logos on the old HHS site.

- **If you don't have a Search box in an obvious place, users will assume that any open field is the Search box.**

- **Users are topic-focused.** Most do not know, or care, how your organization is structured. They do not want to have to know which division has the information they need; they just want the information.

- **The number of ways to get to information is much less important than how easy those ways are to find and use.** A study that came out while we were doing this project rated the HHS site as very usable because it had many ways of navigating – the A-Z list, the Select a Topic box, the search function, the Agency button. The study was done entirely by counting features, not by watching people work with the site! The site had all these features, but, in fact, people did not notice them or could not use them.

What happened?

After 6 months and several rounds of developing and testing prototypes, HHS launched the new site in October 2002. The overall information architecture and design have held up very well since then. Here is the modified site:

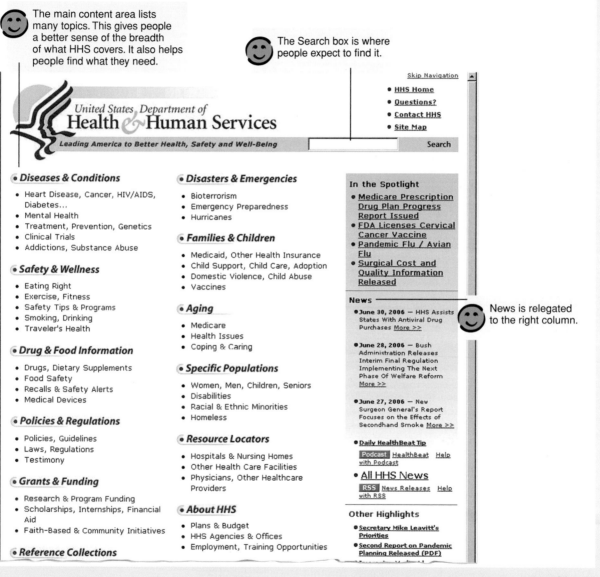

The main content area lists many topics. This gives people a better sense of the breadth of what HHS covers. It also helps people find what they need.

The Search box is where people expect to find it.

News is relegated to the right column.

Did it make a difference?

The new portal allows people to get to what they need much more effectively and efficiently than the old one did. Here are some data points from usability testing:

Success with the new HHS portal site (16 people each doing 12 tasks = 192 attempts)	
Getting off the home page onto a good path	97 percent
Getting off the next menu page still on a good path	87 percent
Completing the scenario successfully	82 percent

See Theofanos, Mulligan, and Redish, 2004, for more on changing the HHS portal site.

Five of the tasks we asked people to do in the usability test of the old site at the beginning of the project and the usability test of the new site at the end of the project were exactly the same. Therefore, we can compare results for those five tasks. (We had 16 participants in each test. The tests were at different times, so the people were different, but they were all recruited by the same group from the same overall pool of people and had similar demographic characteristics.)

Comparing the two sites on the same tasks	
Success using the original home page on five tasks	41 percent
Success using the final home page on the same five tasks	92 percent

Building your site *up* from the content – not only down from the home page

Most web users who come to your site are looking for information that is a few clicks down in the site. If they navigate to the information, they do so by going *down* a path from the home page. But to make those paths – and your home page – work well, you have to build the site the other way, from the information *up* through the pathways to the home page.

To build up from the content, you have to have some sense of the content you have and the content you will need for the site. Do a content inventory/content analysis by listing all the content you now have on the site. You can use a spreadsheet to keep track of the topic, the current URL, who is responsible for that content, and so on. You might also have a column to indicate whether that page should be deleted, revised, or kept as is. You can also add notes about content that needs to be written.

For more on doing a content inventory/content analysis, see www.usability.gov/design/inventory.html.

You can then use card sorting to find out how your web users would organize the content. For a card sorting study, you create a stack of 50 to 60 cards to represent your content with one topic on each card. Representative users sort the cards into groups that are logical to them. In an "open card sort," the users also label the groups they create. That gives you the users' words for your home page. In a "closed card sort," you tell the users the labels you plan to use and they tell you what topics they would look for under each of your labels.

For more on card sorting, see www.usability.gov/design/cardsort.html. Also see Courage and Baxter, 2005, Chapter 10.

You can get help from professional information architects in organizing the content of your web site.

For more on information architecture, see Rosenfeld and Morville, 2006.

SUMMARIZING CHAPTER 3

Here are key messages from Chapter 3:

- Don't expect people to read much on the home page.

- You can make your site's identity and brand obvious with very few words.

- Few people will read long mission statements on your home page.

- You set the tone and personality of your site with your choices of visual style, colors, graphics, typography, writing style, and words.

- A useful home page makes it instantly clear what the site is about.

- A useful home page is mostly links and short descriptions.

- Let people start key tasks right from the home page.

- Make sure forms are visible even on small screens.

- Put the Search box near the top, where people expect it.

- Don't make people fill out forms that they don't want to fill out just to get to the information on your site.

- Send each person on the right way, effectively and efficiently, by using your site visitors' words and by writing clear links.

- Build your site from the bottom up as well as from the top down.

Getting There: Pathway Pages

4

From home pages, let's continue on to thinking about the content for your pathway pages.

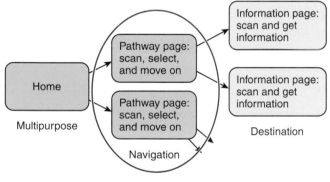

Our focus in this chapter

The key message of this chapter is that your busy site visitors are trying to get to "the good stuff" – to whatever they are looking for – as quickly as possible. They don't want to stop and read on the way. They are still navigating. They aren't "there" yet.

In this chapter, we explore these eight points:

- Most site visitors are on a hunt – a mission – and the pathway is just to get them there.

- People don't want to read a lot while hunting.

- A pathway page is like a table of contents.

- Sometimes, short descriptions help people.

- Marketing is likely to be ignored on a pathway page.

- The smoothness of the path is more important than the number of clicks (within reason).

- Many people choose the first option that looks plausible.

- Many site visitors are landing inside your site.

This chapter is mostly about structuring pathway pages. I touch on how to write links here, but you'll find more about writing links in Chapter 12.

An information page can also be a pathway to related information or more details. We'll consider those pages in the section on layering in Chapter 6.

Most site visitors are on a hunt – a mission – and the pathway is just to get them there

Think of people trying to find the information they are looking for as bloodhounds on a hunt. They try to pick up the "scent" of the information they are looking for and try to follow that "scent of information" to a successful end – the web page that has the information they want.

If a link gives off "good scent," people feel confident that they are on the way to what they want. As Jared Spool shows in his report on *Designing for the Scent of Information,* measuring people's confidence at each page on a pathway is a good way to tell if your links are working well for your web users.

See Spool, Perfetti, and Brittan on the scent of information. www.uie.com.

People don't want to read a lot while hunting

While hunting (foraging) for information, people aren't interested in reading. They are too busy trying to *find* their "food." They are focused on the hunt. It's only when they get to the right place – when the page says "here's the information you came looking for" – that they switch modes from hunting to gathering and are ready to read, to take in the information.

Case Study 4-1 shows that most people want to read very little on pathway pages.

The concept of "scent of information" comes from the work of Pirolli, Card, and their colleagues at Xerox's Palo Alto Research Center (PARC).

The Xerox PARC researchers also talk about people as information foragers – sniffing our way through web sites, hunting for what we need. It's an excellent metaphor for the behavior that we commonly see in usability testing.

Case Study 4-1	What people do on pathway pages

The United States has no national registry for vital records such as birth certificates. To get a copy of your birth certificate, you must find the right office in the state where you were born – although many people do not realize that.

The U. S. government has a portal site that promises to link people to the right place for many needs. In a usability test of that site, we gave people the scenario: "You need a copy of your birth certificate, and a friend said you could get to the right place from this site."

At the time of the test, the portal site was called Firstgov.gov. In 2006, the name changed to USA.gov.

Every one of the 16 people in our usability test found the link they needed easily on the home page. They looked under Online Services for Citizens and clicked on Birth and Marriage Certificates.

That brought up this web page:

What did people do on this page?

Most people clicked on B, often several times. They did this even though they were sophisticated web users and they all knew that gray meant the link was not available. Their need for their birth certificate overwhelmed the message that the gray B was sending.

What could we do to fix this page?

We could greatly improve the page with these three actions:

- Cut the prose drastically.
- Eliminate the alphabet. It just confuses people.
- Think about the essential message of the page. If this is a conversation, what must the page tell the person who comes to it?

What happened?

The people who own this page could have solved the problem in several ways: a map or a drop-down box, for example. But the simplest way was a short instruction and a list of states – and that's what they did.

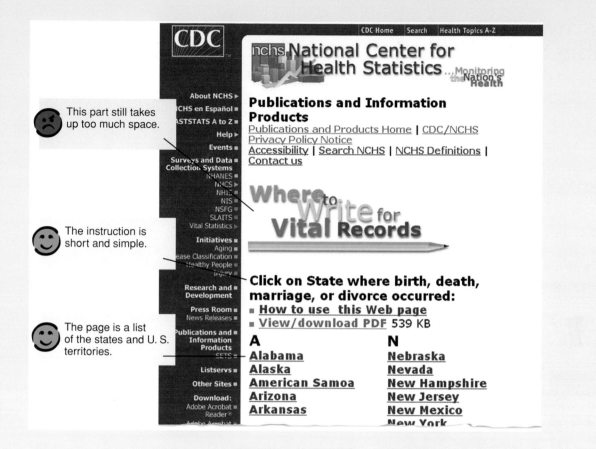

What can we learn from this case study?

Here are a few take-aways that you might find relevant:

- Most people will not read a paragraph of text on a pathway page. They want the page to tell them what to do without having to read.

- Using the letters of the alphabet may work well as the entry to a very long list of topics (like an index), but it does not work well for other uses. (People may not connect the letters to anything other than topics.)

- You are in a conversation with your site visitors. Think of the message that the page must send to keep people on a good pathway.

A pathway page is like a table of contents

You would not expect to see paragraphs of text mixed into a table of contents. You want to scan the table of contents to

- get a quick overview of what's offered
- pick the place that you want to go to

That's exactly what a pathway page is for – whether it is the path to information in a manual or to a section of an e-commerce site.

Figure 4-1, the pathway page for the Kids' section of L.L.Bean.com, shows how you can give site visitors lots of options. On a pathway page such as this, be sure to use your site visitors' words and group the items into categories that make sense to your site visitors.

The next level down in an e-commerce site may need short descriptions. See the next section of this chapter.

Tom Brinck and his co-authors use the term "scope notes" for these descriptions that add "scent" to the link. They also have a very useful table of the different ways that people navigate. See Brinck, Gergle, and Wood, 2002.

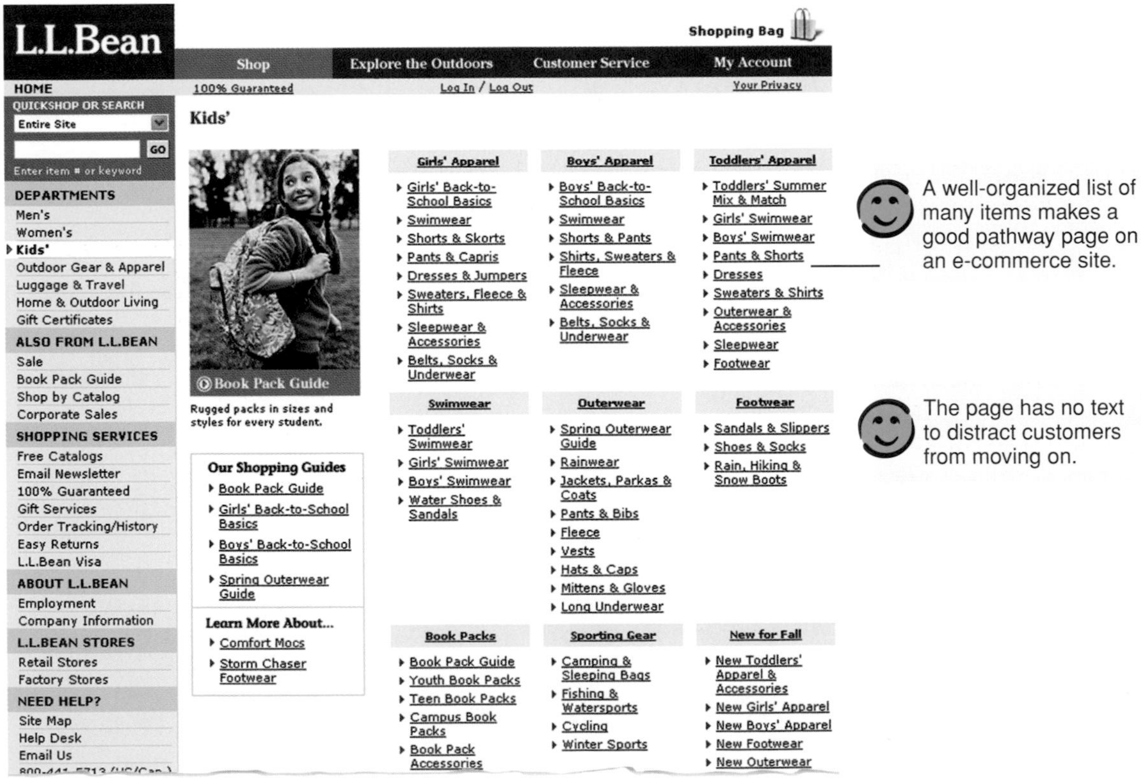

A well-organized list of many items makes a good pathway page on an e-commerce site.

The page has no text to distract customers from moving on.

Figure 4-1 The pathway page helps customers move quickly to what they are looking for – no paragraphs to read and minimal marketing messages.

www.llbean.com

Sometimes, short descriptions help

If the links aren't instantly obvious, a few words of description may help your site visitors find the link they need. Although people don't want to read paragraphs of text or uninformative, welcoming marketing messages on pathway pages, they may want brief help in deciding which link to choose to move toward their goal.

The Coral Cay Conservation organization's page in Figure 4-2 shows how you can use brief, informative descriptions with each link on a pathway page. The descriptions follow the links, and the links stand out on the page. They are not embedded in paragraphs.

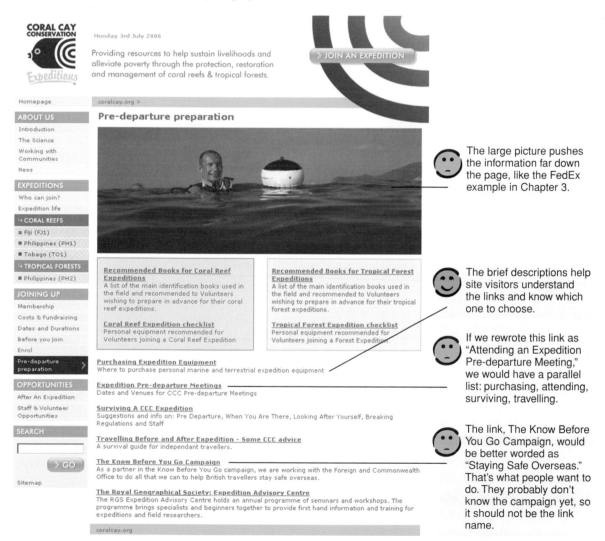

Figure 4-2 The Coral Cay Conservation organization trains volunteers to collect scientific data to aid conservation. Its web site includes several pathway pages with brief descriptions to help site visitors choose the link they need. www.coralcay.org

On e-commerce sites, once people get to the area of the site with the type of product they are interested in, they begin to need some technical information to help them choose which products to consider further. Jared Spool calls this type of page a "gallery." These pages may show a list of items or pictures of the options within the product category. As Spool points out, if it shows only the pictures, it doesn't do enough to help most web users. That can also be true if it lists only the products by model numbers or series names.

See Spool's article at www.uie.com/articles/galleries.

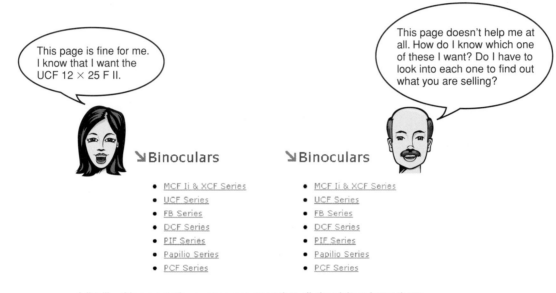

A list like this on a pathway page assumes that all site visitors know these category names and know which one they want.

When you provide information to increase scent on a pathway page, put it in fragments or bullets – not long sentences or paragraphs. Make it useful information that your site visitors will find helpful in deciding how to move ahead. If you write only marketing hype, that's not going to be useful. If you write technical specifications with the pictures, think carefully about whether your site visitors understand the technical language.

Figure 4-3, one of many gallery pages from Dell Computers' web site, has both good features and places where it could be improved. The "help me choose" option leads to a page comparing the three notebook types on several questions. However, Dell might have done more to bring the users' words in those questions onto this gallery page. The information on the page in Figure 4-3 doesn't require a lot of reading, but the words it uses may not mean much to potential buyers.

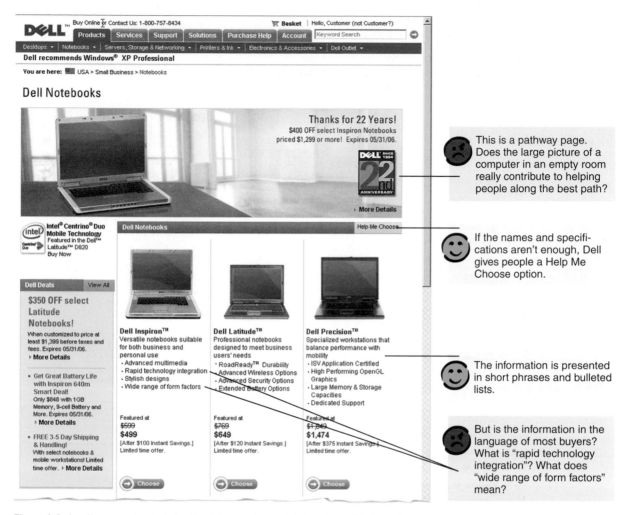

Figure 4-3 A gallery page has to help site visitors make good choices toward their goals.　　www.dell.com

Marketing is likely to be ignored on a pathway page

Short descriptions may help people choose well, but pathway pages are not the time for lengthy marketing messages. You market best when you help your site visitors have successful experiences. Most web users don't want to stop to read even your friendly, welcoming messages while they are still hunting for the page they need.

Consider the pathway page in Figure 4-4. It tells home buyers and home-owners all about the various types of information and help they can get from FannieMae.com.

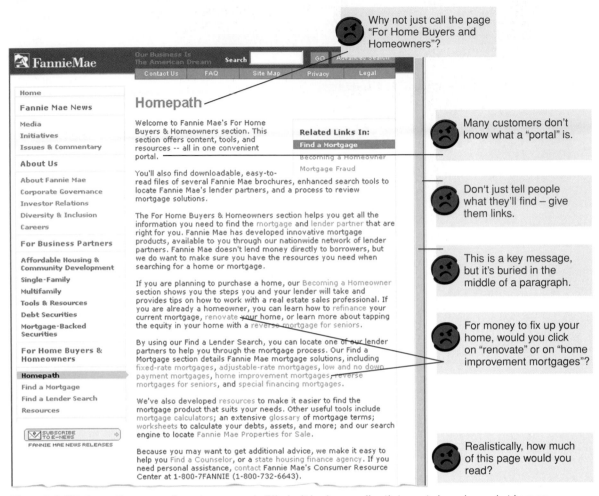

Figure 4-4 This is a pathway page. Its main message is "We don't lend money directly to you to buy a house, but here are many ways we can help you with your mortgage needs."   www.fanniemae.com

Even before getting to the page in Figure 4-4, people have to realize that Homepath is the link they need on the home page. They can't click on For Home Buyers & Homeowners; that's a non-clickable title. "Homepath" is an example of a made-up name that has very little "scent"; it's not likely to mean anything to most people. Site visitors have to guess that it's what they want if they want more information for home buyers and homeowners – and the only reason for that guess is that it's the first link under the more informative title.

If people stay on this pathway page at all, they probably just skim through the links. As with the Aspen Square Hotel home page in Chapter 3, most of the page becomes a blur of words, as in Figure 4-5.

Figure 4-5 What many people see (and want) on a pathway page. There isn't much informative content in the words surrounding the links.

Figure 4-6 might work much better as a pathway page to the information that Fannie Mae has for home buyers and homeowners.

The smoothness of the path is more important than the number of clicks (within reason)

Your site visitors want to get to what they need as quickly as possible. What's the best way to help them do that? Does everything have to be no more than three clicks from the home page?

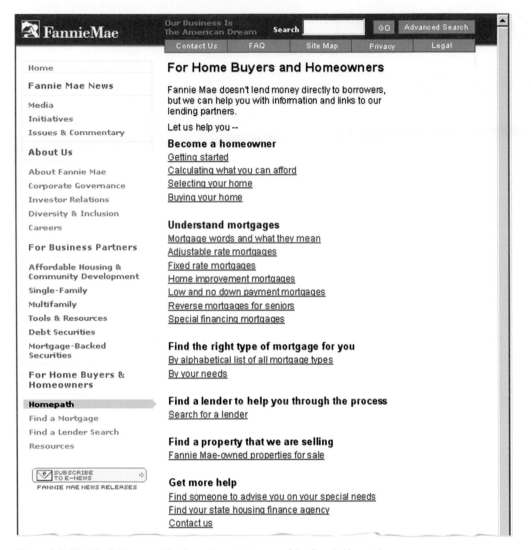

Figure 4-6 What I might suggest for the main content area of the Fannie Mae pathway page.

My answer is "No," and my evidence is watching many hundreds of people work with web sites. The "three click rule" isn't a rule; it's a myth. Three is not a magic number. People will willingly go beyond three clicks if they are confident of the scent of the pathway they are on. In fact, if they are moving steadily on a successful path, they won't realize if it took them four or five clicks rather than three.

A click or two more can indeed make a more successful site. Tom Brinck and his colleagues at Diamond Bullet Design revised a web site through a user-centered design process, taking it from an internal organization focus to a user-task focus. The information on the new site is typically one level deeper – requires one more click – but takes less than half the time to find!

	Old version	New version
Task success	72 percent	95 percent
Average time to complete each task	132 seconds	50 seconds
Number of clicks to get to information: On average, 1 click **more** in new version		

Source: From a study by Tom Brinck and colleagues. www.asis.org/Bulletin/Dec-04.brinck.html.

Don't make people think

People want to get to the right web page quickly *and efficiently.* If they have to stop and think about what to do at each step along the pathway, it's not efficient – nor is it quick. They would rather click one or two more times than have to think along the way.

The wording and the guideline come from Steve Krug's book, *Don't Make Me Think!* (Krug, 2005).

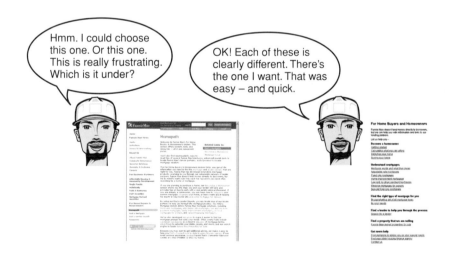

Hmm. I could choose this one. Or this one. This is really frustrating. Which is it under?

OK! Each of these is clearly different. There's the one I want. That was easy – and quick.

Keep people from needing the Back button

If the pathways aren't smooth – if people can't find the right link to move forward easily – they end up hopping part way down one path, back up to try another path, down that one, possibly back up again, and so on. Jared Spool calls this "pogo-sticking" – and both he and I find the people we watch utterly frustrated when they have to do this. If people use the Back button while trying to find information on your site, rethink your pathway pages.

Many people choose the first option that looks plausible

Humans don't act optimally. As Herbert Simon pointed out many years ago, we "satisfice." We trade off time for benefit – often without consciously realizing we are doing it. We make decisions based on what we see, without carefully exploring all the options.

Many busy web users click as soon as they see a link that looks like it might work for what they need. And the younger your web audience is, the more likely they are to jump to act.

Here are some implications of the realization that many people click on the first link they see that might help them:

- Think carefully about the order of information on your pathway pages.
- Put the most important information and links high on the page.
- If you want people to select one link over another, put the one you want them to select first.

 Many web users who listen to the screen also choose the first option they hear that sounds reasonable. Older web users, however, tend to be more cautious clickers, looking over all the options before choosing. If you put the most important information and the links most people want high on the page, you'll be helping all your web users.

Edith, the persona you met in Chapter 2, is an example of an older web user who is a cautious clicker.

For more on older adults as cautious clickers, visit www.aarp.org/olderwiserwired/oww-resources.

Many site visitors are landing inside your site

So far, we've focused on web users who come into your site at the home page and navigate down into the site through your pathway pages to the information they want. Certainly, some of your site visitors do that.

But many web users bypass those pages. In fact, on many web sites, more site visitors come through an external search engine than through the home page. That's a reality. You have to assume that your

Nielsen and Loranger (2006, 27) found that "interior pages accounted for 60 percent of the initial page views."

information pages inside the site are also going to be the starting point for some of your web users.

Yet, I still see many web pages that are dead ends, like the Denver page about schedules for street sweeping in Figure 4-7.

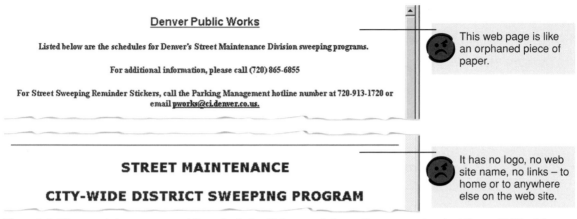

Figure 4-7 When people have no sense of the web site to which a page belongs, they may wonder about the credibility of the page and of the entire site. All pages should share the web site's global features.

Pages like this give people no clue as to what site they are on, where in that site they are, or how to get to the home page or to anywhere else in the site. Sites with pages like these are losing great opportunities to share all the other wonderful information or products they have with site visitors who come directly from an external search engine.

Every page in a site should have

- the site's logo, name, and tag line (the consistent masthead at the top of the page)
- the site's Search box
- the site's global navigation (assuming it has tabs or other ways of indicating the major sections of the site)
- links to relevant information within the same part of the site – and elsewhere on the site
- a clear link to the home page, making it obvious what "home" that is

It's fine to make the logo and site name at the top active as links to the home page; many experienced web users expect that. However, that's not enough. You also need a link that says "home" for those who don't know to click on the logo or name. That can be either a text link or a tab, depending on how you set up your site's global navigation.

If your part of the site is a subsite of a subsite, you may have several home pages going back up a pathway to the main home page. If so, label every "home" link clearly. I've watched usability test participants feel completely lost when a click on "home" takes them to a different home page than the one they expected.

Pages inside a site that have no connection to the rest of the site expose rifts within the organization to the outside world. They send the message that the people doing this part of the site don't feel that they have to cooperate with the larger community of the organization. They indicate that no one is managing the larger organization's site with enough clout to bring everyone together. The web content owner – and the organization – and the site visitors – all lose out on the value the web brings of connecting content in one place to relevant content elsewhere on the web site.

SUMMARIZING CHAPTER 4

Here are key messages from Chapter 4:

- Most site visitors are on a hunt – a mission – and the pathway is just to get them there.

- People don't want to read a lot while hunting.

- A pathway page is like a table of contents.

- Sometimes, short descriptions help.

- Marketing is likely to be ignored on a pathway page.

- The smoothness of the path is more important than the number of clicks (within reason).
  - Don't make people think.
  - Keep people from needing the Back button.

- Many people choose the first option that looks plausible.
  - Think carefully about the order of information on pathway pages.
  - Put the most important information and links high on the page.
  - If you want people to select one link over another, put the one you want them to select first.

- Many site visitors are landing inside your site.
  - Don't let your pages be dead ends.
  - Provide links for site visitors to get elsewhere in the site – home, other major sections, and other relevant content.

Writing
Information,
Not Documents

5

In this chapter, we tackle three important issues:

- Breaking up large documents
- Deciding how much to put on one web page
- PDF – yes or no?

All three issues relate to helping people get just what they need, when they need it, in the amount they need, as quickly as possible.

Right information at the right time in the right amount.

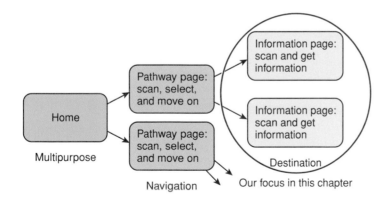

Breaking up large documents

Most people come to the web for information, not for a complete document. They don't want the user manual; they want instructions for the task they are doing. They don't want the handbook; they want the answer to specific questions. They want usable, manageable pieces.

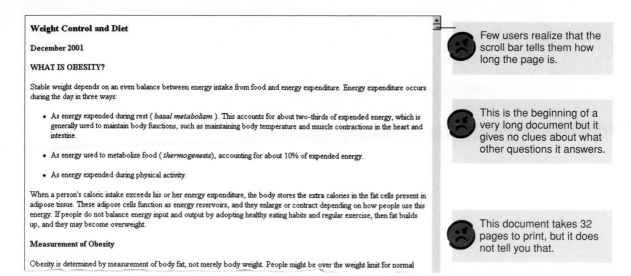

Figure 5-1 A very long document does not work well on the web.   www.reutershealth.com/wellconnected/doc53.html

 What would you do if you were looking for information on obesity and you came across the web document in Figure 5-1? Would you print it out even though it does not tell you how many pages it will take to print it? Would you read it all online, scrolling or paging down many, many times? Or would you decide to go elsewhere for your information, hoping to find something that gave you more clues up front about what topics about obesity it covers?

To present content on the web in the amount that most people want:

- Think "topic," not "book."
- Break large documents into topics and subtopics.

Think "topic," not "book"

Imagine that you've just bought a new cell phone. You open the box and see a stack of index cards in the box with the phone. Each card tells you how to do one task with the phone: set the time and date, choose the ring tone, put a number into memory, and so on.

How would you feel about getting this information on index cards? What would you do with the cards?

You might never open the plastic wrap around the stack of cards because then it would be hard to keep them together. You'd probably worry about losing them or about how messy they would be in your office, your kitchen, or your briefcase.

Books make sense in the world of paper. If each topic were on a separate card, the cards would get lost. On the web, a separate page for each topic makes more sense than a book of many topics.

In the world of paper, a book is more comfortable than a stack of index cards. You know what to do with the book: you put it on an office shelf or in a kitchen drawer or in your briefcase. In the paper world, you need the book so all the pieces don't get lost.

 But when would you ever go to the book? Wouldn't it most likely be to look up just one of the topics in the book? How much of the book would you want to look at? Wouldn't it be just one topic?

Online, we don't need the book. A better model for content on the web is a database with a good search engine and good navigation.

If people come to your site to get information on specific topics, give them those specific topics as separate web pages – not all together in a book or long document.

Figure 5-2 shows how Nokia has broken a user manual into a series of "index cards" on different tasks. Note how Nokia has also taken advantage of the interactivity possible on the web. Each task is not only a separate topic on a separate web page, it is also an animated

Setting the Alarm Clock

The alarm clock feature is based on your phone's internal clock and sounds an alert at a time you specify. Total steps = 4. Click each step below.

Tip: When entering shortcuts on your Nokia phone, press the keys in a quick and timely fashion.

Step 1: Press the Navi key labeled *Menu* and press 7 1. *Set alarm time:* prompt appears.

Step 2: Enter the alarm time. Use two digits for both hours and minutes. Enter 10:30.

Note: The *Clear* key does not work on this screen. If you make a mistake, re-enter all four digits.

Step 3: Press the Navi key labeled *OK.* The *am* and *pm* options appear.

Step 4: Select *am or pm* and press the Navi key labeled *OK.* Select *am* and press *OK.* The alarm is on.

Each task is presented on its own page.

You can read it quickly or click the links and watch it happen.

Each link is a step in an interactive demo that the user controls.

Figure 5-2 Nokia makes good use of the web with interactive "index cards" for each task.

www.nokiausa.com/support/phones

demonstration. You can grab the information quickly by reading, or you can watch what to do by clicking each step in turn.

Break web content into topics and subtopics

Consider breaking up your web content by

- time or sequence
- task
- people
- type of information
- questions people ask

Divide web content by time or sequence

In many situations, time or sequence is a good way to organize information: something happens first, then something else, and so on. Figure 5-3, from Bank of America, shows a pathway page to a series of short articles on

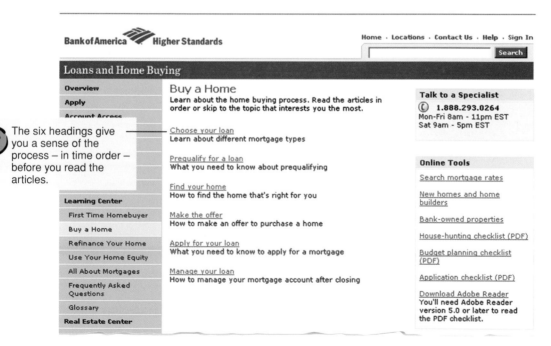

Figure 5-3 Organizing information in a time sequence is often the logical way to break a large topic into useful pieces.

http://www.bankofamerica.com/loansandhomes

buying a home. Just scanning down the article titles (the links) gives prospective home buyers a sense of the tasks involved and the sequence they come in.

Divide web content by task

When you are putting task-based information on a web site, realize that, in almost all cases, a site visitor is looking for information on only one of what may be many tasks that your product lets users do.

Breaking up task-based information into a single web page for each task is the best way to help web users get just the content they need. Of course, you also need a good search engine and a good navigation structure to allow your site visitors to quickly find the right web page.

Figures 5-4 and 5-5, from the Canadian version of Intuit's QuickBooks, show how some companies are breaking up their online manuals into a database of separate articles on different tasks. The first screen invites you to search by keywords, start down a navigation path, or choose one

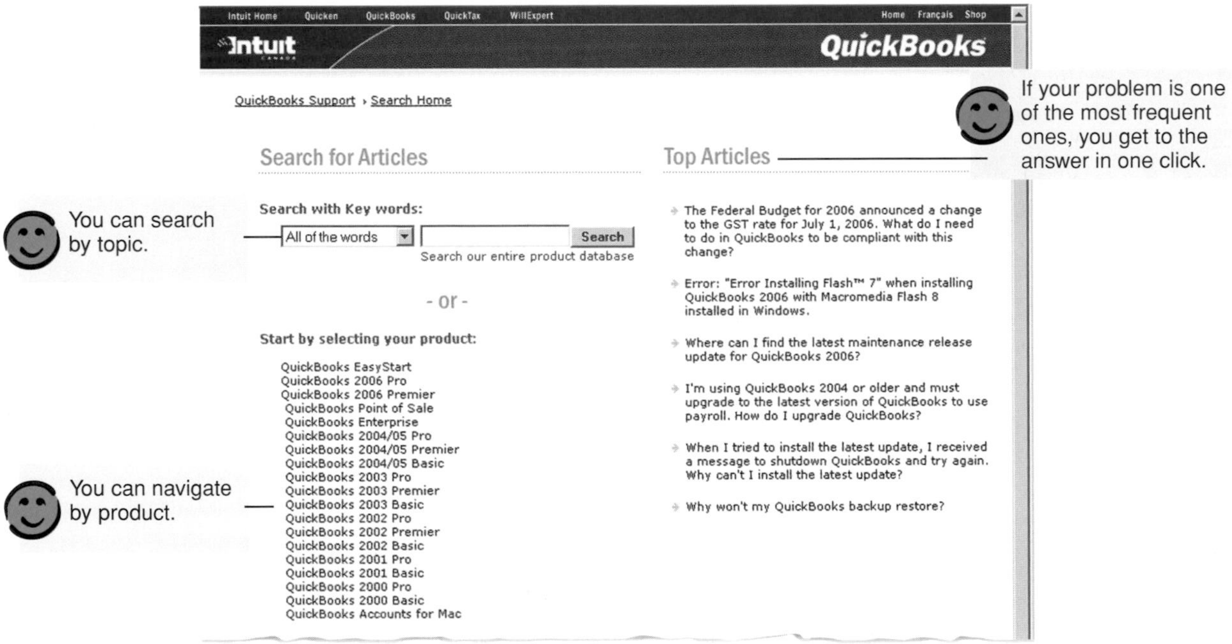

Figure 5-4 A database of articles with good search and navigation is a good model for the web.

http://knowledgebase.quickbooks.ca

If this is your question, you get the answer without having to read extra information.

Figure 5-5 Each article is like a separate "index card" of information.   http://knowledgebase.quickbooks.ca

of the most frequently asked questions. When you get to the information pages, you get just the article on your specific need.

Divide web content by people

Another useful way to break up your web content is to consider who is going to use the information.

Separating information for different site visitors may work well at many levels within a site. The Nokia and Intuit examples earlier in this chapter ask people to self-identify by the product for which they want help. That's typical of support and troubleshooting information on sites that support many products.

On some web sites, information for different people is totally separate and the site helps people self-identify right on the home page. Figure 5-6, from The Pension Service in the U. K., shows how one site helps its web users start down paths that are relevant to their different needs.

Breaking up information by user types works, however, only if people will be able to quickly and clearly self-identify into the right group. If they have to stop and think about which link to choose – or if they are likely to start down a wrong path – dividing the information by user type may be more frustrating than helpful.

Consider also whether some people will feel excluded if you divide infor-mation by user type. They may feel excluded if they do not see them-

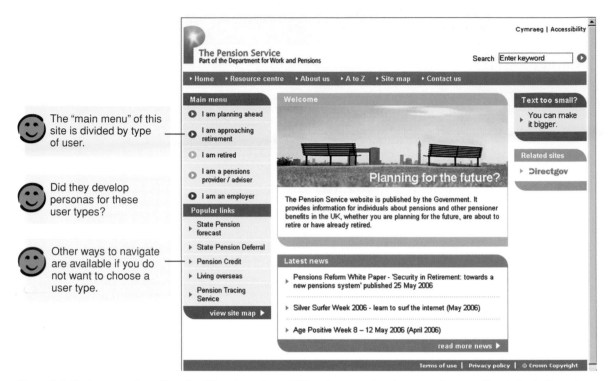

The "main menu" of this site is divided by type of user.

Did they develop personas for these user types?

Other ways to navigate are available if you do not want to choose a user type.

Figure 5-6 Having separate sections for different user types (different personas) makes sense for some sites, but only if people will easily identify which user type to choose.   www.thepensionservice.gov.uk

selves in any of your user types. Even if they find a relevant user type, they may think you are excluding them from information they may want because that information is under a different user type.

If people are likely to want information you have under different user types, make it clear and easy for them to move between different versions or different levels of related information. For example, Figure 5-7 shows how the U. S. National Cancer Institute (NCI) lets people move easily between articles written for the general public and articles on the same topic in more technical detail and more technical language aimed at health care professionals.

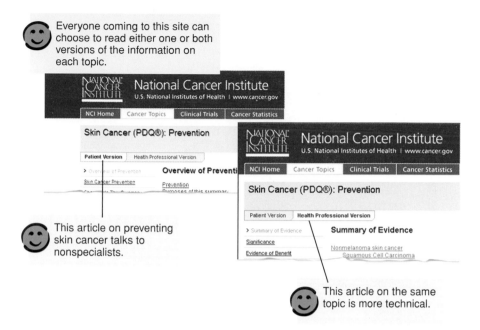

Figure 5-7 Separating information into general and technical articles may work well. If some site visitors want both, make it obvious how to move from one to the other.   www.cancer.gov

The NCI folks learned in usability testing that patients and their families liked starting with the general information in lay language, but they also wanted access to the more technical information when they felt ready for it.

Divide web content by type of information

"How do I . . . ?" defines one big set of questions people come to web sites to ask. "How do I . . . ?" questions are about tasks or procedures. People want the information as step-by-step instructions.

"Can I . . . ?" "May I . . . ?" "Must I . . . ?" "Why should I . . . ?" and "What do I need to know about . . . ?" define another big set of questions. These questions are about rules, policies, concepts, and facts. People want the information as questions and answers or clear chunks of facts with good headings.

"How do I . . . ?" questions are different from "Can I . . . ?" questions, which usually relate to company policies.

In many cases, you have both "can I" and "how to" information about the same topic. You have policies and procedures. Your site visitors may know the "can I" and need the "how to." They may know the "how to" and need the "can I" for a specific situation. Answer the different types of questions on separate, linked pages or on separate sections of the same page.

Figures 5-8 and 5-9 show how the University of Otago in Dunedin, New Zealand, has separate, but linked, pages on facts about enrolling (entrance requirements) and the process of enrolling.

For user manuals and other large documents, many technical writing groups are breaking up their information, using the Darwin Information Typing Architecture (DITA). For more on DITA, see http://www-128. ibm.com/developerworks/ xml/library/x-dita1.

Figure 5-8 Information that answers the question "Am I eligible?" is separate from, and linked to, information on "How do I enroll?"   www.otago.ac.nz/study/entrance.html

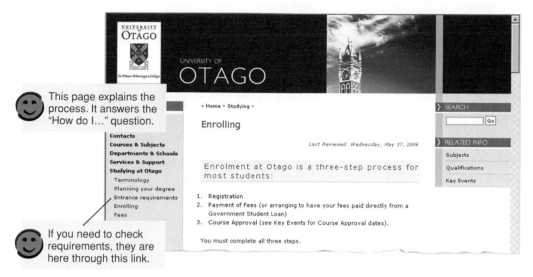

Figure 5-9 Separate, linked pages are a good way to organize related web content while keeping each web page short and succinct.   www.otago.ac.nz/study/enrolling.htm

Divide web content by questions people ask

People come to web sites with questions, so using questions and answers may help people find what they need.

As you write questions, match the way that people would ask the question. You want to help them quickly recognize the question as the place to get the information they need. In fact, an advantage of using questions is that if users come with only a vague sense of what they want, they may recognize a question even if they had not thought of those specific words.

Caroline Jarrett suggests that too often FAQs (frequently asked questions) on web sites are really EAQs (easily answered questions).

Be sure that the questions you include are the ones that your site visitors come with - not just the ones you want to answer.

Writing good questions comes up again in more detail in Chapter 10 on headings.

Figure 5-10, from Briggs and Stratton, a company that sells engines and other machinery, shows how one company organizes its customer support by topic, product, and questions.

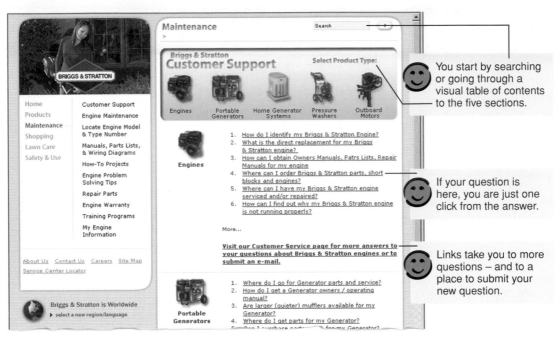

Figure 5-10 Databases of questions organized by users' topics are a useful part of many web sites.
www.briggsandstratton.com

Deciding how much to put on one web page

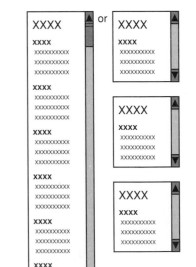

We've been looking at how to break your web content into pieces – by time or sequence, by task, by people, by type of information, and by the different questions that people ask. Once you have the pieces, you have to decide how many topics, articles, questions, or pieces of information to put together on one web page.

One page or separate pages? When faced with that decision, ask yourself these questions:

- How much do people want in one visit? How connected is the information?
- Am I overloading my site visitors? How long is the web page?
- What's the download time?
- Will people want to print? How much will they want to print?

How much do people want in one visit?
How connected is the information?

I see many web pages where topics are stacked together on one web page when they are answers to different questions that different people ask at different times. The topics fit together from the organization's point of view, but the web user wants only one when visiting the site.

For example, you can see in Figure 5-11 that Dymocks, an Australian bookseller, has all of its customer service information in one file – one long web page. Whether you are looking for the company's privacy policy, how to use its shopping basket, or whether you can return an item, you go to the same page. I've been in the Dymocks store in Sydney many times; it's a wonderful bookshop. But this part of the web site doesn't match most web users' needs.

A page like this is built for the scenario, "Mario wants to read all of our customer support policies and procedures at one time." That scenario doesn't seem likely. It's much more likely that site visitors will start conversations like the following with the site.

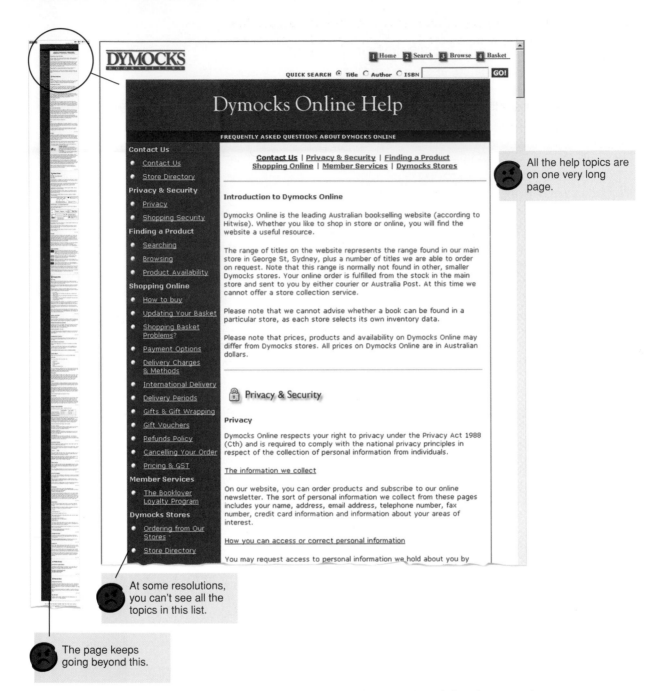

All the help topics are on one very long page.

At some resolutions, you can't see all the topics in this list.

The page keeps going beyond this.

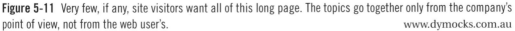

Figure 5-11 Very few, if any, site visitors want all of this long page. The topics go together only from the company's point of view, not from the web user's.   www.dymocks.com.au

These site visitors each want only the answer to the one question they are asking. They don't want to have to wade through other information to get to what they want.

From the web user's point of view, a more useful design would be a pathway page with topics each leading to a much shorter page that covers just that topic – the way it is done by Powell's of Portland, Oregon (Figure 5-12).

In this web site, visitors choose the help topic they need from a pathway page.

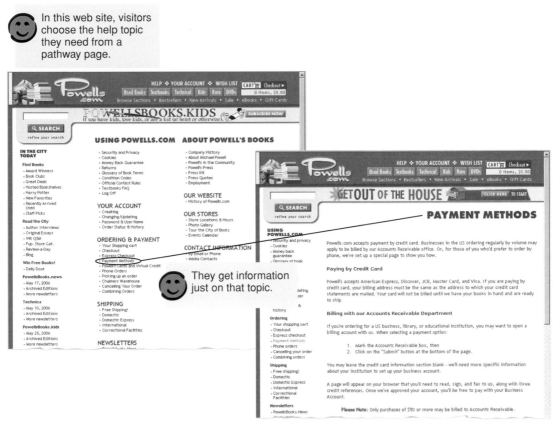

Figure 5-12 If each topic answers a different need, giving each topic its own page makes sense for web users.

www.powells.com

Am I overloading my site visitors?
How long is the web page?

We've just seen when you should break up web pages that cover many different topics. A web page on one topic can also be too long. Consider again the example at the beginning of this chapter: the 32-page document on Weight Control and Diet. That's just too much for any person to absorb at once.

Most people today do scroll vertically if the page layout indicates that the page continues. But they won't scroll forever. Think of three or four scrolls' worth as a maximum length for a web page.

To break up longer pages, use the guidelines earlier in this chapter to find a good way to group and divide the information into subtopics. That way, you can make a series of pages with a table of contents on a previous (pathway) page.

What's the download time?

A third consideration in deciding between putting information together on one web page or separating it onto separate web pages is how long it will take for your site visitors to get what they need. Remember that many people still have slow connections and pay by the minute.

People are going to be annoyed if they wait a long time for a page that has much more than they need. On the other hand, if you break up the information onto many small pages and your visitors want all those pages, waiting for each one to load may be annoying. And the time between pages may interrupt their putting the information together in their heads.

So you have to think about the issue of download time together with the issues of how much of the information people want and how connected it is in their minds.

Will people want to print? How much will they want to print?

And the fourth question to think about in deciding between one page or separate pages is what people might want to print.

- If people want just one section and have to print pages and pages to get it, they waste toner, paper, and time. That's frustrating.

- If the document is broken into pieces that are so small that people have to print several web pages in succession to get what they need, that's also frustrating. They waste paper and time, if not toner – and it takes many clicks to finish the task.

So you have to consider how much people want in any particular visit to your web site.

If you have some people who want to print only a little, some who want to print more, and some who want to print an entire document, offer

Make sure that your pages print well.

Always include a way for people to print the content without losing the end of each line of text.

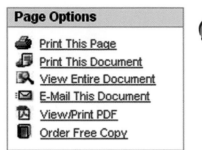

You can let people choose how much to print.

Figure 5-13 This web site, where sections of a document are separate web pages, offers people three printing options (as well as other options). www.cancer.gov/cancertopics/chemotherapy-and-you

options. Figure 5-13 shows how the U. S. National Cancer Institute makes some of its content available.

PDF – yes or no?

You probably already know this, but just in case . . . PDF stands for portable document format. PDF was invented by Adobe Systems, Inc. (www.adobe.com), as a way to publish documents that anyone can read, regardless of whether they are working in the same operating system or using the same software that the document's creator worked in.

A PDF file keeps the layout, page breaks, and fonts of the original document. With PDF, you can have a document that looks the same whether you send a paper copy to someone or that person prints it from the web.

Anyone who has Adobe Acrobat Reader on a computer can open, read, and print the document. Most new computers today come with Acrobat Reader already installed, and Adobe allows free downloads of Acrobat Reader from its web site. Anyone who is comfortable downloading and installing software can have a copy.

Should you rely on PDF files for your web content?

I'm not going to say, "Never put up a PDF file." As always, it comes down to your goals, your audiences, and their scenarios.

However, realize that, with most PDF files, you are providing a paper document on the web rather than web-based information. If the document looks like a paper document or if it is large, people are likely to print it rather than read it on the screen. You have distributed the document; you have saved the printing and shipping cost; you have shifted the cost and effort of printing to your audiences — but have you really met their needs?

When might a PDF file be appropriate?

If you are using the web to distribute journal articles or other material that you expect people to print and use on paper, and if your audiences are comfortable with PDF files, PDF may be the right way to go.

The web is a great distribution mechanism:

- Many people are now more comfortable going to a search engine than trudging down to the library.

- You can get the PDF whenever you want (no need to know when the library is open; no need to work only in the daytime).

- A search engine may find what you want from a few keywords (no need to understand the way the library organizes the journals; no need to go hunting through the stacks; no worries that someone else will have already taken the article).

- You can send the link to colleagues or get the document instantly because someone sent the link to you.

- You can have and give access to the documents to people who might not live near a library or who are in countries where mail delivery is slow or unreliable.

Distribution is the great advantage that the Internet has over paper, even for paper documents.

When is a PDF file not appropriate?

However, PDF documents are often not the best way to create a useful and usable web site. Break documents into non-PDF pieces —

- when people don't want the whole document

- when people want to read from the screen

- when your audiences are not comfortable with PDF files or with downloading software

- when accessibility is an issue — and you should always consider accessibility

When people don't want the whole document

If people come to your web site for information – not for documents as a whole, but for only some of the information in those documents – a PDF file defeats the very purpose and nature of the web.

Yes, PDF files are searchable. But people don't want to first navigate or search to get the document and then search again within the document. They want to navigate or search directly to the specific information that they want. And many people don't know how to search in a PDF document.

And yes, you can divide up a PDF document and give it a linked table of contents so that people who know how to open the index list can jump to a specific place in the document – but only if you have set it up well. Most PDF files are just put up on the web, with no attention to internal links.

A story: I was getting information from the web site of a government agency when I reached a point where I needed the physical address of one of the agency's regional offices. A link on the page said it would take me to a list of the regional offices. What would you have expected to happen by clicking that link? I expected a single page with a list of offices. To my surprise, Acrobat started to open. I waited, as one must, and a document opened that had nothing at all to do with regional offices. It was a report on something totally different from the topic I was getting information about. My first thought was "wrong link," but curiosity led me to at least look quickly through the document. Sure enough, an appendix 20 pages later was the list of regional offices I needed.

That's not a good use of PDF. If the link promises a list of offices, take the page out of the paper document and make it a separate (not PDF) web page.

When people want to read from the screen

Why make the document look just like paper if it is not meant to be used on paper?

For example, a two-column layout works very well on paper. It doesn't work well on the web if you can't see the entire page without scrolling. On the screen, people have to scroll down while reading only halfway across the screen and then scroll up again to read the second column.

A document like the U. S. Department of Agriculture Issue Brief in Figure 5-14 just begs to be printed and read off-line.

Figure 5-14 A two-column PDF document does not work well if readers have to scroll to read the columns.

When your audiences are not comfortable with PDF files or with downloading software

If you have a public audience, don't assume that a PDF file is acceptable. Not everyone has Acrobat Reader. Not everyone is willing or able to download and install software even if it is free.

In usability testing that I did in 2004 on information about cancer, more than half of the public participants – cancer patients and their family members – were unwilling to select the PDF option. They said they saw the PDF symbol all the time, but they didn't know what it was and never chose it. They had never downloaded programs onto their computers, and they were leery of doing so.

Even people who have computers that come with Acrobat Reader may be uncomfortable going to PDF files. For people with dial-up access or slow machines, a PDF file may take a long time to open.

PDF files often open in a second window, and second windows cause problems for many people. They want to back out of the file that came up, but Back isn't available – and they don't realize that they now have two browser windows open.

When accessibility is an issue

For many years, PDF files did not work well for people who use assistive software, such as screen-readers. That has changed. Adobe Acrobat 8.0 supports tagging so that accessibility software can read a PDF file. But . . .

- For Acrobat to work well with a screen-reader, the author has to set up the file well with correctly marked headings, appropriate tags for images, and other elements that the screen-readers need. Most PDFs aren't well set up.

- If you scan a document as a graphic file to get it on the web, even Acrobat 8.0 can't tell what to do with it to make it accessible.

- Many people who use assistive software still bypass PDF files. Experience has taught them that PDF files are not accessible. Even though PDF files can now be made accessible, so few are that people have no reason to change their negative expectations.

- Many people (not only those who use screen-readers) do not update software regularly, even if it is free. It takes time and effort to upgrade. People may be afraid that the upgrade will not work well with something else on their machine. They may not want to take the time to learn new features. They may need authorization from a supervisor or another group in the company to upgrade.

Three more reasons for not using PDFs

PDFs are not the best way to provide information on your web site for at least three more reasons:

- PDF files are optimized for the printed page.
- Acrobat Reader works differently from browsers.
- Most PDF files are not written in web style.

PDF files are optimized for the printed page

A typical PDF page is in portrait orientation. Most web users are looking at landscape-oriented screens.

Acrobat Reader works differently from browsers

Users have to learn yet another way of navigating, another way of printing, another way of searching.

Internet Explorer controls

Acrobat Reader controls

As a web content specialist or a web developer, you may be comfortable going back and forth among different browsers, even though that means changing where and what you click on. Are the people you are writing to all equally comfortable doing that?

PDF files are usually paper documents – not written in web style

Paper   Web
book   topics

If the author was in "paper mode" – in "document mode" or "book mode" – when writing what becomes the PDF file, it's very likely that the writing isn't going to work well on the web. The paragraphs will be too long. The headings will be too sparse. The author will have probably assumed that people coming to the document will read it from first page to last.

In some cases, offer both versions

If some site visitors want information on the screen and others want entire documents, offer both. Many sites do.

When you link to a PDF, tell people that's what they are getting and how large it is or how long it will take to download.

Figure 5-15 shows you how employees at the U. S. Federal Aviation Administration can choose to download a PDF of their entire web content standards or get an HTML page on specific topics in the standards.

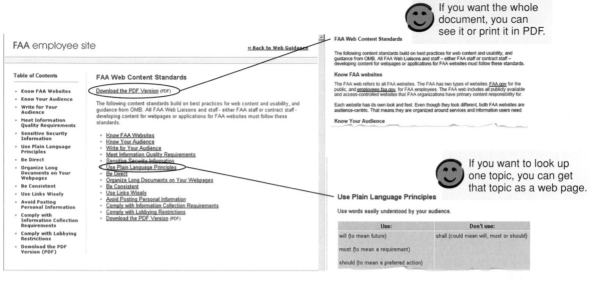

Figure 5-15 This intranet site offers the whole document as a PDF and also offers each topic as a separate web page.

SUMMARIZING CHAPTER 5

Here are key messages from Chapter 5:

- Break up large documents.

- Think "topics," not "book."

- Divide web content by
  - time or sequence
  - task
  - people
  - type of information
  - questions people ask

- Decide how much to put on one web page by considering
  - how much people want in one visit
  - how connected the information is
  - how long the web page is
  - the download time
  - whether people will want to print
  - how much they will want to print

- Think carefully about using PDF files for your web content.

- PDF is more of a distribution mechanism for paper documents than a good way of giving web content.

- PDFs are appropriate in some situations.

- But consider not using PDFs when
  - people do not want the whole document
  - people want to read from the screen
  - your web users are not comfortable with PDF files or with downloading software
  - accessibility is an issue

- In some cases, the best solution is to offer both PDF and HTML versions of your web information.

Focusing on Your Essential Messages

6

In Chapters 3 and 4, we looked at home pages and pathway pages – at "getting to the information." In Chapter 5, we started on information pages by considering how to break up documents and large blocks of information into separate web pages. In this chapter, we'll talk about what to put into each of those information pages.

First, let's expand our picture of how people get to your information pages. The top line in this new picture is the one we focused on as we discussed home pages and pathway pages. The other lines bring in the realities of other ways people reach your information pages, whether you are blogging or writing content deep within a site.

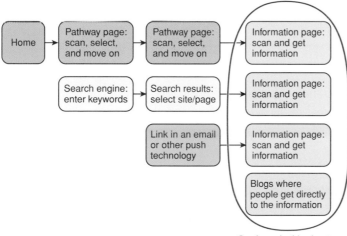

Our focus in this chapter

What do *you* do when you get to information pages? Do you immediately start to read it all or do you first skim and scan?

Most people don't jump right in and read. They skim and scan, even on information pages. They are deciding:

- Did I get where I thought I was going?
- Is what I'm looking for on this page?

They look at the page title, and they look for headings and key words in the text.

For users to know they've gotten where they want to go, links and page titles must match. We'll talk about that in Chapter 12, which is all about links.

Six guidelines for focusing on your essential messages

When they decide they are on the right page, most web users want to focus immediately on the information they came to get. The rest of this chapter gives you six guidelines to help busy web users get what they need.

1. Give people only what *they* need.
2. Cut! Cut! Cut! And cut again!
3. Start with the key point. Write in inverted pyramid style.
4. Break down walls of words.
5. Market by giving useful information.
6. Layer for different needs.

You'll see lots of examples of good headings in web writing throughout the book, and Chapter 10 is all about writing useful headings.

1. Give people only what *they* need

A good mantra for the web is **less is more.**

What do your site visitors want to know? Need to know?

- Do they really care about the entire history of your project? Probably not.
- Do they care about the detailed legal reference for your right to ask them for information? Probably not.
- Do they want to hear how much you welcome them before you show them what you have to offer at what price? Probably not.

That content may be important to *you,* but if it isn't important to your site visitors, drop it entirely, put it at the bottom of the page, or layer it with a link to another page.

How do you know what people need to know? How do you know what counts as an essential message?

One good way is to use the process in Checklist 6-1.

**Checklist 6-1
Process for Selecting Web Content**

1   If you already have a draft or a previous web page, put it aside. (I know this is difficult, but it is the best way to rethink a web page.)

2   Think about the topic from your site visitors' point of view.

3   List the questions that your site visitors ask about the topic. (It's best if you actually know what questions they ask. Use all the sources in Chapter 2 to find out about what your users want to know.)

4   Decide which question your site visitors would ask first – and which they would ask next – and next after that – until you have all the questions in an order that is logical to your site visitors.

5   If you have a draft or previous web page, use it as source material to answer the questions you have written down. (It's okay to cut and paste as long as you edit what you paste so that it's a good answer to the question.)

   If you do not have a draft or previous web page, write answers to the questions in your list. Just answer the question. Don't add fluff.

6   If you are working from a draft or previous web page, look over what is left that hasn't yet gone under a question in your list. Do your site visitors care about any of what is left? Is any of it critical for your site visitors to know? If it is critical, write a question that your site visitors might ask so that you can give them the answer.

7   If you have questions in your list for which you do not have an answer, find the person who can answer the question and include the answer on your web page.

8   Read your new draft. Does it flow logically?

9   Discard what you have not used. If your site visitors neither need nor care about the information, why include it on the web page? This may be the most difficult step to take, but remember that the web is about what people want and need to know, not about saying everything there is to say on a topic.

Case Study 6-1 shows how we might apply this process to create a web page inviting people to participate in an art contest.

Case Study 6-1	Using users' questions to plan a web page

Think like a site visitor: If you saw a link about entering an art contest, what would you expect to find on the page the link takes you to?

> ### International Aviation Art Contest
> "Create an Air Show Poster" is the theme of this year's contest for children ages 6 to 17. Enter now.

Think about the conversations site visitors would want to start about this topic.

Thinking of people's questions is a great way to analyze web content even if you do not end up using the question-and-answer format in writing your web pages.

Continuing in this mode, you might end up with these questions, in this order:

- Who can enter?
- What is the deadline?
- What are the prizes?
- What is the theme?
- What types of art are acceptable?
- What will the judges look for?
- Where do I send my entry?

The answers would make a good web page about the contest. It might look like this:

International Aviation Art Contest

This year's theme: Create An Air Show Poster

Who can enter?
All children from age 6 to age 17 may participate. The child's age on December 31, 2004 is what counts.

What is the deadline?
Entries must be postmarked by **January 10, 2005**.

What prizes are there?
Entries will be divided into three age groups:
6 to 9 years; 10 to 13 years; 14 to 17 years.

The contest starts on the state level.

State prizes
Winners and runners up in each state get a certificate and recognition from their state. The top three entries in each age group from each state go on to the national competition.

National prizes
Judges will pick a national winner and two runners up in each age group. They all get certificates, ribbons, and a framed photograph of their artwork — and their work will be sent on to the international competition. The first place national winners also get a professional work of art from the American Society of Aviation Artists.

International prizes
Winners in the international competition get certificates and gold, silver, or bronze medals.

What types of poster are acceptable?
- Size should be 11 inches by 17 inches.
- **8½ by 11 is not acceptable because of international rules.**
- All artwork must be hand made by the child.

Acceptable media	NOT acceptable media
watercolor	pencil
acrylic or oil paints	charcoal
indelible markers	other non-permanent media
colored pencils	computer generated work
felt-tip pens	collage work involving the use of photocopies
soft ball-point pens	
indelible ink	
Crayola or similar indelible media	

What will the judges look for?
The judges will look for creative use of the theme in relation to aviation.

Who must certify that the child made the poster?
A parent, guardian, or art teacher must certify that the entire artwork is the original work of the child.

Make sure the certificate is fastened to the poster with tape or glue. Also, **please print the name of the artist on the back of the poster and please print legibly**.

Where do we send the poster?
Get the Entry Form for the 2005 International Aviation Art Contest.

When it is ready, send the poster with the appropriate paperwork to your state's sponsor office.

My version; adapted from the facts of the actual art contest

2. Cut! Cut! Cut! And cut again!

Remember that most web users don't want to read much. They want to grab information. The key to successful writing on the web is to let go of the words without losing the essential messages.

Use the process in Checklist 6-2.

Checklist 6-2
Process for Cutting Down to Essential Messages

1   Go through the steps in Checklist 6-1, Process for Selecting Web Content.

2   If you are writing questions and answers, consider whether you have written the shortest, clearest questions and the shortest, clearest answers. If you are writing in another style, consider how well your essential messages stand out on the web page.

3   Focus on the facts. Cut the flab.

4   Focus on your site visitors and what they want to know. Cut out words that talk about you or the organization – unless your site visitors want or need that information.

5   Put your new draft away for a day or two. Then, take it out and see if you can cut some more without losing your essential messages.

6   Read it out loud. Ask a colleague to read it out loud. Ask a few representative people from your audiences to read it out loud. Listen carefully and revise based on what you hear.

Consider Figure 6-1, the web page about a new PlayStation 2 model.
Does the typical potential buyer of this gaming device want to read
these paragraphs of text?

Figure 6-1 This page, labeled "Description," seems to be trying to get people excited about buying the product. Yet it gives people two long paragraphs to read.   www.us.playstation.com

If we let go of many of the words in the description in Figure 6-1, we might end up with Figure 6-2. Doesn't this make the essential messages stand out more?

Figure 6-2 My suggested revision gives the same essential messages in many fewer words.

Leave in enough to be clear

As you write and revise web content, remember that you are conversing with real people. Those people bring all of their previous experience and knowledge – and also their lack of experience and knowledge – to understanding what you are writing.

It is possible to cut so many words that you leave out information that people need in order to understand your messages. Caroline Jarrett and Whitney Quesenbery learned this important lesson when usability testing The Open University's web site.

Here's the relevant piece of a web page that they were testing:

BSc (Honours) **Psychology** Code: B07

You need: **360 points** $\boxed{i}$

Level: **Undergraduate** $\boxed{i}$

"You need: 360 points" – short, simple, plain English words. From the writers' point of view, the essential message here is only "360." The writers assumed everyone would understand what the rest of the words mean.

For anyone already enrolled at the university, that assumption is probably valid. Students know this is saying you need to accumulate 360 course points to get an undergraduate degree in this field (like credits to graduate with a major at a U. S. university).

But Caroline and Whitney were investigating how well the site works for newcomers to The Open University. And many of those people had a different understanding of those few simple words.

For this audience, a few more words are needed: "To get a degree in this field, you must take enough courses to earn 360 points."

This story illustrates how important it is to

- understand what your web users know and don't know
- do usability testing with the web users you are focusing on

3. Start with the key point. Write in inverted pyramid style

Whatever your essential message is, put it first. Many web users read only a few words of a page – or of a paragraph – before deciding if it is going to be relevant and easy for them to get through. If they think it might not be, they move on. They may jump down the page to a heading or a bulleted list or to very briefly try another paragraph. And that may be all the time and attention that they'll give to a page.

Like many other usability specialists, I have seen that behavior with most web users and most web sites over many years. And now our observations have been confirmed with eye-tracking data. Eye-tracking captures exactly where people's eyes go as they work with web pages. We can look at an individual's pathway through a web page. We can also accumulate data over many people and show the most common ways of using a specific web page.

Figure 6-3 shows accumulated eye-tracking data (called a heat map) for a web information page. Notice how people looked in an F pattern – across the lines at the top of the information and then at the beginning of the bulleted list. Notice how, after the first few lines, they looked more at the beginning of lines than all the way across. (That's typical skimming behavior.) Notice how readership trails off down the page.

 Blind web users act similarly. Blind web users scan with their ears. They listen to only a few words before deciding whether to keep going. With their screen-readers, blind web users can jump to the next link or the next heading or the next paragraph – and they do so at an amazingly rapid pace.

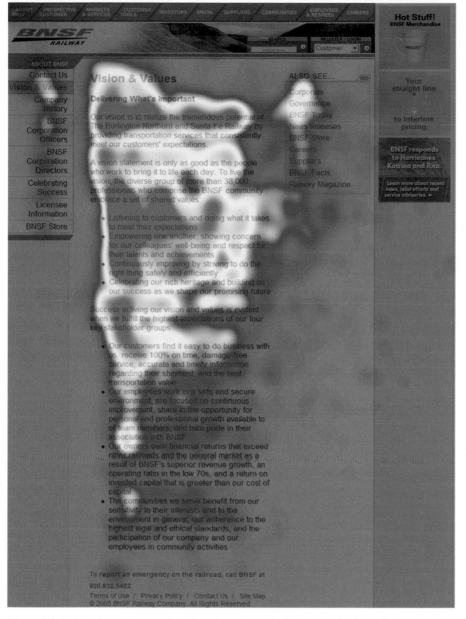

Figure 6-3 This heat map from eye-tracking shows the typical F pattern of web reading on information pages. Readers looked most at the first paragraph and then at the beginning of the bulleted lines.

The colors show the concentration of eye fixations, with red indicating the heaviest concentration and blue the least.

Eye-tracking by Jakob Nielsen and Kara Pernice Coyne, Nielsen Norman Group. Used with permission. For more about the study this picture comes from, see www.useit.com/eyetracking.

Journalists and technical writers know that many readers skim the headlines and the first paragraphs of articles. That's one reason they write in "inverted pyramid" style – with the main point first.

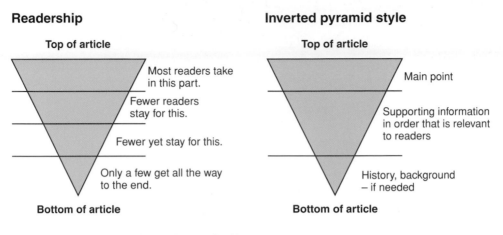

Inverted pyramid writing style matches readership.

For many web content writers, using inverted pyramid style requires a major shift in thinking and writing. For school essays and reports, you may have been taught to write in narrative style, telling a whole story in chronological order and building up to the main point at the end – the conclusion. That's not a good style for the workplace or for the web. Busy web users don't have time for that when they are trying to find information. They want the conclusion first.

Jakob Nielsen has advocated inverted pyramid style since 1996. See his Alertbox column at www .useit.com/alertbox/9606.html

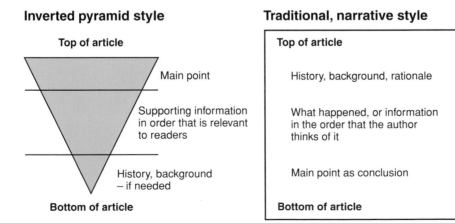

Web users trying to grab and go prefer inverted pyramid style to traditional, narrative style.

Although it may be difficult at first to learn to write in inverted pyramid style, it's a very useful skill. As Chip Scanlan says:

> [Inverted pyramid style] also an extremely useful tool for thinking and organizing because it forces the reporter to sum up the point of the story in a single paragraph. Journalism students who master it and then go on to other fields say it comes in handy for writing everything from legal briefs to grant applications.

And, I'll add, for writing successful web pages.

Figure 6-4, a blog article about insurance, shows a good example of inverted pyramid style.

Inverted pyramid style draws readers into the material right at the beginning – often with a small story or with interesting and relevant facts. To see the impact of starting with information that draws the reader into the material, compare two versions of the same information about literacy levels in Figures 6-5 and 6-6.

Chip Scanlan's web column on inverted pyramid style is at www.poynter.org/column .asp?id=52&aid=38693

If you studied technical writing, you may have the benefit of having already learned the "key message first" style. See for example, Blicq and Moretto, 2001. Ron Blicq has taught this style for many years, calling it "pyramid style" rather than "inverted pyramid style." His emphasis is the same as what I'm calling "inverted pyramid here" – focus on your main reader and put the key message up front.

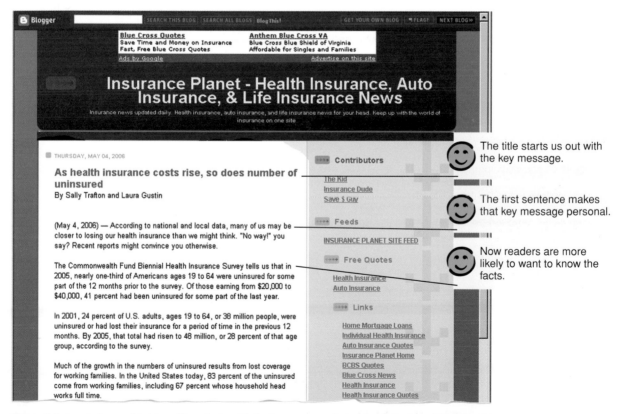

Figure 6-4 Inverted pyramid style writing starts with the key message. (I changed the colors of the text and background from the original to increase contrast and legibility.)   insuranceplanet.blogspot.com

In December 2005, the National Center for Educational Statistics (NCES) released the preliminary findings from its 2003 National Assessment of Adult Literacy. This survey, the most comprehensive measure of adult literacy in the United States since the 1992 survey, reveals how people use and understand information. The power of this survey is that it uses tasks that people need for success in their everyday lives—filling out an order form or balancing a checkbook or reading a prescription label.

The results placed participants in one of four categories and showed
- 14% of the adult population (30 million people) to be at the below basic literacy level;
- 29% (63 million people) at the basic level;
- 44% (95 million people) at the intermediate level; and
- 13% (28 million people) at the proficient level.

In short, over 93 million people are functioning at a basic or below basic literacy levels meaning they have limited ability "to use printed and written information to function in society, to achieve one's goals, and to develop one's knowledge and potential." Over 43% of Americans struggle with basic, everyday tasks that are often taken for granted.

Figure 6-5 Version 1 of an article on literacy levels in the U. S.

More than 43% of Americans struggle with basic, everyday tasks like filling out an order form or reading a prescription label. That's more than 93 million people who find it hard to understand written materials they need.

In December 2005, the National Center for Educational Statistics (NCES) released the preliminary findings from its 2003 National Assessment of Adult Literacy. This survey, the most comprehensive measure of adult literacy in the United States since 1992, reveals how people use and understand information. The power of this survey is that it uses tasks that people need for success in their everyday lives: reading an article about a health problem or balancing a checkbook or understanding a bus schedule.

The results placed participants in one of four categories and showed
- 14% of the U. S. adult population (30 million people) at the below basic literacy level;
- 29% (63 million people) at the basic level;
- 44% (95 million people) at the intermediate level; and
- 13% (28 million people) at the proficient level.

Figure 6-6 Version 2 of an article on literacy levels in the U. S.

Did version 2 do a better job of drawing you in? Were you more likely to stop reading part way through the first paragraph of version 1?

4. Break down walls of words

Even with inverted pyramid style, keep your paragraphs short and use bulleted lists. Break up the text.

Walls are barriers. Large blocks of text that look like wall-to-wall words are barriers to web users. Very short paragraphs or bullet points work best.

If you are moving from writing for paper to writing on the web, think of the pieces you need as even smaller than what you would plan for a paper document. Each small topic needs its own heading. Each question and answer needs the question as a heading and the answer in short sentences or as a bulleted list.

Case Study 6-2 shows how breaking down walls of words increased business for an e-commerce company.

Case Study 6-2   Breaking down walls of words made the difference!

When CompareInterestRates.com tried a variety of changes to their online form, the only change that made a significant difference was moving from paragraphs of text to a bulleted list. Here's how the original web form started:

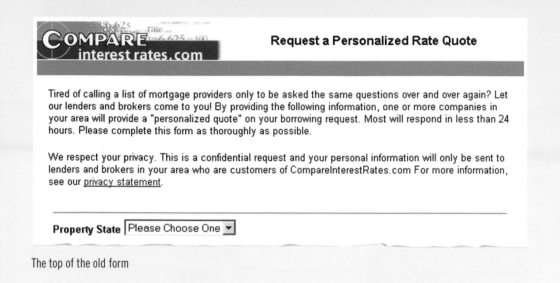

The top of the old form

CompareInterestRates.com is owned by Loanbright, an e-commerce company that helps mortgage companies get business.

What Loanbright tried

Working with Caroline Jarrett, a usability consultant, Loanbright tried several variations of the form, with combinations of these changes:

- including a photo or not (and variations of the photo by size and content)
- placement in the browser window (centered or left-justified)
- color in the fields or no color
- colored background behind the form (blue or yellow) or no color
- reworking the text at the top

How people get to the form – and what the study measured

People get to the form by clicking on a web page ad or through a sponsored link on a search engine page. What matters to Loanbright is the conversion rate: the percentage of users who complete and submit the form compared to those who arrive at it. Loanbright can serve up different versions of the form from the same ad or sponsored link, so they were able to measure conversion rate for different variations of the form within the same "stream of traffic."

What they found

The new forms increased conversion rates from 5 to 7.3 percent in one stream of traffic and from 10 to 12.5 percent in another stream of traffic. In the world of conversion rates, that is excellent improvement.

At first, however, it was not clear which change was contributing most to the success. With detailed statistical analysis, it became clear that **only reworking the text at the top had a significant impact.** Here's one of the variations showing the bulleted list at the top instead of a wall of words.

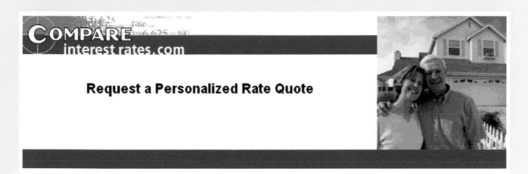

Usability testing with eye-tracking supported the conclusion from the conversion rate study. All the participants in the usability test preferred the bullet points.

See Jarrett and Minott, 2004, for the complete story of this study.

5. Market by giving useful information

On the web, you market best by giving users the factual information they want as easily and quickly as possible. Because web users see so much less at a time on the screen than on a piece of paper, there isn't the same room for non-factual "happy talk" as there is in a brochure or advertising flyer. And because web users are so often goal-oriented, they don't want to be distracted by information that isn't relevant to gathering up all the facts.

In Figure 6-7, the credit union is using lots of space at the top of the page for text that adds nothing to the information in the table. Most web users will go right to the table. What users need at the top are explanations of the terms such as APR and Loan to Value. (Don't expect web users to notice the asterisk in an online table or to scroll to the bottom of the page to read a footnote. That's a major difference between paper and web pages. On the screen, very few people connect an asterisk with footnotes or think of footnotes at all.)

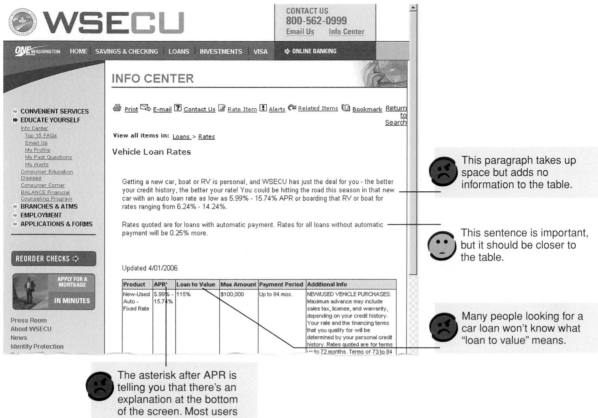

Figure 6-7 People come to financial sites to look up facts. They don't usually read the marketing blurbs on pages like this. They just want the rates.   www.wsecu.org

All sites sell – products or themselves

Some sites sell products. The main purpose of an online store or a travel site or a hotel site is to derive revenue from online sales. E-commerce sites sell best by

- helping site visitors find what they want
- giving them the information they want about the products
- getting them through the buying process effectively and efficiently

Other sites sell themselves. Information-rich sites that aren't primarily "commercial" may not derive direct revenue from their online presence.

But they are, in fact, marketing themselves – usually as *the place* to go for whatever information they specialize in. And they succeed best when site visitors get what they want: reliable, credible, up-to-date, factual information that is easy to find, easy to understand, and easy to use. That's more important to most site visitors than a mission statement, organization chart, or detailed history.

The web is primarily a "pull" technology; marketing specializes in "push"

On paper, companies market by sending information to people. The company starts the conversation. That's a "push" technology – the company is pushing information out to potential customers.

"Push" does exist in the web world. When people register at a site, they often agree to receive notices that come to them in email. Many sites invite people to sign up for newsletters on specific topics that then also arrive "pushed" to them in their email.

Most web contacts, however, are "pull" technology. People come to your web site on their own initiative to "pull" information from the site. As we've seen throughout this book, the web is most often used as a conversation started by the site visitor. If site visitors start the conversation, you must satisfy the need they came for first – before you try to market to them.

Marketing departments are accustomed to thinking in terms of how to draw people *in.* On the web, however, your primary worry should be how not to drive *away* the people who have chosen to come to your site.

Take advantage of "marketing moments" – market after the visitor is at least partially satisfied

The time to market on a web site is *after* your site visitors have satisfied at least part of their need. Many online bookstores are particularly adept at taking advantage of "marketing moments," as in the example from Barnes and Noble in Figure 6-8.

The Founders credit union (Figure 6-9) does a great job of getting people directly to the facts; but then it misses the opportunity to market to them from the facts.

A "marketing moment" is a time and place on the web site when site visitors are ready for a marketing message. A marketing moment is not meant to distract your site visitor. A marketing moment is a natural follow-on or complement to what your site visitor is doing.

Figure 6-8 Barnes & Noble, like other online bookstores, takes advantage of marketing moments – when site visitors are at the information they came for.   www.bn.com

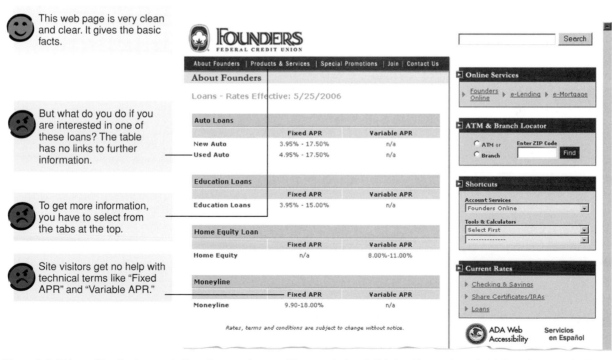

Figure 6-9 This credit union has made the rates easy to see, with no marketing fluff before the numbers; but it has also stranded its visitors. It could market to them now by making the types of loans into links or by putting inviting links next to the loan names.

www.foundersfcu.com

6. Layer information to help web users

Layering is a way of dividing web information. When done well, it's a great way to

- keep web users from being overwhelmed by too much at once
- help different web users each get the amount of information that they want on a topic

To close this chapter, let's look at three typical examples of layering on web sites and then at two case studies that might give you new ideas for using layering in your web site.

Layering from a brief description to the full article

Many web sites entice site visitors with a little bit about an article, a topic, or a product on the home page or on a pathway page and then provide a link that goes to a web page with more information. That's layering. Figure 6-10 shows a well-done example of this typical web layering from the BBC's web site.

Layering from an information page to more on other web pages

Information pages can also be pathways to more information – details, tangential information, or related topics.

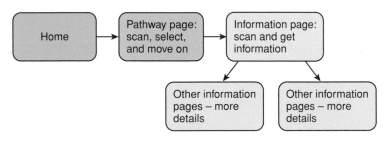

Layering from an information page to other information pages

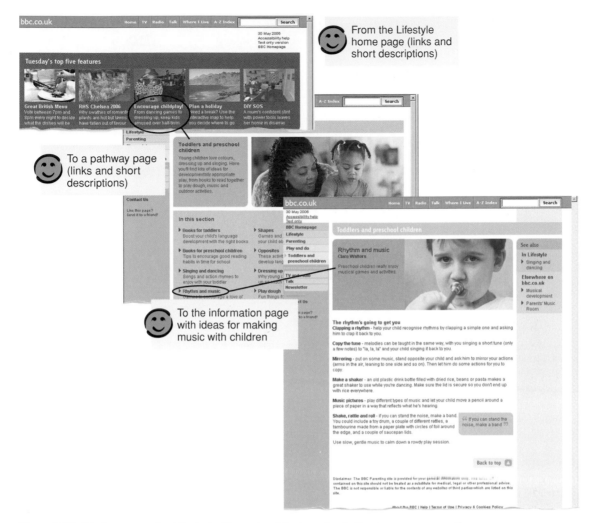

Figure 6-10 This is an example of the typical layered architecture of web sites: home page → pathway page → information page.   www.bbc.com

One of the great advantages of the web over paper is the way that you can make connections for people to information beyond what you want to put on your main page. The links can go to more details on the same topic, related topics, other sites, calculators, lists of providers, message boards, specific contact forms, other online activities, and so on. Figure 6-11 shows just the top few sections of a page from the U. K. government's site, Directgov. Several other sections further down the page also have related links after the brief paragraphs.

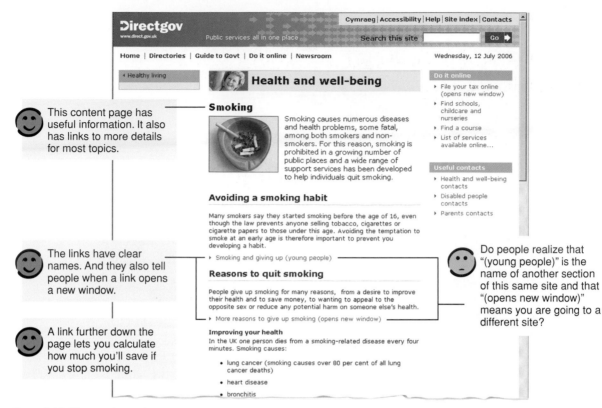

Figure 6-11 Directgov has articles on many topics, and most include links to other relevant pages within the site and to relevant external sites. The links may go to more information, online activities, forms, checklists, and so on.   www.direct.gov.uk

Layering from part of the page to a short explanation

A third type of layering is to provide definitions, technical details, or other "extra" information on top of the main page so that people don't lose the page they are reading. You can do this with a *small* second window that overlays part of the main window or with a rollover.

Figure 6-12 shows how the San Diego Zoo links words some readers may not know to definitions that come up in a small second window.

(A word about definition windows: Make each word and definition its own file. Don't just jump people to the right definition in a very long file that contains the entire glossary. People may not realize what has happened. They may start to scroll in the long file and get lost. Putting all the definitions together is satisfying only the unlikely scenario that

The links in Figure 6-11 all come after the text – not embedded in the paragraph.

The link I'm featuring in Figure 6-12 is embedded in the paragraph, but it opens only a small definition window.

An important issue for information pages is whether and when it's okay to embed links to other topics on other web pages. I cover that issue in Chapter 12 on links.

Figure 6-12 Glossary items are a good use of small secondary windows that allow people to look at the main page and the small window at the same time. Here we are looking at the definition of "prey" from a link in the first paragraph of the San Diego Zoo's article on the cheetah.   www.sandiegozoo.org

someone wants to read your glossary. It is not satisfying the much more likely scenario that the reader wants to quickly understand what a particular word means and then to go on in the original article. If you think that people may want more definitions, include a link to an A-Z index in each definition window.)

Figure 6-13 shows how Traffic.com provides more information on each problem it has marked on the map that the site visitor is looking at.

Bringing up extra information in a rollover or a *small* second window that does not completely overlay the original window has two major advantages:

- The original information and the related extra information are visible together. People can work with both at the same time.
- The small second window is less likely to cause the problems that full-size second windows create for many people. Many people do not realize what has happened when the browser launches a new window and they cannot see their original screen.

When you use small second windows for this type of layering, include a Close Window link, as the San Diego Zoo site does. For many web users, a text link or button reminding them to close the window is faster and easier than having to remember the little x in the corner.

> Be wary of putting information into pop-ups. Many web users have pop-ups turned off.

Figure 6-13 On the maps at traffic.com, you can click on any of the warning triangles and get details of the problem. The new layer opens on the map, so you don't lose the overall information or your sense of place.   www.traffic.com

Layering in innovative ways

Let's turn now to two particularly interesting and useful examples of layering.

- Summarizing archived paper documents into "index card" web pages (the "fresh fish" example, Case Study 6-3)

- Opening layers on the same web page (the "injured workers" example, Case Study 6-4)

Case Study 6-3   Summarizing archived paper documents

Even when you know that a paper document is not going to work well on the web, you may not have the time or resources to change it. Or you may want to keep the old document as it was on paper for historical, archival reasons. And, yet, you may also want to make the key messages in that document more accessible to your web users.

What can you do? One way is to create a new, shorter first layer with the key messages higher in the web hierarchy and link that layer to the old document.

That's what Laurence Dusold at the U. S. Food and Drug Administration (FDA) did when he developed the web site for the FDA's Center for Food Safety and Applied Nutrition (CFSAN). Dusold's team extracted the key messages from old journal articles into short web pages. Here's an example from an article about knowing when fish is fresh:

 ## How can you figure out if the fish is fresh?

The fish's eyes should be clear and bulge a little. Only a few fish, such as walleye, have naturally cloudy eyes.

Whole fish and fillets should have firm and shiny flesh. Dull flesh may mean the fish is old. Fresh whole fish also should have bright red gills free from slime.

If the flesh doesn't spring back when pressed, the fish isn't fresh.

There should be no darkening around the edges of the fish or brown or yellowish discoloration.

The fish should smell fresh and mild, not fishy or ammonia-like.

Email this Page
To a Friend

Source: Excerpted from FDA Consumer, February 1999: Critical Steps Toward Safer Seafood

---

The key messages from a longer article   www.cfsan.fda.gov/~dms/qa-sea5.html

This "key messages" page may be all that most site visitors want. Anyone who wants the full article can get to it from the link at the bottom of the key messages web page.

Over time, Dusold's team has revised the longer articles that the key message pages link to. The original journal article on fish had a title but no internal headings, no lists, no graphics. It was simply long paragraphs of prose. In the years since it first went up, the writers have gone back to the article and put in subheadings, broken the paragraphs up more, turned some sections into bulleted lists (with traditional black circle bullets), and made some parts into lists like the key message summary, with fish as bullets.

U. S. Food and Drug Administration
FDA Consumer
November-December 1997; Revised February 1998 and February 1999

Critical Steps Toward Safer Seafood

by Paula Kurtzweil

A tender tuna steak lightly seasoned with lemon pepper and grilled over a charcoal fire is one way to please a seafood lover's palate. Stuffed flounder, lobster thermidor, and shrimp scampi are others.

But blue marlin served up with a dose of scombroid poisoning or steamed oysters with a touch of Norwalk-like virus are more likely to turn the stomach, instead of treating the palate.

How to Spot a Safe Seafood Seller

Anyone who's ever smelled rotting seafood at the fish counter has a pretty good idea of what a poorly run seafood market smells like. But the absence of any strong odor doesn't necessarily mean that the seller is practicing safe food handling techniques.

Based on FDA's Food Code, here are some other points to consider:

- Employees should be in clean clothing but no outerwear and wearing hair coverings.

- They shouldn't be smoking, eating, or playing with their hair. They shouldn't be sick or have any open wounds.

- Employees should be wearing disposable gloves when handling food and change gloves after doing nonfood tasks and after handling any raw seafood.

- Fish should be displayed on a thick bed of fresh, not melting ice, preferably in a case or under some type of cover. Fish should be arranged with the bellies down so that the melting ice drains away from the fish, thus reducing the chances of spoilage.

The beginning and a piece from the middle of the updated version of the longer, original article — reachable from a link on the "key messages" page.   www.cfsan.fda.gov/~dms/fdsafe3.html

The linked article is now much more usable online than the original journal article was. It has become detailed web information rather than just a paper document archived on the web site.

Dusold tells me that half the pages they work on in a year are new pages and half are updates and reworking of old pages. That way, they continually strive to bring useful layers of information to their site visitors.

Case Study 6-4	Opening layers on the same web page

Layering does not have to take web users from one web page to another. You can keep all of the information on one page, layering it by opening and closing overlays on the same page.

For a user group like injured workers checking on their claims for workers' compensation, this type of layering solves many potential problems.

Think about the web users and their scenarios

The site is for people like Joe.

Joe

- 26 years old
- construction worker
- high school graduate, no college
- married, no children yet
- likes to be outdoors
- has an old home computer his brother gave him
- doesn't use the computer much
- is in pain from his injuries
- is skeptical about whether the government agency is going to be helpful if he tries to get information about what to do

Joe fell off a scaffold on a construction job last week. He knows he's lucky that he's going to be okay. But he sprained his ankle, injured his back, and broke his arm. He won't be able to work for a while.

Joe is worried about money. His wife, Lily, works in retail, but they won't be able to get through the month with just her salary. They're going to be relying on the checks he should get from the government agency that handles benefits for injured workers.

His employer and the doctor both told him he has to file a claim to get paid while he is out of work because he is injured. He wants to be sure that he files the claim correctly so that he starts getting paid quickly.

Think about the web content writers and their constraints

The workers' compensation claim system is a process that the writers cannot change. It has defined steps that they must explain.

Think about how best to provide all this information to these web users

Thinking about Joe, the injured worker, and about the information that they needed to provide, the web team at the Washington State Department of Labor and Industries created a web site with

- each phase in the process as a tab in the content area under the page title

- one page for each step

- layering within the page where links open to more information without changing the underlying page

The three screens that follow show you how this works.

The basic screen for the section on filing a claim

The same screen after you have clicked on "Complete all required paperwork"

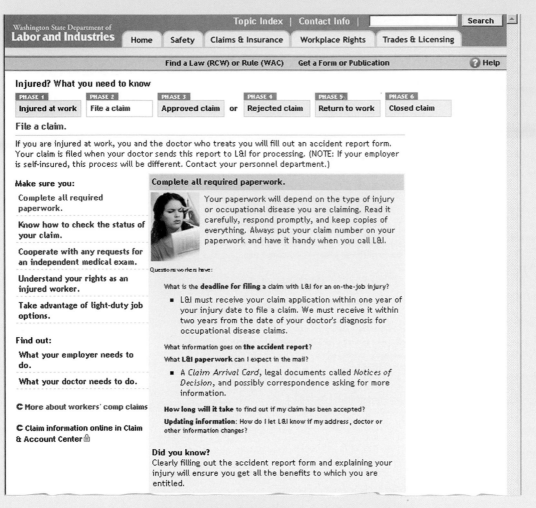

The same screen after you have clicked on two of the questions

 When I show this example, people ask me how it's done and whether it's accessible for people who listen to web sites with screen-readers. The answer is "yes." It's done with Show/Hide using Javascript.

Brian Criss, the webmaster responsible for creating these pages, tells me that 99.99 percent of the people coming to their web site have Javascript enabled. Show/Hide does not reload the page or load a new page.

(Reloading a page is a problem for people with screen-readers because the screen-reader assumes it is a new page and starts reading again from the top of the page.) On these pages, when a screen-reader user clicks on a link that opens text just below or next to the link, the screen-reader continues reading whatever is open – thus, reading the newly shown information as intended.

SUMMARIZING CHAPTER 6

Here are key messages from Chapter 6:

- Give people only what *they* need.

- Cut! Cut! Cut! And cut again!

- Leave in enough to be clear.

- Start with the key point. Write in inverted pyramid style.

- Break down walls of words.

- Market by giving useful information.
  - All sites sell – products or themselves.
  - The web is primarily a "pull" technology, marketing specializes in "push."
  - Take advantage of "marketing moments" – market after the visitor is at least partially satisfied.

- Layer information to help web users.
  - Layer from a brief description to the full article.
  - Layer from a main article to more information on a separate page.
  - Layer from a part of the page to a short explanation.
  - Layer in innovative ways: by summarizing an archived document; by opening layers on the same web page.

Designing Your Web Pages for Easy Use

7

When people come to a web page, they form an impression of the page before they read anything. They react first to the appearance (layout, fonts, colors, and so on). We all do this. You do it on other people's sites. People do it on your site.

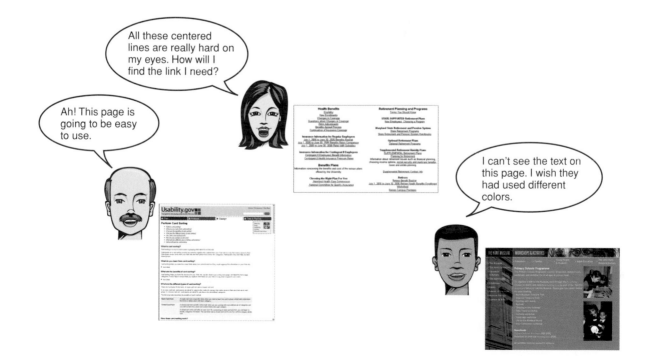

Creating that appearance (designing the web page) is about more than aesthetics. It's also about usability. The design of your web pages can help people find what they need and understand what they find. It can also hinder them.

On successful web sites, the design and the writing style complement and support each other; and designers and writers must work compatibly together to accomplish that.

Designers must understand the needs of the content. If you want a successful web site, you cannot, at the end, pour content into a design that was created without detailed consideration of that content.

Content writers must work together with designers to be certain that decisions on space, font, color, and so on will lead to pages that allow site visitors to easily see and read the content.

If you are a content writer, I hope that you are working with visual designers. If you are a visual designer, I hope that this book makes you appreciate the importance of the content on the web site and that this chapter in particular makes you involve content writers early and continuously in the design process.

This chapter is about how to use layout, space, typography, and color to help people find and understand your web content.

Fourteen guidelines for helpful design

Here are 14 guidelines to design pages that will help – and not hinder – your site visitors:

1. Make the page elements obvious, using patterns and alignment.
2. Consider the entire site when planning the design.
3. Work with templates.
4. Use space effectively. Keep active space in your content.
5. Beware of false bottoms.
6. Don't let headings float.
7. Don't center text.

8. Set a sans serif font as the default.

9. Use a relative type size with a default large enough to read easily.

10. Use a fluid layout with a medium line length as default.

11. Don't write in all capitals.

12. Don't underline anything but links. Use italics sparingly.

13. Provide good contrast between text and background.

14. Think about all your site visitors when you choose colors.

1. Make the page elements obvious, using patterns and alignment

Good design uses creativity to develop usable web pages. On a usable web page, each of the various elements of the page (logo and name, search, global navigation, local navigation, content, ads, and so on) are instantly obvious, allowing people to select what they want effectively and efficiently.

Two critical aspects of making page elements obvious are patterns and alignment.

People are very pattern-oriented. If the Search box is in the upper right on the home page, we expect to see it in that place on all the pages. If bulleted lists are slightly indented on the first few pages we look at, we expect all bulleted lists to be indented in the same way. We are faster at understanding how the page is designed and at finding the specific part we need if the patterns are obvious and consistent across pages.

One of the most effective ways to create patterns that people quickly see and learn is to have only a few places across the page where boxes or text start. When people complain that a site is "cluttered" or "too busy" or "hard to use," they are often reacting to pages where elements are not aligned well.

Figures 7-1 through 7-4 show two very different types of sites with obvious patterns and alignment. Figures 7-1 and 7-2 are from the web site of the investment company JPMorgan Chase.

Figures 7-3 and 7-4 are from the web site of the New York Metropolitan Opera. The designs are different, but each is consistent within itself, with clear patterns and alignment.

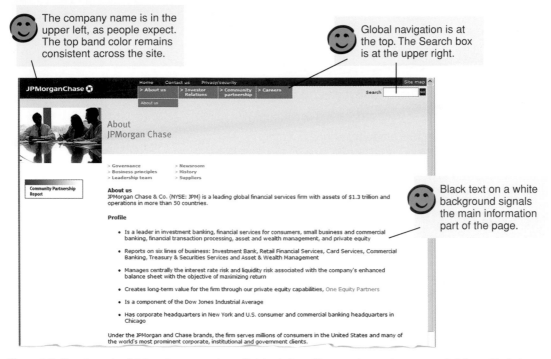

The company name is in the upper left, as people expect. The top band color remains consistent across the site.

Global navigation is at the top. The Search box is at the upper right.

Black text on a white background signals the main information part of the page.

Figure 7-1 The elements of this web page are immediately obvious. The page has a clean, somewhat formal look, in keeping with the image that an investment company wants to portray.   www.jpmorganchase.com

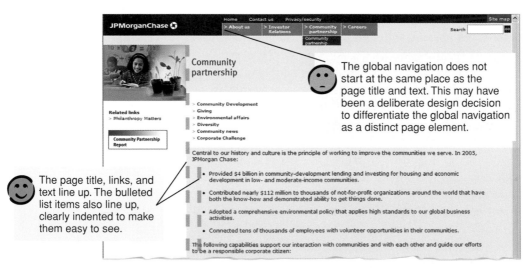

The global navigation does not start at the same place as the page title and text. This may have been a deliberate design decision to differentiate the global navigation as a distinct page element.

The page title, links, and text line up. The bulleted list items also line up, clearly indented to make them easy to see.

Figure 7-2 The design is consistent across these pages. The color changes to indicate which of the main areas you are in. The photo changes to match the topic of the page. (I added the light gray overlay and the dotted lines to make the alignment more obvious to you.)

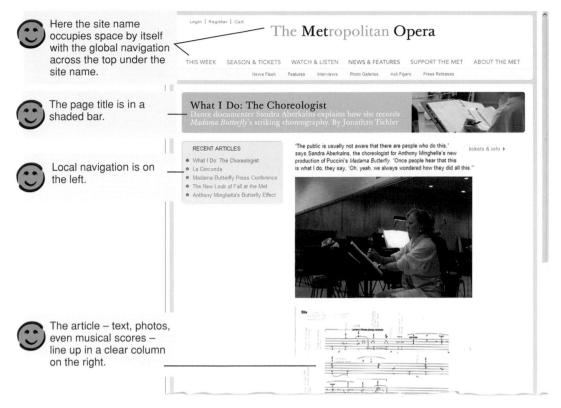

Here the site name occupies space by itself with the global navigation across the top under the site name.

The page title is in a shaded bar.

Local navigation is on the left.

The article – text, photos, even musical scores – line up in a clear column on the right.

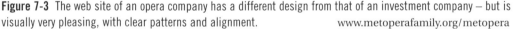

Figure 7-3 The web site of an opera company has a different design from that of an investment company – but is visually very pleasing, with clear patterns and alignment.   www.metoperafamily.org/metopera

2. Consider the entire site when planning the design

From your site visitors' point of view, your home page, pathway pages, and information pages are all part of the same site. Your site visitors don't know – or care – that different people may be responsible for different parts of the site. To them, it's all part of the same experience – getting the information they need or buying the product they want.

The design challenge is how to maintain patterns and alignment across different types of pages while making each type of page serve its purposes well. To see how this can be done, let's look at an e-commerce example and an information site example.

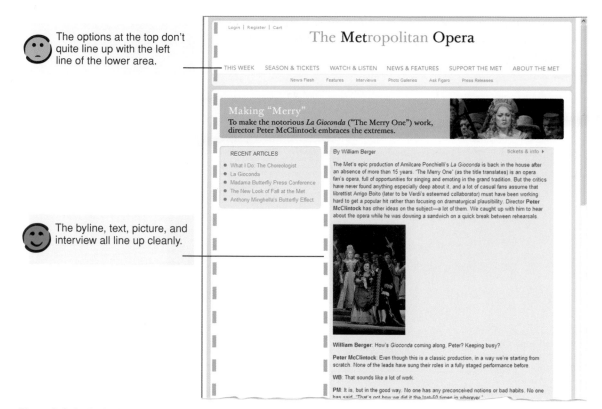

The options at the top don't quite line up with the left line of the lower area.

The byline, text, picture, and interview all line up cleanly.

Figure 7-4 Again, I added the light gray overlay and the dotted lines to show the text area and the alignment.

An e-commerce example

An e-commerce site has at least these page types in addition to its home page:

- gallery pages (showing several items of the same type)

- item description pages

- a series of pages in the checkout process

- information pages about the company, policy pages (such as when and how you may return items), and perhaps other pages with stories or instructions

Figure 7-5 shows four pages about Godiva chocolates. Notice how well
the web site maintains patterns, alignment, and consistency across
different types of pages.

A gallery page

An item description page

Part of the checkout process

An information page

Figure 7-5 This site does an excellent job of maintaining consistent patterns and alignment across different types of pages
while allowing each page type to serve its purpose.   www.godiva.com

An information site example

An information site should also maintain consistency in patterns and alignment across different types of pages. Figure 7-6 shows how this is done at www.usability.gov, from the U. S. Department of Health and Human Services – a great resource on usability for everyone on your web team.

Plan a consistent design across the web site

Use the process in Checklist 7-1 to plan for a consistent design across the different types of pages in your web site.

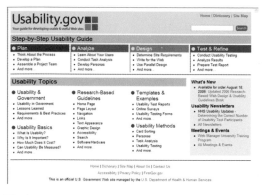

The home page

A pathway page

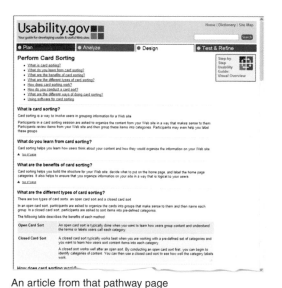

An article from that pathway page

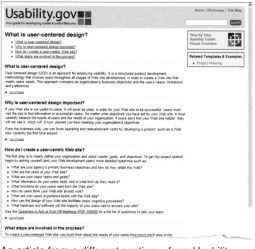

An article from a different section – from Usability Basics

Figure 7-6 Sites that are primarily for information can also develop clean, clear patterns with alignment and consistency.

> **Checklist 7-1**
> **Process for creating a consistent design**
>
> 1. List all the types of pages the site will have, including all the different types of information pages and forms.
>
> 2. Minimize the number of page types. For example, for an e-commerce site, pages with company information, pages with policies, and perhaps even pages with informative articles would probably work well as one page type rather than as three different page types.
>
> 3. Give each page type an informative name so that the entire team can talk about the pages.
>
> 4. For each type of page, list all the elements that will appear on that page type.
>
> 5. Check with people who might contribute to or use the pages to be sure you have all the page types and all the elements for each page type.
>
> 6. Plan the entire set of page types together, developing designs that work as broadly across page types as possible.
>
> 7. Where pages need different patterns or alignment, make those as compatible as possible.

Understand the process that moves from plan to launch

Content writers should be aware of the design process that takes a web site from planning to final pages. Most teams move from sketches showing the elements of each page type (wireframes) through several rounds of ever more finished prototypes. The final version of each page type becomes a template that content writers, designers, and coders use to develop the actual pages in the web site.

Figure 7-7 shows four steps (out of at least 9 or 10) in one team's process from wireframe to prototype to template to final web page. The site is for people who are new to and contemplating attending The Open University in the U. K. Whitney Quesenbery and Caroline Jarrett, who were part of the project team, shared these with me, with permission from Ian Roddis.

You should be doing iterative usability testing throughout this process, with several versions of your prototypes.

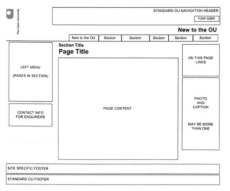

Wireframe, showing which elements will be on this type of page and where they will go.

Prototype with draft content for a second round of usability testing.

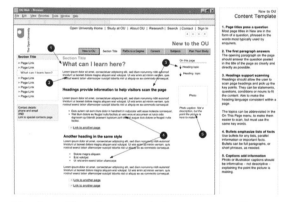

Template with explanations of what goes where. The words in the content area are just showing where text will go. (This is called "greeking," although the words, starting with "Lorem ipsum," come from Latin.)

Page in the live site.

Figure 7-7 How one team moved from wireframe to prototype to template to final web site. This set shows only two of many iterations of wireframes and prototypes. Example courtesy of The Open University web team, led by Ian Roddis.

Integrate content and design from the beginning

Every step in this process involves meshing content and design. Even the list of page elements requires decisions about content. What will the content be like on each page type? Will there be in-page links on information pages? If so, where should they come? How much information will there be about each item in the catalogue? How long will typical headings be in the content? What patterns will the content writers use for their information? And so on.

As design progresses, more and more decisions must be made that affect web content. The placement and space allotted for different pieces of content on each page type constrain what writers can do. And so, writers must be involved in decisions about that placement and space. Decisions about font and color usually belong to the visual designer, but designers must work closely with content specialists to be certain that the choices will produce web pages that are both aesthetically pleasing and easy for people to skim, scan, read, and use.

3. Work with templates

At the end of the process, the final prototypes become templates for each page type. If you are a content writer, accept the templates with enthusiasm and use them.

Templates make life much easier for everyone. You can concentrate on the information, knowing how it will fit into and what it will look like on the web page. Writing to fit the constraints of a web template can help you learn to let go of words, break information into small pieces, focus on your key messages, write good headings, and use all the other guidelines in this book.

The other great aid for writers besides templates is a style guide. See the interlude later in this book on Creating an Organic Style Guide.

4. Use space effectively. Keep active space in your content

Space is not just emptiness. Space is an important design element – both on paper and on web pages. If you are used to writing and designing for paper, however, you may need to think about space somewhat differently for your web content.

Most web users are still looking at screens that show much less than a typical sheet of paper. (Even people with monitors large enough to show an entire sheet of paper often don't maximize each window.) So we want to make good use of the screen "real estate" that we have.

Too little space on a web page can make information very difficult to skim, scan, find, and read. Too much space in the wrong places can mislead people about whether the page is finished and about how headings fit with the text.

We'll look at examples of all of these problems. But, first, I must introduce the concepts of passive space and active space because the problems are primarily related to poor use of active space.

Understand passive space and active space

Information designers distinguish between passive space and active space. Passive space is outside of the main content area, for example, the margins on a piece of paper. Active space is inside the main content area, for example, the space between paragraphs on a piece of paper. You need active space to help readers both separate and group information. Figure 7-8 shows you passive space and active space in a typical paper document, such as a draft page from this book.

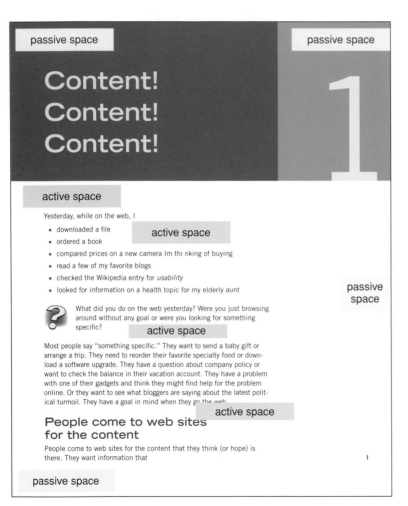

Figure 7-8 A book page showing active space and passive space. The space between the bullets and the bulleted text, the space at the end of each bulleted item, and the space between the question mark icon and the text after it are all examples of active space.

For your web content, focus on active space

On the web, we can reduce passive space, but we must keep active space to help people make sense of the information. And we must use active space appropriately for the medium.

You can create useful active space by:

- breaking the text into small chunks
- using lots of headings
- keeping paragraphs short and putting space between them
- turning sentences into more visual forms, like lists and tables
- putting space into lists
- including pictures and other graphics with a little space around them

Compare Figure 7-9, advice from Purina, the pet food company, with Figure 7-10, about parking permits at Stanford University. The Purina page needs a little active space after each list item.

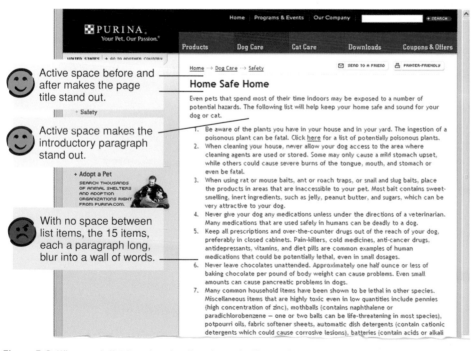

Figure 7-9 When each list item is a few lines long, the list needs space between the items. People are much less likely to even try to read a page with too little active space than a well-spaced page.

www.purina.com

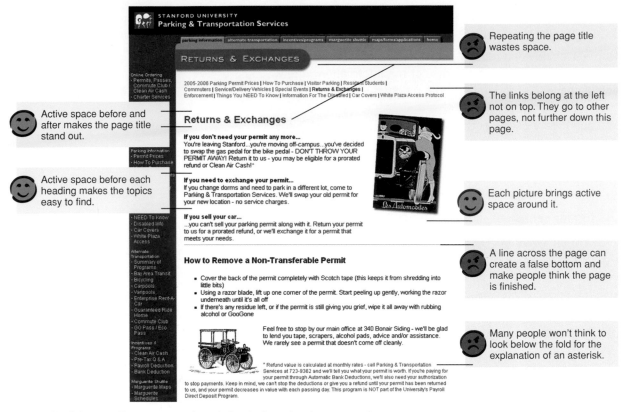

Figure 7-10 This page, like so many on the web, has both good and poor uses of space.   www.transportation.stanford.edu

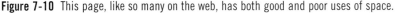

It would be even better if the list in Figure 7-9 were organized into sections with bold headings and written so that each list item started with a bold statement that summarized the main point.

5. Beware of false bottoms

You don't control how much of your web page any particular site visitor is looking at. What they see depends on their monitor size, their screen resolution, and the size of the window they have open.

Over and over in usability testing, I've seen people stopped by a horizontal line or a block of space at the bottom of their screen. Even if the scroll bar shows that there's much more, the message that the horizontal line – and even more a large block of space – seems to be sending overwhelms the message of the scroll bar. For example, the Franklin Institute page in Figure 7-11 is likely to lead many people to conclude that the site has no search function.

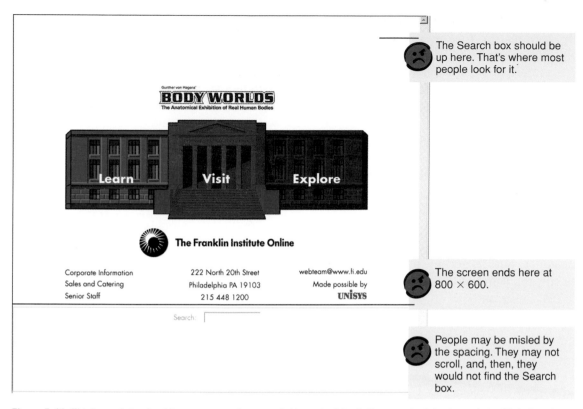

Figure 7-11 Think carefully about how your use of space might create false bottoms and mislead people to think that the page is finished.

sin.fi.edu/

Don't create false bottoms on web pages. Don't put a horizontal line or large blocks of space across the page. They stop people. Check out your site on different size monitors, at different resolutions, and in different browsers to be sure that your spacing is not likely to mislead people.

6. Don't let headings float

Space should help people see what goes with what on web pages, and one important relationship is that between headings and text. One of the most serious problems on many web pages is that the headings are the same distance from the text before them as they are from the text after them. The headings float in space, seemingly unconnected to the text they cover.

When headings come right on top of the text, you have no question about what text each heading goes with. Look back at the Stanford University page in Figure 7-10 and notice how clear the relationship is between headings and text.

The headings on the web page in Figure 7-12 from a New Zealand health site, however, don't do as well. When I show a page like this one in my workshops, people find lots to like about it. It's broken into small pieces. The sentences are short. It has bold headings. But they also complain that it's hard to know what goes with what. They have trouble putting the headings and text together properly.

What's wrong? The problem is that the headings float in space. To make headings work well, you need to put the active space above the heading and not between the heading and the text it goes with.

For more about headings, see Chapter 10.

Floating headings come naturally with ordinary HTML. To put the headings directly on top of the text they cover, use cascading style sheets (CSS). You get much more with a CSS than just solving the problems of floating headings, but it's worth learning about and using a CSS even if this is the only problem that you have. Keeping the headings from floating is that important!

The space between the introduction to a list and the first list item is a similar problem. Use CSS to remove that space, too. For more on lists, see Chapter 9.

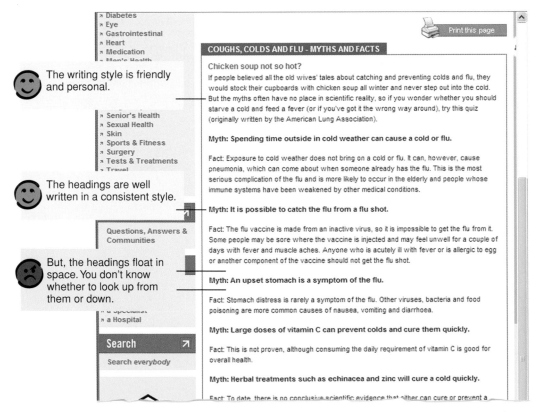

Figure 7-12 Put headings closer to the text they go with than to the text of the previous section. Don't let them float in space. Use cascading style sheets to control how you place the headings.   www.everybody.co.nz

7. Don't center text

I began this chapter talking about the importance of patterns and alignment. Centered text violates our need for pages with obvious alignment, clear places where different types of text start.

Compare Figures 7-13 and 7-14. Figure 7-13 is the original, a pathway page from a university web site. Figure 7-14 is a revision, where the only difference is moving from centered text to left-aligned text.

Text with each line centered is hard to read.

Our eyes don't know how far back to come to start each new line.

Health Benefits
Eligibility
New Enrollments
Changes in Coverage
Questions about Changes in Coverage
Retro Adjustments
Benefits Appeal Process
Continuation of Insurance Coverage

Insurance Information for Regular Employees
July 1, 2005 to June 30, 2006 Benefits Booklet
July 1, 2005 to June 30, 2006 Benefits Rates Comparison
July 1, 2005 to June 30, 2006 Rates with Subsidies

Insurance Information for Contingent II Employees
Contingent II Employees Benefit Information
Contingent II Health Insurance Premium Rates

Benefits Plans
Information concerning the benefits and cost of the various plans offered by the University

Choosing the Right Plan For You
Maryland Health Care Commission
National Committee for Quality Assurance

Retirement Planning and Programs
Terms You Should Know

STATE-SUPPORTED Retirement Plans
New Employees: Choosing a Program

Maryland State Retirement and Pension System
State Retirement Programs
State Retirement and Pension System Handbooks

Optional Retirement Plans
Optional Retirement Programs

Supplemental Retirement Annuity Plans
SUPPLEMENTAL Retirement Plans
Planning for Retirement
Information about retirement issues such as financial planning, choosing income options, social security and medicare benefits, taxes and estate planning.

Supplemental Retirement Contact Info

Retirees
Retiree Benefit Booklet
July 1, 2005 to June 30, 2006 Retiree Health Benefits Enrollment Worksheet
Retiree Campus Privileges

Figure 7-13 Centered text is harder on the eyes than text that lines up on the left. Don't center text.   www.umd.edu

The page is much neater and easier to use because the lines all start at the same place on the left.

Health Benefits
Eligibility
New Enrollments
Changes in Coverage
Questions about Changes in Coverage
Retro Adjustments
Benefits Appeal Process
Continuation of Insurance Coverage

Insurance Information for Regular Employees
July 1, 2005 to June 30, 2006 Benefits Booklet
July 1, 2005 to June 30, 2006 Benefits Rates Comparison
July 1, 2005 to June 30, 2006 Rates with Subsidies

Insurance Information for Contingent II Employees
Contingent II Employees Benefit Information
Contingent II Health Insurance Premium Rates

Benefits Plans
Information concerning the benefits and cost of the various plans offered by the University

Choosing the Right Plan For You
Maryland Health Care Commission
National Committee for Quality Assurance

Retirement Planning and Programs
Terms You Should Know

STATE-SUPPORTED Retirement Plans
New Employees: Choosing a Program

Maryland State Retirement and Pension System
State Retirement Programs
State Retirement and Pension System Handbooks

Optional Retirement Plans
Optional Retirement Programs

Supplemental Retirement Annuity Plans
SUPPLEMENTAL Retirement Plans
Planning for Retirement
Information about retirement issues such as financial planning, choosing income options, social security and medicare benefits, taxes and estate planning.

Supplemental Retirement Contact Info

Retirees
Retiree Benefit Booklet
July 1, 2005 to June 30, 2006 Retiree Health Benefits Enrollment Worksheet
Retiree Campus Privileges

Figure 7-14 Text should start lined up on the left and end with the right margin ragged – wherever the words end.

I don't know why I see so much text on the web where each line is centered. We don't read centered text well. We expect each line of a paragraph or a related set of text to start at the same place on the left.

When the text is centered, our eyes have no "anchor" – no steady place to come back to at the start of each line. So centered text is much more tiring to read than left-aligned text.

Even menu items in a left or right navigation column are easier to skim and scan when they are lined up on the left. Indeed, column headings in a table work better with the items in the column if the heading starts at the left column edge rather than being centered over the column. Use left-aligned, ragged right for all your web content.

8. Set a sans serif font as the default

Most web sites use sans serif type, such as Arial or **Verdana** or Tahoma. That's a difference between modern web sites and what has traditionally been used for paper documents.

A brief primer on fonts and type families

If you open the font list in your word processing program, you'll see a long list of available fonts. That list could be even longer; your list probably shows only some of the hundreds of fonts that have been developed.

All those hundreds of fonts, however, fall into two major categories (plus the unusual, artistic fonts that you would consider only for very special situations): serif and sans serif.

To appreciate the difference, look at a capital T in Times New Roman and in Tahoma.

serifs
Times

no serifs
Tahoma

Serifs are the "arms" and "feet" that extend down and out on the letters of serif fonts. "Sans" is the French word for "without." Sans serif fonts don't have the arms and feet.

The old research on paper

Research with paper documents in the mid-twentieth century generally found that serif fonts were better for sustained reading. The explanation was that the serifs at the bottom of the letters draw the eye horizontally along the line of type.

However, relying on that research for your web content may not serve your site visitors well. Here are several reasons why that research may not carry over to modern web content:

- The research is now more than 50 years old.

- Serif fonts were the norm then. People had little familiarity with sans serif fonts.

- With just a point or two more space between lines of type ("leading" – a word from the days when printers put a slug of lead between rows of type), you can make even a paper document in sans serif very readable.

- Not all documents are meant for sustained reading. On the web, we break information into small pieces with small paragraphs, short sentences, lists, and tables.

(An aside: Even on paper, you may want to use sans serif. Brochures, forms, and instructions usually do very well in sans serif. This book is printed in Trade Gothic, a sans serif font.)

Researchers who work with low-vision readers recommend sans serif for both paper and web.

The new research on the web – no winner for reading speed or comprehension, but people prefer sans serif

Research on web content has not shown a consistent result for either reading speed or comprehension. Some studies found that people did better with serif fonts; others found that people did better with sans serif fonts; still others, that it made no difference.

In most of these studies, no matter which font people read fastest or comprehended best, people preferred sans serif. It may be familiarity; people see most sites in sans serif. It may be that a site in serif font looks like a paper document; it seems old-fashioned.

Choose an easy-to-read sans serif

Serif compared with sans serif is not the whole story.

Within each of those broad categories, typefaces differ in other features, such as how wide the rounded parts of letters like "b" and "d" are, how high lowercase letters like "x" are compared to the overall height of letters like "h," how clearly the typeface distinguishes between the letter "l" and the number "1," how close together the letters are to each other, and so on.

Even at the same point size, different fonts take up different amounts of space on the screen. Try it for yourself by typing the same sentence several times and then changing the font but not the point size for each rendition of the sentence.

Of course, you do not entirely control what your site visitors see. They may have their browser set to always show a particular font. However, as the default, select a highly legible sans serif font. Select one that most of your site visitors are likely to have available on their computers. If you choose an unusual font, most people won't see your pages in that font because browsers use only what the specific computer has available. Do usability testing to make sure your default results in legible pages.

9. Think broadly about users and their situations when setting type size

Type size for the web is not as simple an issue as type size for paper. Whatever you specify for type size, it may be rendered differently on a Windows machine and a Macintosh. It may be different on different monitors and through different browsers. Furthermore, your site visitors may need to adjust the size. They may need to enlarge it because they have vision problems or because they want to let someone looking over their shoulder also see what is on the screen. They may want to make the type smaller to fit more on their screen.

Set the default large enough for your site visitors

Very small text is difficult to read, even for small amounts of text.

Very large text is also difficult to read, especially for large blocks of text.

On paper, you are probably using 12-point type as the standard. That's a good idea for the web, too. It's still more difficult to read from the screen than from paper, so making the type at least as large as what people see on paper is a good idea. (A book like this one can use smaller type because it is printed at extremely high resolution. Typical output from a desktop printer is 600 dots per inch. Typical screen resolution is on the order of 100 dots per inch.)

If your audience is predominantly teenagers or 20-somethings, you can probably use the equivalent of 10-point type as your default, but be sure it is resizable for other site visitors. If your audience is predominantly older, you might want to set the default at the equivalent of 14-point type, again making it resizable.

Many content writers, visual designers, and developers creating web sites today are young and have great eyesight. If that's you, think of your parents and grandparents. Look around and notice how many people wear eyeglasses. Vision declines with age. Make the default type size large enough so that people want to stay on your site and read your content.

Adjust your content so that you can use large enough type and get your message into the space you have

On the web, you are balancing how much to say and the type size for saying it. If you have only a certain amount of screen real estate for your content, you either have to write fewer words or make the type smaller. That's a good reason to let go of the words and focus on your key messages.

Let people choose their own text size

Use relative type size so that people can adjust it for their own needs. For example, you can specify type as percentages. Headings should always be larger than the regular text, so you might set a level-one heading as 150 percent of the regular text and a level-two heading as 125 percent of the regular text. (That would be equivalent to having 18-point level-one headings and 15-point level-two headings with 12-point text. Separating heading levels by about 3 points works well.)

 Make it easy for people to adjust the type by giving them buttons on the web page. Many sites now do this, as Wired Magazine has for several years. (See Figure 7-15.) Most people do not know that they can do it with the browser controls, and, even for those who do know, the buttons are a clear indication that a site has this feature, a reminder that they can adjust the size, and an easy way to do it.

Clicking on a different size letter A changes the size of the text on the page

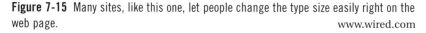

Figure 7-15 Many sites, like this one, let people change the type size easily right on the web page.   www.wired.com

Make all the text adjust, not just the main content area

All the text on the web page should get larger or smaller as people adjust the type size. On many sites, unfortunately, only the main content area adjusts with these changes, not the side columns of navigation and other information. But navigation is also critical. Don't make people squint – or leave your site – because they can't read the sides of your pages. Also make sure that your page is still usable when people enlarge the type. For example, make sure that people can still get to the control of a drop-down box and that they can still use the fields in your online forms.

10. Use a fluid layout with a medium line length as default

People not only adjust the text size, they adjust the width of the window they are looking at. This is another huge difference between paper and the web. Monitor sizes vary; screen resolutions vary; how much screen space people give to each window varies. For your web pages to be readable and useful, the text must adjust and wrap well from line to line as people resize their windows. So set your text to be fluid (also called a "liquid layout").

However, you should consider what your web page will look like if someone just opens it in a full window at whatever screen resolution you are designing for, such as 800 × 600 or 1024 × 768. For that default, use a medium line length (50 to 70 characters or about 8 to 10 words).

The problem with very long lines of type is physical. People's eyes have to move more to get through the line. They have to move their eyes to get back to the beginning of the next line, and sometimes they miss a line or go back up to a line they have already read. Long lines are tiring to read.

The problem with very short lines is semantic – related to the meaning of the words. If the line is so short that people don't get a whole phrase or set of words that go together on each line, the material is hard to understand.

This is a paragraph of information written in Verdana with a line length of 100 characters per line. Although university students in one research study read lines that were this long faster than shorter lines, in another study, other students read the medium lines fastest. And students preferred the medium line lengths in both studies. Do you find this comfortable to read?

This is a paragraph of information written in Verdana with a line length of 50 characters per line. This is the length that students preferred even when they read longer lines faster. Research on paper over many years found that people did best with lines that were about this long. Do you find this comfortable to read?

This is a paragraph of information on the web written in Verdana with a line length of 25 characters per line. Whole paragraphs in very short lines are difficult for people because it's hard to get the meaning with so few words on a line. Do you find this comfortable to read?

11. Don't write in all capitals

ALL CAPITALS TAKE UP 30 PERCENT MORE SPACE ON THE PAGE. THEY SLOW READING SPEED BY ABOUT 15 PERCENT. THEY ARE ALSO BORING. PEOPLE'S EYES GLAZE OVER, AND THEY TEND TO STOP READING. IN EMAIL AND ON THE WEB, PEOPLE THINK YOU ARE SHOUTING AT THEM WHEN YOU WRITE IN ALL CAPITALS.

All capitals take up 30 percent more space on the page. They slow reading speed by about 15 percent. They are also boring. People's eyes glaze over, and they tend to stop reading. In email and on the web, people think you are shouting at them when you write in all capitals.

 Which paragraph did you read? Do you agree that all capitals are more difficult and less interesting to read?

Using capital letters for headings and emphasis is a carry-over from typewriter days, when writers had very few options for varying the type in a document. You have better options today.

For web sites, follow these guidelines:

- Use all capitals only for a single word or short phrase in specific circumstances where people expect it.
- Use **bold** or **color** for headings, not all capitals.
- Use uppercase and lowercase (like normal sentences) even for important information. If you put a whole paragraph in capital letters to make people pay attention to it, you will achieve exactly the opposite. Most people will ignore it.

The traditional explanation for why all capitals are more difficult to read is that the shape of a word in lowercase give us more information than the shape of the same word in all capitals. The letters that stick up (have "ascenders"; b, d, f, for example) and the letters that go down (have "descenders"; g, p, y, for example) give words different shapes. Those differences in shape are present in lowercase letters but not in capital letters.

For other theories on why all capitals are more difficult to read, see Larson, 2004.

Which of these is easier to read quickly?

12. Don't underline anything but links. Use italics sparingly

On web pages, most people assume that anything that is underlined is a link, no matter what color it is. So reserve underlining for links. Underlining for emphasis or to indicate a book title is an old-fashioned technique that comes from typewriter days.

Italics have always been the way to show a book title in printed documents. Use that on your web pages. Otherwise, use italics sparingly. Italics work as a light form of emphasis, but you don't want to overemphasize too much at once. An entire paragraph in italics would be very hard to read.

(There's also a difference between a font that was designed to be italic and the italic versions of many typefaces, which just slope the letters of the regular font.)

Don't use italics for headings. First, they do not stand out on the page nearly as well as bold. Second, people do not all agree on how to put italics into a hierarchy in a set of headings. When I show people sets of headings all at the same point size where one is in bold type, one is in italic type, and one is in regular type, people always say the bold one is the highest level – the most important heading. But then I get mixed results as to whether the heading in italic is more important or less important than the heading in regular type. Use bold or color for all your headings. Change the size and possibly the placement to show which is the more important level of heading.

13. Provide good contrast between text and background

In the early days of desktop publishing, we talked about the "ransom note" effect – with so many different fonts and colors on the page that you couldn't tell what went with what.

In the early days of the web, we saw the same phenomenon – an exuberance of design that made for colorful, but not usable, web pages. And a common problem with those web pages was a colored or patterned background that made the text virtually unreadable.

Design exuberance can still be wonderful – if it matches the personality of your site. But it has to work with and not against the content. If you want people to read what you are putting on the web, you have to make it legible. Legibility requires high contrast between text and background.

Keep the background clear so that the text is readable

Patterned backgrounds obscure the text, as in Figure 7-16. Don't do it. You defeat your business goals if you make the page hard to see and the text hard to read.

Keep the background light and the text dark

High contrast requires a light background and dark text (or vice versa). Many color combinations are difficult to read because they don't provide enough contrast between the text color and the background color, as you can see in Figure 7-17.

Are you focusing on the building or the words?

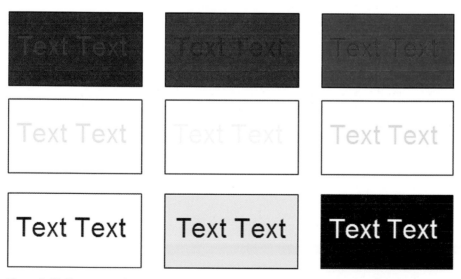

Figure 7-16 When the foreground (the words) and the background compete for attention, it's hard to read the words. Plain backgrounds don't compete. Textured backgrounds or backgrounds with pictures, such as the building here, do compete.

www.huntmuseum.com

Figure 7-17 You can see for yourself that some combinations of text and background are very difficult to read.

Dark backgrounds and dark type are often very hard to distinguish. Blue text on red may even seem to vibrate on the screen, making that combination very hard on the eyes. Light colors (including light gray) are hard to see on a white background. Figure 7-18, an overview about asthma, shows you how some of these combinations look on an actual web page.

Figure 7-18 High contrast between text color and background color is essential for legibility. If people have to struggle, will they stay on your site?   aafa.org

By far the best combination for contrast and legibility is black type on a white or very light background. That's what most web teams are using today for parts of the web page that must be easy to read. It's a smart way to go.

Use light text on a dark background sparingly

Light text on a dark background is often called "reverse text." Most people find reverse text difficult to read, especially for sustained periods.

Don't use reverse text for the main content area of your web site. Look again at Figures 7-16 and 7-18. You can see how difficult reverse text is to read. (Also look at the case study at the end of the chapter.)

You can often make reverse text work well for small bits on the page, if you keep the contrast high, the size large enough, and the font bold enough. For example, many designers use reverse text on tabs, as you can see in Figure 7-19, from a Canadian site about diabetes.

Figure 7-19 White type on a colored background is often used for tabs, where people are reading only one or two words at a time.   www.diabetes.ca

14. Think about all your site visitors when you choose colors

As you choose colors, also keep in mind that different cultures attach different meanings to colors and be sensitive to the needs of people who are color blind.

Above all, never let color be the only indicator of a feature, function, or information. Make sure your site works in monochrome, even if you think no one will ever look at it without the color. Print your pages in grayscale so that you can check that all the page elements are obvious and readable.

Think about the cultural meaning of colors

Some graphics and colors are pretty much universal. You can drive almost anywhere and assume that a traffic light has red, amber, and green; that red means stop and green means go.

Colors also evoke connotations, like calm, aggressive, soothing, cheerful, luxurious – and those connotations are different in different cultures. Colors are sometimes associated with political parties – and, again, those associations vary with the culture. Rather than spout a few factoids about specific colors in specific cultures, the best advice I can give you is to test your site with people from the different cultures that you want to reach.

Some colorful hats

As seen by a person with deuteranopia, a form of red/green colorblindness.

Figure 7-20 What you see as bright and different colors may not appear that way to everyone else.   www.vischeck.com

Check your colors to avoid problems for color-blind users

About 5 to 8 percent of males have some form of color deficiency, most often that they cannot distinguish red or that they cannot distinguish green. (Some women are color-blind, too; but the percentage is very small.)

Consider what would happen on your web site if someone cannot tell that items on the page are in red or in green (or in other specific colors). In the example from the Vischeck web site (Figure 7-20), if you only want people to see a row of hats, it may not matter that some people can't tell that the hats are different colors. If it is important that people see hats with five different colors, however, these colors won't work for everyone.

Selecting colors that work for the different varieties of color blindness is not simple. It isn't as easy as just avoiding all reds and all greens. The shade of red or green matters. Other colors can be problematic when used in combination with certain reds and greens.

The best way to know if your web page is going to cause problems is to check your design before you finalize it. Sites like www.vischeck.com and colorfilter.wickline.org let you see how your web pages will look to people with different types of vision problems.

Putting it all together: A case study

In the following case study, I take a web page through a series of changes so that you can see the effect of each design guideline.

Case Study 7-1   **Revising a poorly designed web page**

Consider this page about the White-naped Crane as it originally appeared
on a web site about birds:

White-naped Cranes *Grus vipio*

White-naped Cranes breed in northeastern Mongolia, northeastern China, and
adjacent areas of southeastern Russia.

Breeding habitat includes shallow wetlands and wet meadows in broad river
valleys, along lake edges, and in lowland steppes or mixed forest-steppe areas.
White-naped Cranes nest, roost, and feed in shallow wetlands and along wetland
edges, foraging in adjacent grasslands or farmlands. During migration and on
their wintering grounds, they use rice paddies, mudflats, other wetlands and
agricultural fields. White-naped Cranes are excellent diggers. The White-naped
Crane is often found in the company of other crane species , including Red-
crowned, Hooded, Demoiselle, and Eurasian Cranes.

Mated pairs of cranes, including White-naped Cranes, engage in unison calling,
which is a complex and extended series of coordinated calls. The birds stand in a
specific posture, usually with their heads thrown back and beaks skyward during
the display. In White-naped Cranes, the female initiates the display and utters
two calls for each male call. The male always lifts up his wings over his back
during the unison call while the female keeps her wings folded at her sides. All
cranes engage in dancing, which includes various behaviors such as bowing,
jumping, running, stick or grass tossing, and wing flapping. Dancing can occur
at any age and is commonly associated with courtship, however, it is generally
believed to be a normal part of motor development for cranes and can serve to
thwart aggression, relieve tension, and strengthen the pair bond.Nests are
mounds of dried sedges and grasses in open wetlands. Females usually lay two
eggs and incubation (by both sexes) lasts 28-32 days. The male takes the
primary role in defending the nest against possible danger. Chicks fledge (first
flight) at 70-75 days.

www.ornithology.com

? Do you agree that it is not as well designed as it might be?

You can probably identify several ways to make it easier for people to
see it, read it, and get the information from it.

First, let's make it easier just to see by increasing the contrast between the background and the text.

White-naped Cranes *Grus vipio*

White-naped Cranes breed in northeastern Mongolia, northeastern China, and adjacent areas of southeastern Russia.

Breeding habitat includes shallow wetlands and wet meadows in broad river valleys, along lake edges, and in lowland steppes or mixed forest-steppe areas. White-naped Cranes nest, roost, and feed in shallow wetlands and along wetland edges, foraging in adjacent grasslands or farmlands. During migration and on their wintering grounds, they use rice paddies, mudflats, other wetlands and agricultural fields. White-naped Cranes are excellent diggers. The White-naped Crane is often found in the company of other crane species , including Red-crowned, Hooded, Demoiselle, and Eurasian Cranes.

Mated pairs of cranes, including White-naped Cranes, engage in unison calling, which is a complex and extended series of coordinated calls. The birds stand in a specific posture, usually with their heads thrown back and beaks skyward during the display. In White-naped Cranes, the female initiates the display and utters two calls for each male call. The male always lifts up his wings over his back during the unison call while the female keeps her wings folded at her sides. All cranes engage in dancing, which includes various behaviors such as bowing, jumping, running, stick or grass tossing, and wing flapping. Dancing can occur at any age and is commonly associated with courtship, however, it is generally believed to be a normal part of motor development for cranes and can serve to thwart aggression, relieve tension, and strengthen the pair bond.Nests are mounds of dried sedges and grasses in open wetlands. Females usually lay two eggs and incubation (by both sexes) lasts 28-32 days. The male takes the primary role in defending the nest against possible danger. Chicks fledge (first flight) at 70-75 days.

Serif font; white background

And then let's change from centered text to left-aligned and break it up more.

White-naped Cranes *Grus vipio*

White-naped Cranes breed in northeastern Mongolia, northeastern China, and adjacent areas of southeastern Russia.

Breeding habitat includes shallow wetlands and wet meadows in broad river valleys, along lake edges, and in lowland steppes or mixed forest steppe areas. White-naped Cranes nest, roost, and feed in shallow wetlands and along wetland edges, foraging in adjacent grasslands or farmlands. During migration and on their wintering grounds, they use rice paddies, mudflats, other wetlands and agricultural fields. White-naped Cranes are excellent diggers.

The White-naped Crane is often found in the company of other crane species, including Red-crowned, Hooded, Demoiselle, and Eurasian Cranes.

Mated pairs of cranes, including White-naped Cranes, engage in unison calling, which is a complex and extended series of coordinated calls. The birds stand in a specific posture, usually with their heads thrown back and beaks skyward during the display.

In White-naped Cranes, the female initiates the display and utters two calls for each male call. The male always lifts up his wings over his back during the unison call while the female keeps her wings folded at her sides.

All cranes engage in dancing, which includes various behaviors such as bowing, jumping, running, stick or grass tossing, and wing flapping. Dancing can occur at any age and is commonly associated with courtship; however, it is generally believed to be a normal part of motor development for cranes and can serve to thwart aggression, relieve tension, and strength the pair bond.

Nests are mounds of dried sedges and grasses in open wetlands. Females usually lay two eggs and incubation (by both sexes) lasts 28-32 days. The male takes the primary role in defending the nest against possible danger. Chicks fledge (first flight) at 70-75 days.

Serif font; white background; left-aligned; seven paragraphs instead of three

Now let's change from serif font to sans serif at the same point size.

White-naped Cranes *Grus vipio*

White-naped Cranes breed in northeastern Mongolia, northeastern China, and adjacent areas of southeastern Russia.

Breeding habitat includes shallow wetlands and wet meadows in broad river valleys, along lake edges, and in lowland steppes or mixed forest steppe areas. White-naped Cranes nest, roost, and feed in shallow wetlands and along wetland edges, foraging in adjacent grasslands or farmlands. During migration and on their wintering grounds, they use rice paddies, mudflats, other wetlands and agricultural fields. White-naped Cranes are excellent diggers.

The White-naped Crane is often found in the company of other crane species, including Red-crowned, Hooded, Demoiselle, and Eurasian Cranes.

Mated pairs of cranes, including White-naped Cranes, engage in unison calling, which is a complex and extended series of coordinated calls. The birds stand in a specific posture, usually with their heads thrown back and beaks skyward during the display.

In White-naped Cranes, the female initiates the display and utters two calls for each male call. The male always lifts up his wings over his back during the unison call while the female keeps her wings folded at her sides.

All cranes engage in dancing, which includes various behaviors such as bowing, jumping, running, stick or grass tossing, and wing flapping. Dancing can occur at any age and is commonly associated with courtship; however, it is generally believed to be a normal part of motor development for cranes and can serve to thwart aggression, relieve tension, and strength the pair bond.

Nests are mounds of dried sedges and grasses in open wetlands. Females usually lay two eggs and incubation (by both sexes) lasts 28-32 days. The male takes the primary role in defending the nest against possible danger. Chicks fledge (first flight) at 70-75 days.

Sans serif font; white background; left-aligned; seven paragraphs instead of three

And finally, let's revise it by reorganizing, letting go of words, putting in bold headings, and adding a picture. The page may grow a little longer, but isn't it more inviting and easier to get the information?

White-naped Cranes – *Grus vipio*

Breeding Area
Northeastern Mongolia
Northeastern China
Adjacent areas of southeastern Russia.

Habitat
Shallow wetlands and along wetland edges, foraging in adjacent grasslands or farmlands.

White-naped Crane

During migration and on their wintering grounds, White-naped Cranes use rice paddies, mudflats, other wetlands and agricultural fields.

Breeding habitat includes shallow wetlands and wet meadows in broad river valleys, along lake edges, and in lowland steppes or mixed forest steppe areas.

Nests
Mounds of dried sedges and grasses in open wetlands.

Eggs
Usually two.

Nesting behavior
Both sexes incubate the eggs, which hatch in 28-32 days. The male takes the primary role in defending the nest against possible danger. Chicks fledge (first flight) at 70-75 days.

White-naped Cranes are often found with other crane species
The White-naped Crane is often found in the company of other crane species, including Red-crowned, Hooded, Demoiselle, and Eurasian Cranes.

White-naped Cranes dance, as do other cranes
All cranes engage in dancing, which includes various behaviors such as bowing, jumping, running, stick or grass tossing, and wing flapping. Dancing is commonly associated with courtship; but it can occur at any age. Dancing is generally believed to be a normal part of motor development for cranes and can serve to thwart aggression, relieve tension, and strength the pair bond.

Mated cranes call and display
Mated White-naped Cranes, like other crane pairs, engage in unison calling, which is a complex and extended series of coordinated calls. The birds stand in a specific posture, usually with their heads thrown back and beaks skyward during the display.

In White-naped Cranes, the female initiates the display and utters two calls for each male call. The male always lifts up his wings over his back during the unison call while the female keeps her wings folded at her sides.

SUMMARIZING CHAPTER 7

Here are key messages from Chapter 7:

- Make the page elements obvious, using patterns and alignment.

- Consider the entire site when planning the design.
  - Plan a consistent design across the web site.
  - Understand the process that moves from plan to launch.
  - Integrate content and design from the beginning.

- Work with templates.

- Use space effectively. Keep active space in your content.
  - Understand passive space and active space.
  - For your web content, focus on active space.

- Beware of false bottoms.

- Don't let headings float.

- Set a sans serif font as the default.
  - The research with paper that said serif is best is very old and does not apply to web sites.
  - The new research on the web has mixed results for reading speed and comprehension, but people prefer sans serif.

- Think broadly about users and their situations when setting type size.
  - Set the default large enough for your site visitors.
  - Adjust your content so that you can use large enough type and get your message into the space you have.
  - Let people choose their own text size.
  - Make all the text adjust, not just the main content area.

- Use a fluid layout with a medium line length as default.

- Don't write in all capitals.

- Don't underline anything but links. Use italics sparingly.

- Provide good contrast between text and background.
  - Keep the background clear so that the text is readable.
  - Keep the background light and the text dark.
  - Use light text on a dark background sparingly.

- Think about all your site visitors as you choose colors.
  - Think about the cultural meaning of colors.
  - Check your colors to avoid problems for color-blind users.

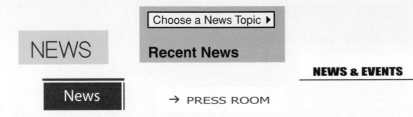

The Internet has radically changed the audiences, the life span, the distribution, and the use of press releases, but press releases haven't changed to meet the needs of web users. They should.

If your web site includes news briefs in any of their various forms – press releases, news items, announcements – this interlude is for you.

The old – and ongoing – life of a press release

A typical press release is one or two pages about a key event, a key person, new results, or new information. Press releases were originally designed to get information to newspaper and broadcast reporters in a timely manner, with the hope that the news would be featured that day – or shortly after that day – in the paper or on radio or TV. Most press releases include the name and phone number of someone in the organization's press office so that reporters can call for more information. Press releases are often meant to entice reporters to call so that a public relations person can expand on the information, connect the reporter to people to quote, and so on.

Newspapers, radio, and TV are still there. And reporters still need press releases – delivered to them electronically or on paper. But those very same press releases are also now posted on the organization's web site – not just for a day, not just for the "press," not just to entice people to call for more information.

What has changed?

Once that press release is posted to a web site, it becomes part of an entirely different world. The following table shows the incredible difference between the traditional life of a press release (or any type of news item or news announcement) and its life on a web site:

	Old world: print and broadcast	New world: web
Audience	Media people: journalists and reporters	Everyone!
Life Span	One day? Less? May be filed for future use	Forever!
Distribution	Sent only to specific people	Available through home pages and search engines – including external search engines
Use	Often expanded by talking to a media relations specialist and other people	As a summary, fact sheet, or basic information, either standing alone or linked to more details elsewhere in the web site

How do people use press releases on the web?

Story 1: Press release as summary

The new life of press releases hit home to me when I was usability testing a web site meant for researchers and research librarians. The first scenario went something like this: "You have heard that researchers at . . . just released a new report on . . . and you want to see what they have to say on that topic."

We thought that participants would look for the new report. Some of them did. But half of the participants first clicked on the tab for Press. One said: "I always look for a press release first. A good press release summarizes the key findings. Then I'll decide if I really want the report."

Great idea. But, at the time, the press releases on this web site were just copies of paper documents; they didn't even link to the full report. They do now!

Link press releases to relevant information on the web site – full reports, pages about people, production information, and so on.

Think about the long life, new users, new uses of today's press releases.

Story 2: Press release as fact sheet

I started to be more alert to how and when press releases show up on web sites. In another usability test – this time of a health information site for the general public – some people searched for information. Old news items (press releases) showed up in the search results.

Several participants selected the link to a press release, without realizing that's what it was – or even knowing anything about press releases. They assumed the links were to web information and they treated the press releases as fact sheets.

For these participants, the old press releases were simply information on a relevant topic. They wondered why the pages didn't have headings, why the pages had wall-to-wall text, why the pages looked different from other pages on the site.

Participants also assumed that the contact name on the page was the researcher when it was really someone in the organization's public relations office. The press release page did not say who the person was.

Consider a new format for press releases – one that matches the web site and typical web writing. Or plan for two versions – one for print and one for the web.

Include a date on all press releases.

Think about whose name and contact information should go on a document that may live a very long time on the web site.

State clearly who the people you name are.

Story 3: Press release as basic information

I was helping another web team do a content inventory of what they had available on each of the main topics the site covers. To everyone's surprise, most of the information was in old press releases.

 What are your press releases like? How well do they serve as summaries for the public? as fact sheets? as basic information? How well do they fit into the look and feel of your site? How well do they work as web writing?

Story 4: The press call up

I once had several reporters as participants in a usability test. They all said they had no time or patience for trying to use the organization's web site. They knew whom to call. *They* were not reading news items on the web site.

What should we do?

Plan and write press releases with the web audiences and web life span in mind. Write them as web information. Use subheadings, short paragraphs, bulleted lists, tables, graphics, and links.

Think of both the print and the web life of press releases. If you must keep the paper version in its traditional style, produce a second version for the web – one that will work well for its long web life.

Typical press release	Web-based information
No headings after the title	Broken into sections with bold headings
Long paragraphs	Very short paragraphs, bulleted lists, tables, graphics
No links	Links to full report, additional information, other relevant pages on the site, relevant people
Full page, looks like a paper document	Fits into the template of other information pages on the site
Name and phone number of media relations specialists, often without saying who they are	Clearly indicates who each person named is; links to email or information about the person

Also remember that today's press releases are going to people who write for other web sites, not only to people who write for print newspapers, magazines, newsletters, and broadcast radio or TV. Your press release may show up just as you created it through a link in a blog or copied onto someone else's web site – all the more reason for putting out the press release in a version that follows guidelines for good web writing.

Does it make a difference?

Yes. A client let me test different styles in a usability study. We took a press release that had all the features in the table under "typical" and redrafted it to have the features under "web-based information."

For more on this study, see Redish, 2005.

In one scenario of the usability test, participants got to a press release that we had not changed. In another scenario, they got to the one we had changed. (The two press releases were on different topics, but they were similar in length and level of detail. Both were information based on studies that researchers in the organization had done. Both came up as primary choices when people searched the site for their respective topics. So both were acting like fact sheets.)

Many participants noticed the difference and commented spontaneously and favorably about the one that was more like web-based information:

At the end of each session, we pointed out the two press releases again and asked the participants which they preferred. All but one preferred the one with headings and links that was formatted like the rest of the site. The one who differed said: "I always print the web pages I want."

What would the difference look like?

Look at the press releases in Figures Interlude 1-1 and Interlude 1-2.
Both are from Jiffy Lube, a company that takes care of cars. The first
figure is in traditional press release style. The second is much more like
the type of page that people expect on the web.

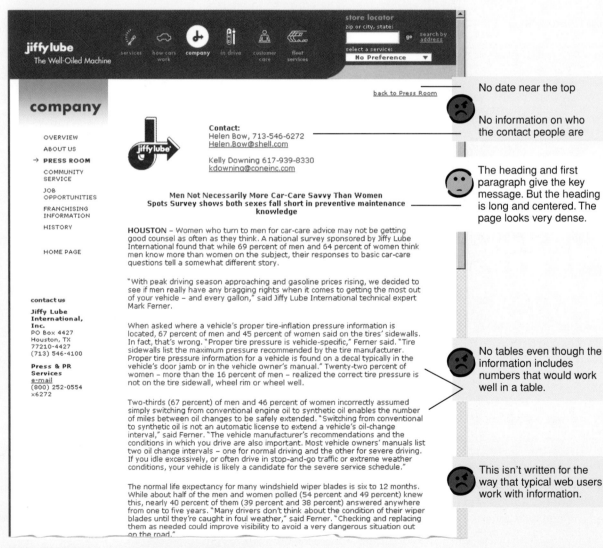

Figure Interlude 1-1 A press release in traditional style.   www.jiffylube.com

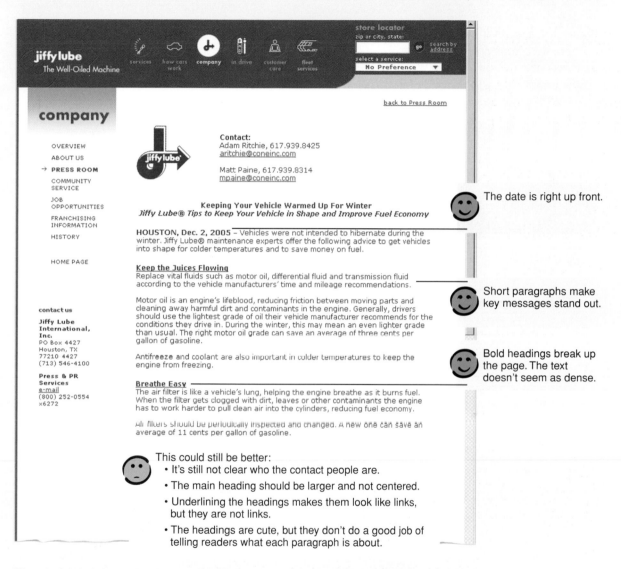

Figure Interlude 1-2 A different press release from the same site. This one is much closer to good style for web information.   www.jiffylube.com

On the Jiffy Lube site, both of these are found only under the link to Company and then to Press Room. However, I found them by Googling for information on how to get my car ready for winter. So press releases, even when deep in a site, are web information that is readily reached by ordinary people asking a search engine for help on their topic.

Press releases show up as web information through searches — at your site or through an external search engine.

And the search results from Google led me to the same press release on many other sites. Your press releases may have a very long life as web information – not only on the site you maintain, but on other sites as well. Think about this new life and consider writing press releases to serve better as web information.

For an example of how a press release became web information – and needs to be updated and managed as web information – see Case Study 8-4 at the end of Chapter 8.

Tuning Up Your Sentences

8

Now that you've planned your content, broken up your documents, decided on your essential messages, and designed your web pages, let's talk about writing the paragraphs, sentences, and words of your web content.

As you write, remember these three principles from Chapter 1:

- Good web writing is like a conversation.
- Good web writing answers people's questions.
- Good web writing lets people "grab and go."

As you write:

- Picture the people you are talking with. If you have personas, think of them as you write.
- Ask yourself: What would people ask me about this topic on the phone?
- Reply to them as if they were on the phone.

> You might keep photos and short descriptions of your personas on your cubicle corkboard or on your desk. If you are part of a team, the team might keep persona posters on the wall of the conference room that you use to review draft web content.

Writing informally is not "dumbing down"

Language changes over time. It always has. Standards for good writing also change over time. They always have.

Style in nineteenth-century novels differs from style in twentieth-century novels, which, in turn, differs from the emerging style of twenty-first-century novels.

Similarly, people's expectations of appropriate style for information (instructions, notices, short essays) have changed over time. Over the past 100 years, writing style for communicating useful information has become much less formal. And that trend is accelerating with the web.

This is not "dumbing down"! It's communicating clearly. It's writing so that busy people can understand what you are saying the first time that they read it.

Ten guidelines for tuning up your sentences

These 10 guidelines will help you write clear and effective paragraphs, sentences, and words:

1. Talk to your site visitors. Use "you."
2. Show that you are a person and that your organization includes people.
3. Write in the active voice (most of the time).
4. Write short, simple, straightforward sentences.
5. Cut unnecessary words.
6. Give extra information its own place.
7. Keep paragraphs short.
8. Start with the context – first things first, second things second.
9. Put the action in the verbs, not the nouns.
10. Use your web users' words.

Lists and tables – great ways to tune up your sentences – get their own chapter after this one.

1. Talk *to* your site visitors. Use "you"

If you are telling people something about themselves or something that applies to them, talk *to* them. Use "you." That makes the information inviting and personal.

You can convey serious and important messages – even legal rules and notices – using "you." In fact, people are much more likely to take in those messages if you write with "you" because they can see themselves in the text.

 Compare Figures 8-1 and 8-2. Which version of the information about Australians sending food to the U. S. is easier to read? Which would you rather read? Which would you pay more attention to?

> The new ruling requires the person sending the food to electronically file a "prior notice" with the U.S. Food and Drug Administration. A confirmation of the FDA receipt of "prior notice" must be presented to Australia Post along with the parcel. The "prior notice" form is available at: http://www.access.fda.gov

 This talks about the new ruling even though it is really instructions for what "the person" must do.

Figure 8-1 The original text of one paragraph from the middle of new requirements for mailing food from Australia to the U. S.   www.auspost.com.au

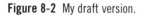

What must I do?

1. Go to the U.S. Food and Drug Administration's <u>prior notice web page</u>.

2. Fill out the form there about the food you are sending to the U.S.

   The system verifies that your information is complete and then shows you a confirmation page with a confirmation number and the information you submitted.

3. Print the confirmation page.

4. Take the confirmation with you when you go to Australia Post to mail your package.

This talks to the web user.

Figure 8-2 My draft version.

Writing that has no personal pronouns often has other problems as well. Just in this one paragraph, we also find passive voice, nouns that hide verbs, and a step that is implied but not clearly stated. The notice that this bit came from also has information in the wrong order, outdated information, and other problems. As you write and revise web content, think about all the guidelines together.

I analyze and rewrite the entire notice as Case Study 8-4 at the end of this chapter.

Be consistent; don't mix nouns and "you" when talking about the same person

In Figure 8-3, instructions for registering for classes, people may be confused because one sentence talks about "the student" and the next talks about "you." If these are the same people, why not use "you" throughout?

Use appropriate nouns to talk about others

If you are talking about other people, things, or situations, use a name or description rather than "you." You can still keep the sentences short and active, as in Figure 8-4.

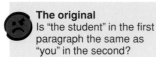

The original
Is "the student" in the first paragraph the same as "you" in the second?

THE STUDENT MUST REGISTER AND THE FEE PAYMENT PROCESS STARTED BEFORE THE FIRST DAY OF CLASSES EACH SEMESTER OR THE STUDENT WILL BE PURGED FROM CLASSES. A late fee is assessed if a student registers or is re-registered after the first day of classes.

You will also need to apply for admission and signup for your classes through ETSU. You may do so at

www.storynet.org/etsu/2005/summer

A revision
Now it's clear that we are talking to the same person – and it's friendlier.

You must register and arrange to pay for your classes before the first day of class. If you don't, you will be dropped from the classes. We charge a late fee if you register or re-register after the first day of class.

You must also apply for admission and sign up for the class through…. Apply at

Figure 8-3 Using "you" whenever you are talking to your site visitors makes information both friendlier and easier to grasp quickly.

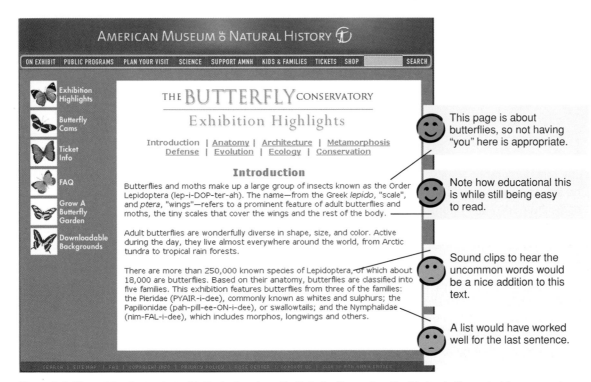

This page is about butterflies, so not having "you" here is appropriate.

Note how educational this is while still being easy to read.

Sound clips to hear the uncommon words would be a nice addition to this text.

A list would have worked well for the last sentence.

Figure 8-4 When giving facts, start with the topic – here, that's butterflies and moths. That sets the context for your readers and helps you write active sentences.

www.amnh.org

Use the imperative in instructions

If you are giving hints or tips or instructions, use the imperative. That's just the verb by itself without "you." For example, "Run!" "Think!" and "Do!" are all imperatives. Figure 8-5 shows you a list of imperatives in tips about house hunting.

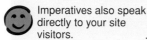

Imperatives also speak directly to your site visitors.

Here are some good house hunting tips:

> Take pictures inside and outside the home.
> Bring a spouse, family member, or friend.
> Make sure the house fits into your budget.
> Ask about utility and maintenance costs.
> Think of commuting time and costs.

Figure 8-5 These tips are easy to read and remember because they each start with a short, plain English imperative verb.   www.freddiemac.com

Use "you" rather than "he or she"

Using "you" also has another advantage: It saves you from gender-specific writing. In English, the third-person singular pronouns (he, she, him, her, his, hers) are gender specific. When you use one of these pronouns, some readers will think that you mean only people of that gender. To avoid even the perception of being exclusionary, avoid gender-specific writing when you are writing about or to both men and women.

If you write "employee," "customer," or "contractor," you may have a problem referring to that person later in the sentence or paragraph. Workarounds, such as combining the two genders into "s/he" or "he or she," are awkward.

"You" is not gender-specific. As you can see in Figure 8-6, the sentences with "you" or the imperative avoid the gender pronoun problem and also speak more directly to site visitors.

Of course, if you are talking about a specific person, it's fine to name the person and to use the appropriate gender-based pronoun to refer to that person. Figure 8-7 is a brief item about how well Jimmy Rollins was doing playing baseball.

If the customer wants to read this article,
he or she must become a registered user of this site.

Long, not direct, and needs
"he or she" – pronouns
with gender.

If you want to read this article, you must become
a registered user of this site.

Better – speaks to the site
visitor. But it's still long
and it's not inviting.

Not Yet Registered?

**Please take a moment to complete this one-time required
registration. Once registered, you gain access to
washingtonpost.com.**

Another good option:
A question heading and a
friendly imperative.

Figure 8-6 Using "you" also avoids the need for "he or she."

SEPTEMBER 27, 2005

BASEBALL: Double Your Pleasure

The most amazing number about Jimmy Rollins' 31-game hitting streak entering
tonight's game - which apparently ties the club record set by Ed Delahanty - is that he
has hit 17 doubles in 31 games.

The "he" here is fine because
the writer is talking about
a specific person.

Posted by Baseball Crank at 07:58 PM | Baseball 2005 | Comments (1) | TrackBack (0)

Figure 8-7 Gender pronouns are okay if you're talking about a specific person.
www.baseballcrank.com/archives2/baseball_2005/index/php

More on gender-neutral writing

Here are four techniques for gender-neutral writing:

- Use "you."

     The customer may return any item she is not satisfied with.

    You may return any item you are not satisfied with.

- Use the plural.

     A contractor must renew his insurance every year.

     Contractors must renew their insurance every year.

- Turn a noun phrase into a verb phrase.

   A prospective student must turn in his or her application at least two weeks before classes start.

   A prospective student must apply at least two weeks before classes start.

- Use "a," "an," or "the" instead of a pronoun

   Your supervisor must explain her decision in writing.

   Your supervisor must explain the decision in writing.

2. Show that you are a person and that your organization includes people

Let's turn to the other side of the conversation. In web writing, it's appropriate to use "I' or "we" for yourself and the organization you are writing for.

If you are blogging, "I" is fine

Bloggers often write about personal experiences and opinions. The singular pronoun "I" is appropriate. Figure 8-8 is a Tunisian blogger's admiration for local craft work.

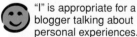

📦 Tunisian Handicrafts

"I" is appropriate for a blogger talking about personal experiences. ── I really admire handicrafts and think they're marvellous works of art.

I remember when I was a kid, after school, I'd go to my grandmother's house where I'd have lunch then go for my Arabic lessons. After I was done with my Arabic lessons, I'd just go wandering around discovering new places in the city.

One of the places I discovered and loved passing by every now and then was a little workshop where a number of men would be sitting on stools working on these beautiful copper plates. With a small hammer and chisel, they tapped away, carving all these amazing shapes and texts with magnificent calligraphy.

I'd just say hi and stand there watching and admiring their work. It was really so inspiring. To this day, whenever I pass through the souks in the old medina of Tunis and see all the copper plates with their different designs, my memories take me back to that little workshop where I saw that art being created.

Figure 8-8   www.subzeroblue.com

If you are writing your own articles, "I" is fine

You may be the sole author of an article or opinion piece or a story. "I" is appropriate; it's your voice as author; your voice in the conversation with the people coming to see what you are saying. In Figure 8-9, Lou Manfredini makes ladder safety very personal.

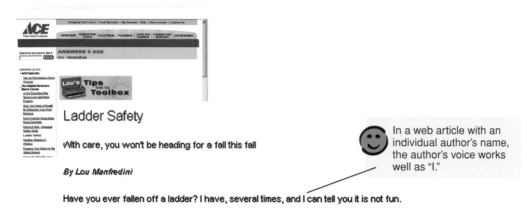

In a web article with an individual author's name, the author's voice works well as "I."

Figure 8-9   www.acehardware.com

If you are writing for an organization, use "we"

When you are writing for an organization, use the plural pronouns: "we," "us," "our." Most web sites do this at least on the Contact Us page, as Lego does in Figure 8-10.

You should use "we," "us," and "our" throughout the site, not just on the Contact Us page. A major goal of most web sites is to have people get information for themselves without calling or using a live chat option. The more you do to make your site visitors feel that you are in the conversation with them on all your web pages, the more comfortable most people feel.

Figure 8-11 shows you how Bed Bath & Beyond puts small conversational notes on the pages with items it is selling. Figure 8-12 shows you how even a government agency (the U. S. Social Security Administration) can be friendly and conversational.

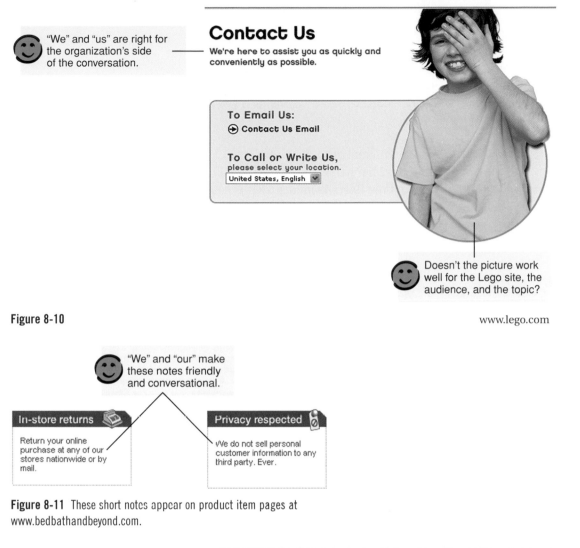

"We" and "us" are right for the organization's side of the conversation.

Contact Us
We're here to assist you as quickly and conveniently as possible.

To Email Us:
⊕ Contact Us Email

To Call or Write Us,
please select your location.
United States, English ▾

Doesn't the picture work well for the Lego site, the audience, and the topic?

Figure 8-10   www.lego.com

"We" and "our" make these notes friendly and conversational.

In-store returns
Return your online purchase at any of our stores nationwide or by mail.

Privacy respected
We do not sell personal customer information to any third party. Ever.

Figure 8-11 These short notes appear on product item pages at www.bedbathandbeyond.com.

Social Security Online
www.socialsecurity.gov

Disability & SSI

Home | Questions? ▾
Contact Us ▾

Search [   ] GO

Qualify and Apply
Updated: July 2005

Find out if you're eligible for Social Security Benefits

Benefit Eligibility Screening Tool (BEST)

Use our screening tool to help identify all the different Social Security programs for which you may be eligible.

When you use "we" and "our," you invite people into the conversation with you.

Overview

We pay disability benefits under two programs: the Social Security disability insurance program and the Supplemental Security Income (SSI) program.

Figure 8-12 Even government agencies can use "we" and "our."   www.ssa.gov

Sometimes, it's okay to talk about the organization by name

If policies or standards in your company or agency don't allow you to use "we," push to change the policies or standards. If you can't – or if, in fact, it makes sense to refer to the company or agency by name – you can still write clear, active sentences.

Sears could have changed some of the references in Figure 8-13 to "we," but they may have repeatedly used the name and not the pronoun to emphasize that they want you to join the Sears team.

Learn more about Sears, Roebuck and Co.
Business Opportunities - Dealer Stores

Sears invites you to join one of America's leading retailers of appliances, electronics, hardware and lawn and garden equipment through its unique Authorized Retail Dealer Store Program.

Have you always wanted to own your own business? Be your own boss? If being in charge of your own future is what you dream of but you're not sure how to make that dream a reality, the Sears Authorized Retail Dealer Store Program may be the opportunity you've been looking for.

"We" would have worked on this web page instead of "Sears," but the writer may have wanted to emphasize which team you would be joining.

Sears celebrates the entrepreneur in you and also supports your goals of achieving success as a business owner by offering the strength and dependability of the Sears name. Sears provides **in-depth training** plus **on-going support** from our dedicated team based in the field and at the company's headquarters.

Figure 8-13 In some situations, naming the company rather than using "we" is appropriate.   www.sears.com

For questions and answers, use "I" and "you" for the site visitor, "we" for the organization

If you follow the advice in this book, you'll find yourself writing in question-and-answer style for at least some of your web content. Web writers often ask me how to use pronouns in these questions and answers.

When the site visitor is asking the question, I suggest using

- "I" and "my" in the question (the voice of the site visitor)
- "you" and "your" in the answer for that same person
- "we" and "our" for the company or agency that is answering the question

www.Expedia.com

When the site is asking the question, I suggest using

- "you" and "your" in the question (addressing the site visitor)
- "I" and "my" in the answer (the voice of the site visitor)
- "we" and "our" for the company or agency that is asking the question

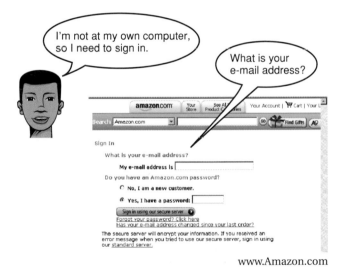

www.Amazon.com

3. Write in the active voice (most of the time)

When you write in conversational style, you'll also find yourself writing mostly active sentences. Active sentences help people grab information quickly and easily.

Sentences in the active voice (active sentences) describe "who does what to whom." In an active sentence, the person or thing doing the action (the actor) comes before the verb. That's the logical word order for English sentences.

Sentences in the passive voice (passive sentences) start with the object that is acted on rather than with the actor. They either put the actor after the verb in a "by . . ." phrase or they leave the actor out entirely. Figure 8-14 gives you examples of active and passive sentences.

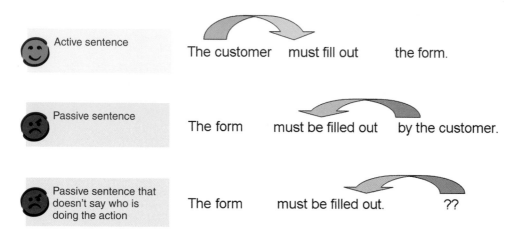

Active sentence — The customer   must fill out   the form.

Passive sentence — The form   must be filled out   by the customer.

Passive sentence that doesn't say who is doing the action — The form   must be filled out.   ??

Figure 8-14 Sentences in the active voice put the actor (the "doer") before the verb. In most situations, active sentences are easier to understand than passive sentences.

I am not saying that every sentence must be in the active voice. When you want to focus on the object or when it really does not matter who is responsible for doing the action, the passive voice may be appropriate.

When an entire web page is in the passive, however, people have a very hard time reading it. Their eyes glaze over; they lose interest. Too much of the passive voice is both boring and really difficult to understand.

 Figure 8-15 is a set of instructions from a university web site about ordering laboratory supplies. If you had to order something, what would you do? Would you ask a colleague to show you how to do it rather than try to make sense of this web page?

In a fascinating study some years ago (with pages from a published document that was very much like the web example in Figure 8-15), the researchers asked people to read the pages and say everything they were thinking out loud. The people in the study translated what they read as they went along, turning the writing into active sentences with actors and action verbs. That's a lot of mental work. And the readers misinterpreted many of the passive sentences; their translations were wrong.

"The Scenario Principle" by Flower, Hayes, and Swartz. You'll find the full reference in the bibliography.

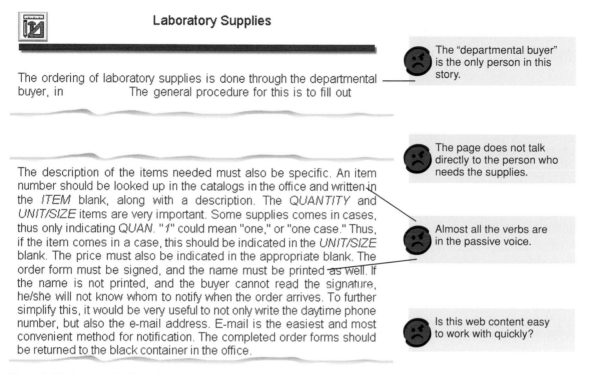

Laboratory Supplies

The ordering of laboratory supplies is done through the departmental buyer, in   The general procedure for this is to fill out

The "departmental buyer" is the only person in this story.

The page does not talk directly to the person who needs the supplies.

The description of the items needed must also be specific. An item number should be looked up in the catalogs in the office and written in the *ITEM* blank, along with a description. The *QUANTITY* and *UNIT/SIZE* items are very important. Some supplies comes in cases, thus only indicating *QUAN*. "*1*" could mean "one," or "one case." Thus, if the item comes in a case, this should be indicated in the *UNIT/SIZE* blank. The price must also be indicated in the appropriate blank. The order form must be signed, and the name must be printed as well. If the name is not printed, and the buyer cannot read the signature, he/she will not know whom to notify when the order arrives. To further simplify this, it would be very useful to not only write the daytime phone number, but also the e-mail address. E-mail is the easiest and most convenient method for notification. The completed order forms should be returned to the black container in the office.

Almost all the verbs are in the passive voice.

Is this web content easy to work with quickly?

Figure 8-15 An example of how the passive voice can make web content difficult to understand and use.

Remember that we are trying to help busy people grab what they need. In most situations, people get the information from active sentences more quickly and more accurately than from passive sentences. And writing in the active voice pressures you to find out who is responsible for actions – information that your site visitors often need to know.

Figure 8-16 shows how we could make the web content in Figure 8-15 easy for people to use quickly and accurately.

Ordering Laboratory Supplies

The departmental buyer in .... handles all orders for laboratory supplies. If you need supplies, fill out the .... form. You can get the form from the buyer in ......

1. Fill out the form

To assure that you get the correct supplies, fill out the form carefully and correctly. Please pay special attention to these parts of the form:

- ITEM: Look up the item in the catalogs in the office. Put in both the item number and a specific description.

- QUANTITY and UNIT/SIZE: Be sure to tell us both quantity and unit/size. If you write "1" for quantity but don't tell us the unit / size, we won't know if you want 1 piece or 1 case.

- PRICE: You must fill out the space for price. The catalog you are ordering from should tell you the price.

2. Sign and print your name on the form

When you have filled out all the information about the supplies you need, be sure to sign the form and print your name. We want to get the supplies to you, but if we can't read your name, we won't know to whom to deliver them.

3. Give us your phone number and email address

We need to know how to reach you. Please give us both a phone number and an email address; we find email is the easiest way to contact people.

4. Turn in the completed form

Put your completed order form in the black container in ...... The buyer will handle your order and notify you when your supplies arrive.

Figure 8-16 My suggestion for revising Figure 8-15.

4. Write simple, short, straightforward sentences

Busy web users have no time to untangle long, convoluted sentences. Try to keep your sentences to about 10 to 20 words.

Here are three critical tips for keeping sentences short and simple:

- Cut the fluff.
- Say it once clearly.
- Keep each sentence to one thought – or two tightly connected thoughts.

If people have to read a sentence more than once to understand it, rewrite it.

Very short sentences are okay, too

Sentences do not need even 10 words to be meaningful and sharp. If you write in questions and answers, a short answer may be all that people need.

Fragments may also work

The personality, tone, and style of your site may make sentence fragments acceptable to your readers. Consider the description of a blog in Figure 8-17. The sentence fragments work well here.

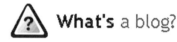 **What's** a blog?

A blog is a personal diary. A daily pulpit. A collaborative space. A political soapbox. A breaking-news outlet. A collection of links. Your own private thoughts. Memos to the world.

Your blog is whatever you want it to be. There are millions of them, in all shapes and sizes, and there are no real rules.

Fragments work well in the informal style of this site.

Figure 8-17 Blogger.com's explanation of a blog.

www.blogger.com/tour_start.g

Even in very serious writing, busy web users need sentences they can understand easily

Simple, short, and straightforward sentences are critical for serious topics. In fact, the more complex the topic, the more you need to be sure that you are writing in a clear, coherent way so that your web site visitors understand your essential messages.

Figure 8-18 shows how the writers at Revenue Canada use short, active sentences to explain what a corporation is and that corporations must pay tax.

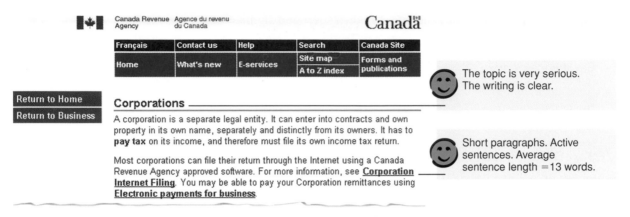

Figure 8-18 You can let go of the words and be clear even for highly technical information.   www.cra-arc.gc.ca

Finding your voice and style

Clear and simple writing need not be monotonous. Your writing can have character and flavor and also be clear. The writing style you use should match the overall personality and tone of your site: formal/informal/irreverent/fun/serious, and so on.

For example, doesn't the "Huh? What does that mean?" in this excerpt from GasPriceWatch.com give you a sense of the writer's personality and style? Does it make you want to continue to read – to continue to be in a conversation with this site?

Why is GasPriceWatch.com Different?

We are database driven. (Huh? What does that mean?) All of the 128,000+ stations in GPW are part of huge inventory of gas stations that our spotters have submitted over the years. If you find a station that is not in GasPriceWatch.com, you can submit it with the street address, city, zip code and other

5. Cut unnecessary words

Sometimes, sentences are longer than necessary because the writer uses several words where one (or none) will do.

The San Francisco Zoo could cut many words from Figure 8-19 without losing any meaning. As you can see in Figure 8-20, the heading and the links are all you need to give the essential messages. Today, colored underlined words send the message "click on me."

Figure 8-19   www.sfzoo.org/visit/

Figure 8-20 This would be quicker and easier for site visitors.

6. Give extra information its own place

In English, once we find the subject of the sentence (the noun or pronoun at the beginning), we expect to find the verb close by. If extra information takes us off on a tangent, we may lose track of what the sentence is all about. When the extra information ends, and we are back in the main sentence, we may get back on track – and then forget the tangential information.

Don't put extra "stuff" between the subject and the verb. Case Study 8-1, Untangling a convoluted sentence, shows you both how tangled a sentence can get in web content and how you can untangle it.

Case Study 8-1   Untangling a convoluted sentence

Do you find it easy to grab the information from the following sentence?

> **Interested persons, on or before June 15, 2007, may submit to the Hearing Clerk, 1000 Pennsylvania Avenue, NW, Washington, DC 20000, written comments regarding this proposal. Faxed comments will be accepted at 202-555-1234. To submit comments electronically, go to this site:**

 The first sentence is 26 words – not overly long, but it has too many tangents in the middle.

Finding the underlying sentence in all these tangles

Let's untangle the overstuffed sentence by finding the subject, verb, and object of the sentence.

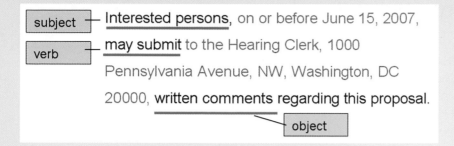

Now you can see that the writer has stuffed the date between the subject and the verb and the address between the verb and the object.

Revising the sentence into good web writing

Wouldn't it be easier for your site visitors if we gave the information like this?

We invite you to comment on this proposal.

Deadline: June 15, 2007

Submit written comments

 by mail to
Hearing Clerk
1000 Pennsylvania Avenue, NW
Washington, DC 2000

 by fax to
202-555-1234
Attn: John Jones

 electronically at
www........

Considering the site visitors' scenarios

The revised version also matches the order in which the site visitor needs the information. It matches different people's scenarios.

Learning from this case study

A sentence with many commas probably has extra information stuffed into it. This case study shows us how to untangle sentences like this.

- Think of your web users and how and when they will use each piece of information.

- If people need different pieces of the information at different times, separate those pieces.

- Keep the main parts of the sentence (subject, verb, object) together.

- Put the key message first.

- Pull out extra information and make each piece its own sentence.

- Consider using visuals, fragments, and lists where they convey the information quickly and accurately.

7. Keep paragraphs short

Your seventh-grade teacher probably never wrote for the web. The type of writing that you did in school (essays, reports, stories) was different from typical writing for the web. For a traditional essay, you were probably taught to write with at least three sentences and more likely five or six sentences in each paragraph. That's too long for a web paragraph.

On the web, a one-sentence paragraph is fine

Keep your web paragraphs very short. On many web news sites, you see paragraphs that have only one or two sentences each, as in Figure 8-21, reporting on a soccer match.

Figure 8-21 Very short paragraphs work well on the web.   soccernet.espn.go.com

Lists and tables may be better than paragraphs

In many cases, you can take information out of sentences and make it more scannable with lists or tables. That's what the next chapter is all about. Before we get there, however, let's consider the last 3 of the 10 guidelines for tuning up your sentences.

8. Start with the context – first things first, second things second

Start each paragraph with a topic sentence – a sentence that sets the context, that tells readers what the paragraph is about.

Even within a sentence, always set the context first. Research shows that people jump to act as soon as they see something that tells them to act. They don't always read on to see if more information restricts the action. That's the problem with a sentence like the one in Figure 8-22, from *e*How's instructions on getting wine stains out of fabric.

For a fascinating study showing that people don't wait for the context, see Dixon, 1987.

Putting the "if" clause first gives people the restricting (context) information *before* they find out how to act (Figure 8-23).

You'll see the whole *e*How page that this piece comes from in the next chapter on lists (Figures 9-18 and 9-19).

6. If washing by hand, rub the table salt into the stain. Then pour boiling water onto it from a height of 12 to 36 inches if the stain persists and if the fabric can tolerate high heat.

 People may start pouring boiling water without reading the last part of the sentence.

Figure 8-22 Putting the context after the action may cause sad consequences. Research shows that people act without reading the whole sentence.   www.eHow.com

If the stain persists and if the fabric can tolerate high heat, pour boiling water onto it from a height of 12 to 36 inches.

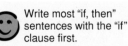 Write most "if, then" sentences with the "if" clause first.

Figure 8-23 My suggested revisions.

Carroll and his colleagues also noted this "jump to act" behavior when they watched people using software manuals. See Carroll, 1990.

Your first reaction to the paragraph in Case Study 8-2 may be "huh?" As you consider it, however, I think you'll quickly see that it has the same problem as the example in Figure 8-22.

Case Study 8-2   **Starting with the context – the topic**

 Is the following paragraph instantly clear? If not, consider what you would do with this information if you were telling it to someone on the phone. Which part of this sentence would you say first? What would come next? How would you break up the information?

> Approved fumigation with methyl bromide at normal atmospheric pressure, in accordance with the following procedure, upon arrival at the port of entry, is hereby prescribed as a condition of importation for shipments of yams.

Slightly simplified from a U. S. Department of Agriculture regulation

Reversing the order

If you were to say the content of this sentence to someone, you would probably reverse the order of the information. You would start with the yams because that's the answer to the question, "What are we talking about?" The yams are the context, the topic, the connection to what the web user came looking for. The yams belong at the beginning, as in this suggested revision:

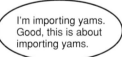

I'm importing yams. Good, this is about importing yams.

If you are importing yams into the United States, — Context; what the reader knows

they must be fumigated when they arrive at the port of entry. — New information for the reader

The approved fumigation method is to use — "Fumigation" is now "old" information because it's already been introduced.

methyl bromide at normal atmospheric pressure, following this procedure: — New information for the reader

Now the reader expects information about the procedure and how to use the methyl bromide.

Learning from this case study

Once again, we see how focusing on the reader helps you write well for the web. When you are writing specific web content, think about the specific knowledge your site visitors come with.

- Think about what your site visitors do and do not know.
- Start with what they know. Then introduce new information.
- Consider using the pattern "if, then." It follows the reader's logic and makes you put first things first, second things second. (You almost always need the "if" in the "if clause," but you don't actually have to write the word "then" in the "then clause." For example, write "if it's raining, take an umbrella.")

The principle of "context, topic, known" before "new" is sometimes also called "given — new." See the work of linguists H. H. Clark and Susan Haviland on "Comprehension and the given-new contract."

9. Put the action in the verbs, not the nouns

Much of the web is about action, and verbs are the action words. Even in essays and articles, you are probably talking about people doing things. Doing = action = verbs.

If you bury the action in a noun, the verb often becomes just an uninteresting placeholder. Take the action out of the noun and put it in the verb, where it belongs.

		noun hiding a verb		weak verb

😠 Weak sentence   The Commission's <u>recommendations</u> for changes <u>were</u> few in number.

strong verb

😊 Strong sentence   The Commission <u>recommended</u> few changes.

noun hiding a verb ... weak verb ... noun hiding a verb

😠 Weak sentence   <u>Retention</u> of these records for seven years <u>is</u> a <u>requirement</u> for licensees.
requirement → require → must
retention → retain → keep

strong verb

😊 Strong sentence   Licensees <u>must keep</u> these records for seven years.

Here's a table of the most common endings for nouns that hide verbs.
Use this to help you keep the action in the verb and not in the nouns.

Look for this	As in this example	Which should be this verb
-al	deni**al**	deny
-ance	mainten**ance**	maintain, keep up
-ence	concurr**ence**	concur, agree
-ment	assign**ment**	assign
-sion	transmis**sion**	transmit, send
-tion	recommend**ation**	recommend
-ure	fail**ure**	fail, if you don't

10. Use your web users' words

Think about your audience! is a good mantra on every level of web
writing – deciding what content to cover, constructing sentences and
paragraphs, and choosing words.

Your web users may not know words that are commonplace to you. How
many web users are likely to understand the instruction for using the
Search function on the Express Order site in Figure 8-24?

Some writers try to sound impressive by using big words. If those big
words aren't ones your readers know, they won't be impressed. They'll
give up on your web site and go to someone else who speaks their
language.

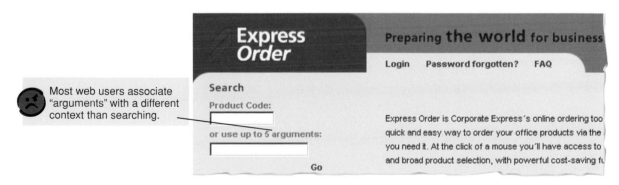

Figure 8-24 This search interface is likely to confuse, not help, most web users.

Compare the words in two versions of information for parents on child-hood asthma (Figures 8-25 and 8-26). Both say they are meant for parents, but one uses clinical, medical words; the other talks in ordinary people's words. Both have questions as headings, but one says, "What is the incidence of asthma?" and the other says, "How common is asthma in children?"

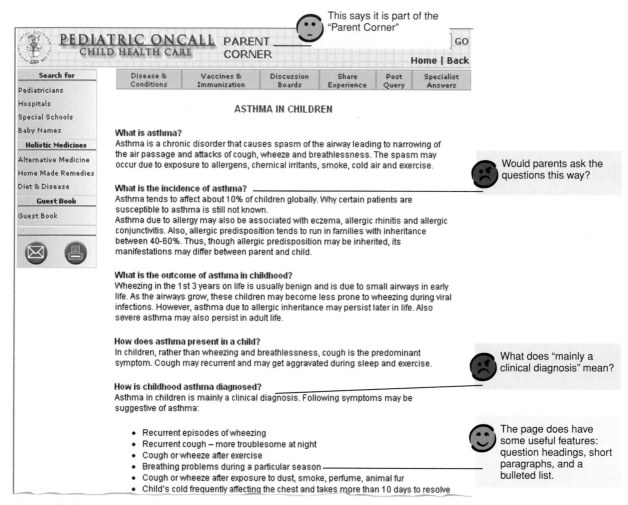

Figure 8-25 This article on asthma in children is addressed to parents but uses doctors' language.   www.pediatriconcall.com

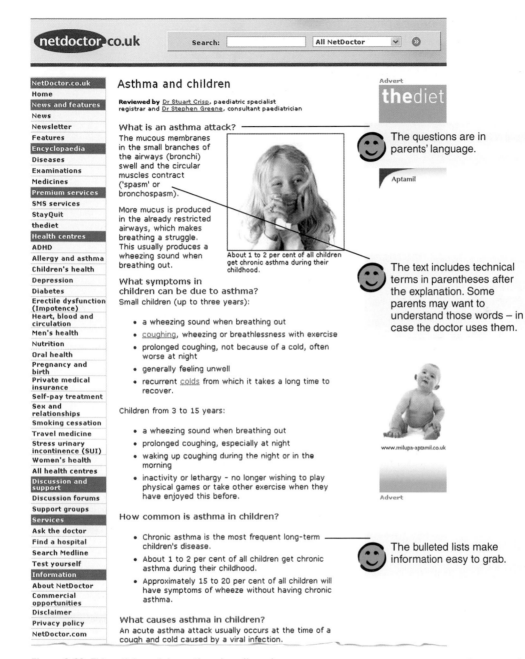

netdoctor.co.uk   Search: [   ] [All NetDoctor ▼] ➡

NetDoctor.co.uk
Home
News and features
News
Newsletter
Features
Encyclopaedia
Diseases
Examinations
Medicines
Premium services
SMS services
StayQuit
thediet
Health centres
ADHD
Allergy and asthma
Children's health
Depression
Diabetes
Erectile dysfunction (Impotence)
Heart, blood and circulation
Men's health
Nutrition
Oral health
Pregnancy and birth
Private medical insurance
Self-pay treatment
Sex and relationships
Smoking cessation
Travel medicine
Stress urinary incontinence (SUI)
Women's health
All health centres
Discussion and support
Discussion forums
Support groups
Services
Ask the doctor
Find a hospital
Search Medline
Test yourself
Information
About NetDoctor
Commercial opportunities
Disclaimer
Privacy policy
NetDoctor.com

Asthma and children

Reviewed by Dr Stuart Crisp, paediatric specialist registrar and Dr Stephen Greene, consultant paediatrician

What is an asthma attack?

The mucous membranes in the small branches of the airways (bronchi) swell and the circular muscles contract ('spasm' or bronchospasm).

More mucus is produced in the already restricted airways, which makes breathing a struggle. This usually produces a wheezing sound when breathing out.

About 1 to 2 per cent of all children get chronic asthma during their childhood.

What symptoms in children can be due to asthma?

Small children (up to three years):

- a wheezing sound when breathing out
- coughing, wheezing or breathlessness with exercise
- prolonged coughing, not because of a cold, often worse at night
- generally feeling unwell
- recurrent colds from which it takes a long time to recover.

Children from 3 to 15 years:

- a wheezing sound when breathing out
- prolonged coughing, especially at night
- waking up coughing during the night or in the morning
- inactivity or lethargy - no longer wishing to play physical games or take other exercise when they have enjoyed this before.

How common is asthma in children?

- Chronic asthma is the most frequent long-term children's disease.
- About 1 to 2 per cent of all children get chronic asthma during their childhood.
- Approximately 15 to 20 per cent of all children will have symptoms of wheeze without having chronic asthma.

What causes asthma in children?

An acute asthma attack usually occurs at the time of a cough and cold caused by a viral infection.

Advert
thediet
Aptamil

☺ The questions are in parents' language.

☺ The text includes technical terms in parentheses after the explanation. Some parents may want to understand those words – in case the doctor uses them.

www.milupa-aptamil.co.uk

Advert

☺ The bulleted lists make information easy to grab.

Figure 8-26 This article explains asthma in ordinary language.   www.netdoctor.co.uk

We all read the simple, short, common words faster

Even highly educated, sophisticated readers do best with plain English writing. They are often the busiest and most impatient of your site visitors, so words that they recognize most quickly work best. And we all recognize and read the most common words more quickly than less common ones. Here's a very short list of just a few words to change. You can create your own much longer list.

Instead of this	try this
obtain	get
prior to	before
purchase	buy
request	ask for
subsequent	next
terminate	end
utilize	use

Consider your broad web audience

You may be saying: "We have special words that have specific meaning in our field. We have to use them." If everyone you are communicating with shares your technical language, then it's fine to use it.

But think about these facts:

- Most writers greatly overestimate the knowledge and vocabulary of even their professional audiences. A lawyer in one specialty may not know the terminology of another specialty – and people coming to the web for information about wills or leases may not be lawyers. A doctor in one specialty may not know the terminology of another specialty – and many health care workers are not doctors. How broad is your web audience?

- The web is almost certainly bringing you a broader audience than you were communicating with on paper. Your Internet site is available to a global audience. As companies go global, even intranet sites must serve people from many countries. Many of your site visitors may not be native speakers of the language of your web site.

You should offer your web content in many languages and in culturally appropriate ways for audiences in other countries and for diverse audiences in your own country. Localizing web sites is an important topic, but it is beyond the scope of this book.

- In your own country, the audiences for your web site may include many immigrants who speak and read your language as their second, third, or fourth language.

Putting it all together

Let's close this chapter with two case studies that bring together several of the guidelines. In Case Study 8-3, I apply several guidelines to a paragraph for doctors about getting a medical license. In Case Study 8-4, I return to the example that started this chapter and show you the entire page about Australians shipping food to the U. S.

Case Study 8-3   Applying several guidelines to one paragraph

As you write or revise your web content, you will often find yourself using many guidelines at the same time.

Consider this paragraph from the American Medical Association's web site. It is advice to doctors who are considering moving and getting licensed in a new area.

 The advice starts with an implied task. It doesn't tell the reader to do the task.

 "Ask" is an imperative verb. It addresses the reader directly.

When contacting a licensing board for the first time, ask for a copy of its current licensing requirements and the average time it takes to process applications. This will provide the physician with a solid idea of when to consider closing an existing practice and/or plan a move as well as with information about the potential problem areas to be addressed in completing an application.

 The second sentence is 39 words long and includes several points.

 The "physician" is the person the writer is talking to. The writer has already spoken directly to the physician with the imperative "ask." Why not continue to speak directly to the physician with "you"?

 The first sentence has two points: ask for (1) requirements and (2) average time.

The second sentence tells why to do that, but it gives the rationale for asking about time before the rationale for asking for the requirements.

www.ama-assn.org/ama/pub/category/2644.html

By attending to all these problems together, we can make this web content much easier for very busy doctors to grab quickly and go on to getting the task done.

 Start with an imperative rather than just implying that the doctor should do this.

 Talk directly to the doctor. Use "you."

Contact the licensing board where you want to practice. Ask for a copy of its current licensing requirements and the average time it takes to process applications.

Separate contacting from asking. Make two short sentences from one long one.

Reading the requirements will help you understand any potential problems you may have in applying. Finding out about the processing time will help you plan when to close your current practice or when to move.

Divide the information into two shorter paragraphs.

Break the original second sentence into two short sentences. Put them in the same order as the two tasks in the first paragraph.

Give each reason its own sentence. The average sentence length drops from 33 to 16 words.

www.ama-assn.org/ama/pub/category/2644.html

Case Study 8-4   Revising an entire web article

An important aspect of web management is keeping information up to date. Plan to review and revise regularly. Take the opportunity when you are bringing information up to date to also rethink your web content based on what you have learned in this book.

Consider the article from the Australia Post site that you saw in Figure 8-1. Here is the entire page as I captured it in 2006:

New requirements for mailing food to the US

The heading is not very informative.

The following media release was issued by the US Embassy in Canberra on Monday December 19.

December 19 of what year?

Australians planning to send food to the United States should be aware of the new "prior notice" requirement under the U.S. Bioterrorism Act.

Here, "the person" should be "you."

The new ruling requires the person sending the food to electronically file a "prior notice" with the U.S. Food and Drug Administration. A confirmation of the FDA receipt of "prior notice" must be presented to Australia Post along with the parcel. The "prior notice" form is available at: http://www.access.fda.gov

"Confirmation" and "receipt" are nouns that hide verbs.

"Must be presented" is passive voice.

However, although this requirement came into effect on December 12, the U.S. Food and Drug Administration has advised that food mailed to the United States will not be refused entry if the parcel does not include the "prior notice" form from now until August 12, 2004. Australia Post has been advised of this change.

This paragraph is not needed in 2006.

The only exemption to this requirement is food that was made by an individual in his/her home and sent by that individual as a personal gift (for non-business reasons) to an individual in the United States.

The exception is at the bottom.

The text of the FDA press release outlining the transitional arrangements can be viewed at: http://www.fda.gov/bbs/topics/NEWS/2003/NEW00995.html.

This paragraph is not needed in 2006.

More information on the Bioterrorism Act is available on the FDA website at: http://www.cfsan.fda.gov/~dms/fsbtact.html

What would we want to fix?

Bringing the article up to date allows us to drop information that was needed only in the transition period that ended in August 2004.

While we are doing that, we can also make the article much easier for people to understand and use.

First, we would bring the exception to the top of the article. Never make people read a lot only to discover that the information does not apply to them!

Then, we would make the process much more obvious by addressing the reader directly and by breaking out each of the three steps. For writing rules, the appropriate style is to tell the reader, "you must. . . ." If we were not stating a legal requirement, but were instead just giving instructions, the appropriate style would be the imperative, "Fill out a 'prior notice' form. . . ."

Note that the original page was a news release. The Australia Post web site managers put it up exactly as it came from the U. S. Embassy. But we can ask whether, 4 years later, it must stay exactly as originally written. Why can't we revise it to be a better explanation for people who need the information?

This is an example of how press releases live forever on web sites. I talk about this interesting issue in the Interlude on the New Life of Press Releases.

What might a revised article look like?

Here is my suggested revision.

The effective date is in a fragment at the top.

The three questions give the page a clear structure.

Australians mailing food to the United States may have to fill out a prior notice form
Starting date: August 12, 2004

Must I do this?
There is one exception: If you made the food yourself in your home and are sending it as a personal gift (not for business reasons) to an individual in the United States, you do not have to fill out the prior notice form.

In all other situations, Australians must fill out the prior notice form.

What must I do?

1. Go to the U.S. Food and Drug Administration's prior notice web page.

2. Fill out the form there about the food you are sending to the U.S.

    The system verifies that your information is complete and then shows you a confirmation page with a confirmation number and the information you submitted.

3. Print the confirmation page.

4. Take the confirmation with you when you go to Australia Post to mail your package.

Why must I do this?
The U.S. Bioterrorism Act requires this.

The key message is in the heading.

The exception comes first, so many people won't have to read the whole page.

Each step gets its own paragraph.

What do we learn from this case study?

Think about these points as you write your web content:

- **Put a full date on every web page.** Include the year. And, by the way, write the date with the month spelled out. That's the best way to avoid misunderstandings because people in different countries read dates differently. As you may know, 5/1/2007 is May 1, 2007, in the United States and January 5, 2007, in much of the rest of the world.

- **Think about the life span of the web page.** If the web page has information that will not be needed after a certain date, revisit it to update it when that information is no longer needed.

- **In fact, have a maintenance schedule for all your web pages.**

- **Think about "holes" in the information.** What questions will people have that the information does not answer? Get the information. You'll avoid phone calls if you do.

- **Over time, turn press releases into pages of web information,** if that information is still needed.

- **Help people see very quickly if they need the information on the page.** Don't make people read a lot only to find out that what they read is not for them. Try to state exceptions first – in a positive way. Don't start with "Except for..." That's negative. You can always find a positive way to help people find the information that's right for them.

SUMMARIZING CHAPTER 8

Here are key messages from Chapter 8:

- Writing informally is not "dumbing down"!

- Talk to your site visitors.
  - Be consistent; don't mix nouns and "you" when talking about the same person.
  - Use appropriate nouns to talk about others.
  - Use the imperative in instructions.
  - Use "you" rather than "he or she."

- Show that you are a person and that your organization includes people.
  - If you are blogging, "I" is fine.
  - If you are writing your own articles, "I" is fine.

- – Organizations should use "we" throughout the site.
- – Sometimes, it's okay to talk about the organization by name.
- – For questions and answers, use "I" and "you" for the site visitor, "we" for the organization.

- Write in the active voice (most of the time).

- Write simple, short, straightforward sentences.
  - – Very short sentences are okay, too.
  - – Fragments may also work.
  - – Even in very serious writing, busy web users need sentences they can understand easily.

- Cut unnecessary words.

- Give extra information its own place.

- Keep paragraphs short.
  - – On the web, a one-sentence paragraph is fine.
  - – Lists and tables may be better than paragraphs.

- Start with the context – first things first, second things second.

- Put the action in the verbs, not the nouns.

- Use your web users' words.
  - – We all read the simple, short, common words faster.
  - – Consider your broad web audience.

- Apply all the guidelines together.

- Keep pages up to date.

- When you update pages, revise them to be better writing for the web.

- When you make web pages clearer, you may realize that people have questions the page does not answer.

Using Lists and Tables

9

A great way to let go of the words without losing essential meaning is to use lists and tables. Lists put active space around each item so that people can skim through the information. Tables take away words that aren't necessary and let people easily scan for what they need.

Nine guidelines for writing useful web lists

I'll start the chapter with nine guidelines to help you write useful and usable lists:

1. Use lists to make information easy to grab.
2. Keep most lists short.
3. Format lists to make them work well.
4. Match bullets to your site's personality.
5. Use numbered lists for instructions.
6. Turn paragraphs into steps.
7. Give even complex instructions as steps.
8. Keep the sentence structure in lists parallel.
9. Don't number list items if they are not steps and people might confuse them with steps.

Six guidelines for creating useful web tables

After the section on lists, we'll move to tables. With these six guidelines, you can help your web users easily grab information about comparisons and relationships:

10. Use tables when you have numbers to compare.

11. Use tables for a series of "if, then" sentences.

12. Think about tables as answers to questions.

13. Think carefully about what to put in the left column of a table.

14. Keep tables simple.

15. Format tables on the web so that people focus on the information and not on the lines.

1. Use lists to make information easy to grab

If you want to tell people about several items, set them out as a list. A list is easy to skim and scan.

Major tourist attractions in Beijing include the Great Wall, the Forbidden City, the Summer Palace, and Tiananmen Square.	Major tourist attractions in Beijing include: • The Great Wall • The Forbidden City • The Summer Palace • Tiananmen Square

 When you were reading the paragraph version, did you find yourself making a mental list?

Compare Figures 9-1 and 9-2. By replacing the paragraph in the original Adventure Women page with lists, we help people

• see how many items there are

• check off items (mentally, even if they can't write on the screen)

• find a specific item quickly

Figure 9-1 Information is more difficult to extract from a paragraph than from a list.
www.adventurewomen.com

Figure 9-2 A possible revision with the information in lists.

2. Keep most lists short

How long can a list be and still work well? It depends.

Short (5–10 items) is necessary for unfamiliar lists

If the list is not one that people immediately recognize, providing two or more shorter lists may be better. Here are two ways to shorten lists:

- Separate the list with a space or a short line after each logical group or after about five items.

- Make several lists, giving each a heading or an introduction.

Look again at Figure 9-2 where the 11 items are in two short lists.

Long may be okay for very familiar lists

Some lists can be long because users immediately understand what is in the list and where the item they want is. For example, a drop-down list of the U. S. states and territories has more than 50 entries. If the states and territories are in alphabetical order, however, the length of this drop-down list is not a problem for most people. They find the right entry quickly.

In Figure 9-3, you see how the Saint Bernard Rescue Foundation offers both a drop-down list and a map for people to select a state.

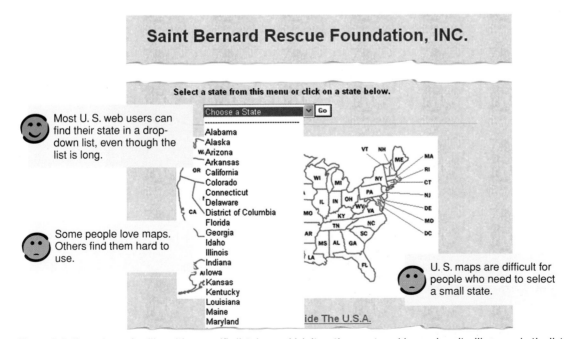

Figure 9-3 If people are familiar with a specific list, know which item they want, and know where it will appear in the list, a long list may be okay.

www.saintrescue.org

A useful way to set out a long list is to group it in a logical way for your web users.

A	N
Alabama	Nebraska
Alaska	Nevada
American Samoa	New Hampshire
Arizona	New Jersey
Arkansas	New Mexico
	New York
C	(except New York City)
California	New York City
Canal Zone	North Carolina
Colorado	North Dakota
Connecticut	Northern Mariana Islands
D	O
Delaware	Ohio
District of Columbia	Oklahoma
	Oregon
F	
Florida	P
Foreign or high-seas events	Pennsylvania
	Puerto Rico
G	
Georgia	R
Guam	Rhode Island
H	S
Hawaii	South Carolina
	South Dakota
I	
Idaho	T
Illinois	Tennessee
Indiana	Texas

Figure 9-4 With a list like this, web users will scroll quickly vertically to the item they need.
www.cdc.gov/nchs/howto/w2w/w2welcome.htm

If you have enough web page space, group the items in a long list like an index with a letter heading for each part of the alphabet. Figure 9-4 brings back the pathway page of states you saw in Chapter 4 in the case study about getting a copy of a birth certificate.

If some of your web users want to print the list, don't put it in a drop-down box.

For printing, put a long list in two columns, as shown in Figure 9-4.

3. Format lists to make them work well

The way you present lists can help or hinder people from using them easily. You want people to be able to connect the list with its introduction, see at a glance that you are giving a list, and find each list item easily. To help users do that,

- eliminate the space between the introduction and the list

- put a space between long items

- wrap lines under each other, not under the bullet

Eliminate the space between the introduction and the list

Plain HTML puts a line of space between the text before a list and the first item in the list. However, you want people to continue directly from the introduction into the list. Eliminate that extra space. Compare Figures 9-5 and 9-6 from an Australian mortgage company's web site.

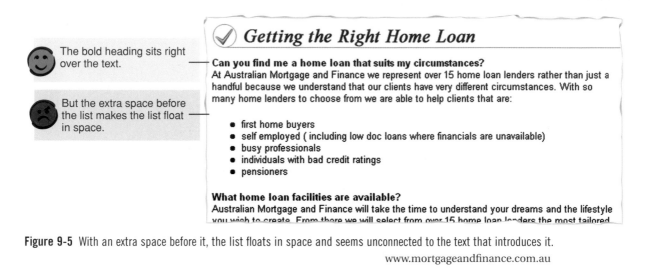

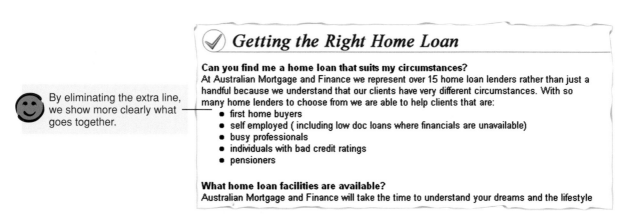

The bold heading sits right over the text.

But the extra space before the list makes the list float in space.

Figure 9-5 With an extra space before it, the list floats in space and seems unconnected to the text that introduces it.

www.mortgageandfinance.com.au

By eliminating the extra line, we show more clearly what goes together.

Figure 9-6 A suggested revision with no space before the list.

Put a space between long items

The lists up to here in this chapter all have very short lines of text. You can also have lists where each list item is a sentence – or more. When list items become long, putting them one on top of the other can make it very difficult for web users to tell that you are, in fact, giving them a list.

Figure 9-7 shows you an example from a page about getting a commercial driver's license in the U. S.

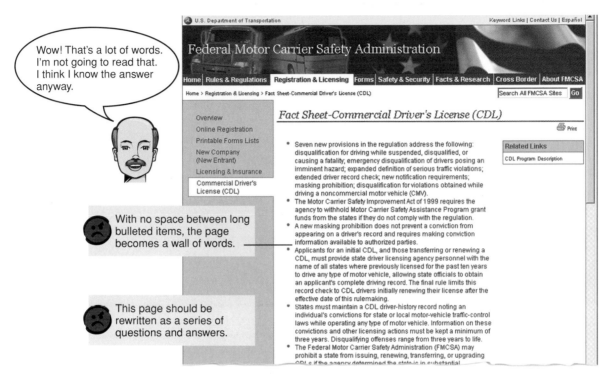

Figure 9-7 When usability test participants got to this page, they gave up. They would not read the page. They guessed the answer to the question they were researching. The bullets did not help because each item is long, and the items are all jammed together with no space between them.   www.fmcsa.dot.gov

Wrap lines under each other, not under the bullet

To make your lists look and work as lists, the bullets have to stand out. If the text wraps back to the beginning of the line under the bullet, each list item looks like a paragraph with a funny symbol at the beginning. It doesn't look like a list.

Where a list item wraps to a second line, start the second line – and all other lines – under the text, not back under the bullet.

If you code text as list items, HTML puts in a round circle bullet and wraps the text correctly. However, if you use graphics or other symbols for bullets, you have to be careful to get the text to wrap correctly.

Also, occasionally, I still see what looks like a regular list with regular bullets and yet it doesn't wrap well. Compare Figures 9-8 and 9-9, which show the top of a Lands' End information page. Figure 9-9 has the same information with changes to the format that make the list much more obvious.

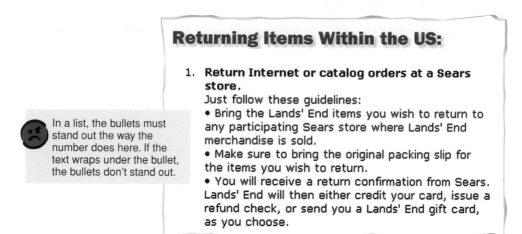

In a list, the bullets must stand out the way the number does here. If the text wraps under the bullet, the bullets don't stand out.

Figure 9-8 When the text wraps back under the bullets, it may not be obvious that you are giving a list.

www.landsend.com

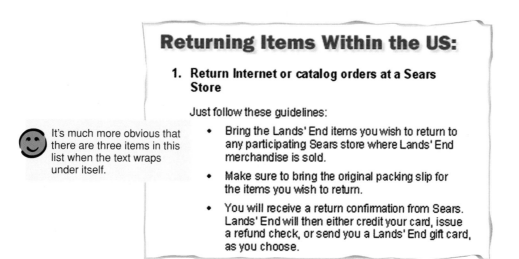

It's much more obvious that there are three items in this list when the text wraps under itself.

Figure 9-9 Notice how much more like a list this seems with the text wrapped well.

4. Match bullets to your site's personality

To indicate each list item, ordinary bullets (round dark circles) are fine; but you don't have to restrict yourself to them. If your site's personality allows something more innovative, you have many ways of showing that personality in your lists. Because the web is such a visual medium, it has expanded our definition of bullets to include many other symbols, icons, and even small photos or illustrations.

You can use a relevant symbol instead of ordinary bullets. Remember the fish as bullets in the case study from the Food and Drug Administration at the end of Chapter 6?

You can use a series of icons as "bullets." In Figure 9-10, the American Museum of Natural History uses different butterflies for each navigation option on the page. (This is from the example you saw as clear writing in Figure 8-4.)

These butterflies even "flutter" a bit within their white boxes as you mouse over them.

That's okay because they move only slightly, they stay within their boxes, and they move only when you hover over them. They don't wander around the screen.

The fluttering butterflies on this site's home page, however, are distracting because they interfere with what people are trying to do. (I'll talk more about this in Chapter 11 on graphics.)

Figure 9-10 Using pictures of butterflies for an exhibit of butterflies fits well with the personality the site is presenting — and may entice more people to the exhibit.

www.amnh.org

Figure 9-11 Small pictures can do well as bullets if it is clear what the picture shows.   www.nsf.gov/news

You can use photos or illustrations in place of bullets. In Figure 9-11, the U. S. National Science Foundation news site uses a small picture related to each news item both as a "bullet" and as part of the overall visual statement about the item.

Work with colleagues to establish the personality to use for bullets

As I mentioned in Chapter 3 when talking about how the home page reflects a site's personality, if you are the sole owner of the site (your blog, your site as a consultant), it's your decision. If you are part of an organization, however, it's not your decision alone. The site (including

See the sidebar in Chapter 3 titled Who decides on the site's personality?

the way you use bullets) has to send a consistent message about its personality. The bullets do not have to be identical throughout the site, but they should be equally relevant, innovative, and in the same overall design scheme.

Don't make people wonder if the bullets have more meaning than they do

I had to spend a few minutes deciding that the abcteach site in Figure 9-12 is using colors randomly.

If you use pictures as bullets, make sure that people can easily see and instantly understand the picture.

People should not have to stop and think about bullets.

Chapter 11 is all about guidelines for pictures.

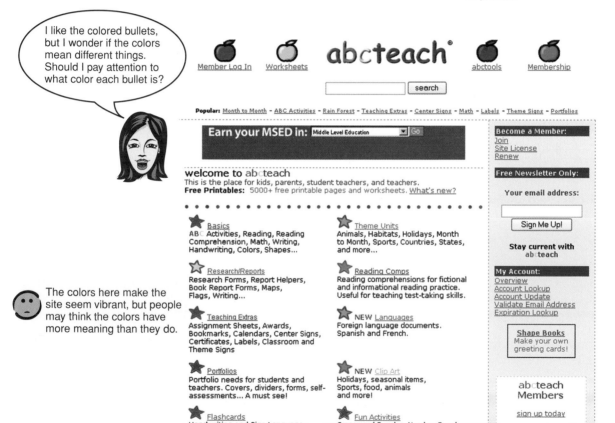

Figure 9-12 Interesting and different bullets can be a great addition to a site, but not if they make people spend time trying to find meaning for the differences. Also, this page may set up incorrect expectations. The pages beyond this home page are much more serious than this page of colored stars as bullets indicates.

www.abcteach.com

I wondered at first whether the colors of the stars or the links had specific meaning. Did all the green stars lead to similar types of pages? Did the yellow stars match the yellow apple at the top?

5. Use numbered lists for instructions

Much of the web is about completing tasks: arranging a loan, returning a package, booking travel, and so on. Tasks require instructions. Instructions imply sequence. Sequence = numbered steps in a list.

Create a blog in 3 easy steps: 1. create an account; 2. name your blog; 3. choose a template.

Create a blog in 3 easy steps:

1. Create an account.
2. Name your blog.
3. Choose a template.

Just as with the bulleted list at the beginning of this chapter, did you find yourself turning the paragraph version of these three steps into a visual, vertical list? Or did you skip the paragraph version entirely and look only at the list?

Figure 9-13 is the original of the "create a blog" page. Note how the writer uses bold, colored text, and big colored numbers to make the instructions stand out.

Create a **blog** in 3 easy steps:

Instructions work best as numbered steps.

1 Create an account

2 Name your blog

3 Choose a template

Figure 9-13 A colorful enticement to start a blog.   www.blogger.com

Always give instructions as a numbered list of the steps that people must do to complete the task. Figures 9-14 and 9-15, from *e*How and Amazon.com, present numbered steps for instructions that are longer and more complex than the blogger.com example.

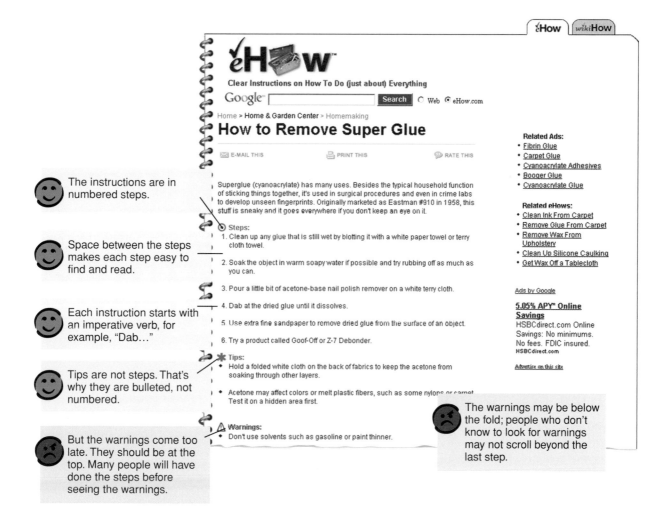

The instructions are in numbered steps.

Space between the steps makes each step easy to find and read.

Each instruction starts with an imperative verb, for example, "Dab…"

Tips are not steps. That's why they are bulleted, not numbered.

But the warnings come too late. They should be at the top. Many people will have done the steps before seeing the warnings.

The warnings may be below the fold; people who don't know to look for warnings may not scroll beyond the last step.

Figure 9-14 *e*How uses numbered lists to give step-by-step instructions.   www.eHow.com

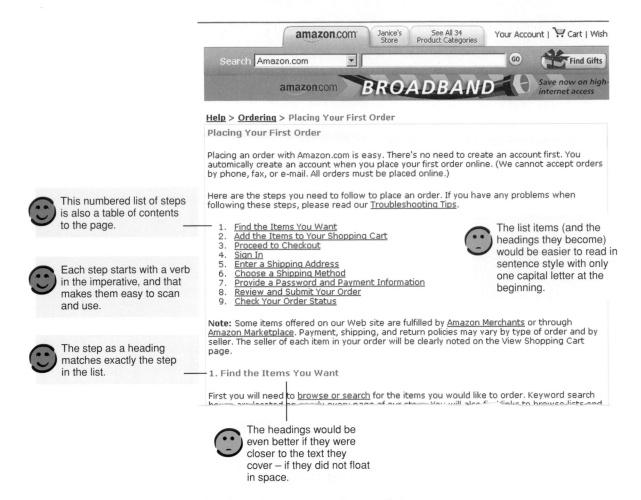

Figure 9-15 Numbered steps help people understand processes as well as specific tasks.   www.amazon.com

6. Turn paragraphs into steps

Have you ever been frustrated by instructions that aren't easy to follow?
Don't frustrate your web users. Realize when you should be giving
instructions. I see far too many pages that are paragraphs of facts when

what people really want are instructions on how to do something. If your
site visitors are asking, "How do I . . . ?" give instructions.

In Figures 9-16 and 9-17, on how to prepare concrete for a particular
type of bonding, notice how I've turned three dense paragraphs into
sections on why, what, and how. The suggested revision with headings
and lists is slightly longer than the original, but it is likely to be much
more effective.

Numbered lists for instructions help both site visitors and writers. They
help site visitors

- see how many steps there are
- check off steps (mentally, even if they can't write on the screen)
- read one step, do it, and find the next easily when they come back
  to the web page
- do the steps in the correct order
- do all the steps (without inadvertently missing a step)

You cannot easily tell that the page has both "why" and "how" information.

 The second and third paragraphs give instructions, but they don't read like instructions.

Surface Preparation for Strain Gage Bonding

Surfaces Requiring Special Treatment

Concrete

Concrete surfaces are usually uneven, rough, and porous. In order to develop a proper substrate for gage bonding, it is necessary to apply a leveling and sealing precoat of epoxy adhesive to the concrete. Before applying the precoat, the concrete surface must be prepared by a procedure which accounts for the porosity of this material.

Contamination from oils, greases, plant growth, and other soils should be removed by vigorous scrubbing with a stiff-bristled brush and a mild detergent solution. The surface is then rinsed with clean water. Surface irregularities can be removed by wire brushing, disc sanding, or grit blasting, after which all loose dust should be blown or brushed from the surface.

The next step is to apply <u>Conditioner A</u> generously to the surface in and around the gaging area, and scrub the area with a stiff-bristled brush. Contaminated Conditioner A should be blotted with <u>gauze sponges</u> , and then the surface should be rinsed thoroughly with clean water. Following the water rinse, the surface acidity must be reduced by scrubbing with <u>Neutralizer 5A</u> , blotting with gauze sponges, and rinsing with water. A final thorough rinse with distilled water is useful to remove the residual traces of water-soluble cleaning solutions. Before precoating, the cleaned

 People who are following the instructions may be surprised to get this far before learning that they need distilled water.

Figure 9-16 It's hard to find the steps in paragraphs like these, and most people won't try.   www.vishay.com

Numbered lists help writers

- make sure they have listed all the steps
- put the steps in the correct order
- check that the procedure works well (by reviewing or trying out the steps)
- save their web users from potentially disastrous mistakes of doing steps in the wrong order

I broke the information into "why," "what," and "how."

Preparing Concrete for Strain Gage Bonding

Why must concrete be specially prepared?

Concrete surfaces are usually uneven, rough, and porous. To develop a proper substrate for gage bonding, the concrete must have a leveling and sealing precoat of epoxy adhesive. Before applying the precoat, you must first prepare the concrete surface with a procedure that accounts for the fact that it is porous.

What do I need to prepare concrete for precoating?

You need

The bulleted list tells people what they must have ready so that they aren't surprised while completing the steps.

- Conditioner A
- Neutralizer 5A
- gauze sponges
- a stiff-bristled brush
- a mild detergent solution
- distilled water
- a wire brush or a disc sander or a grit blaster

How do I prepare concrete for precoating?

Clean the surface

1. Remove contamination from oils, greases, plant growth, and other soils by scrubbing vigorously with a stiff-bristled brush and a mild detergent solution.
2. Rinse the surface with clean water.
3. Remove surface irregularities by wire brushing, disc sanding, or grit blasting.
4. Blow or brush all loose dirt from the surface.

I divided the 12 steps into 3 logical groups. A 12-step list with no breaks is long.

Apply Conditioner A

5. Apply Conditioner A generously to the surface in and around the gaging area.
6. Scrub the area with a stiff-bristled brush.
7. Blot contaminated Conditioner A with gauze sponges.
8. Rinse the surface thoroughly with clean water.

I reorganized sentences so that the action verb is always at the beginning of the step.

Apply Neutralizer 5A

9. Scrub the surface with Neutralizer 5A to reduce the surface acidity.
10. Blot with gauze sponges.
11. Rinse with clean water.
12. Rinse again with distilled water to remove the residual traces of water-soluble cleaning solutions.

Each step is one action.

Figure 9-17 Think of recipes when you are giving instructions — even for information as technical as bonding to concrete surfaces. Isn't this much easier to use than the original in Figure 9-16?

In paragraph form, it's just too easy to forget a step and never realize that you've done that. It's just too easy to put down the steps in haphazard order and create problems for people who don't realize they should have done something first until it's too late.

7. Give even complex instructions as steps

Instructions are not always a straightforward list where everyone must do all the steps. Sometimes, you have to explain branching – where the next step depends on which of two or more conditions are true.

You can still present clear instructions even for complex situations. Consider Figures 9-18 and 9-19, where I suggest a revision to the *eHow* instructions on removing wine stains from fabric.

If the process is very long and complex, think about it as a little web site rather than as one web page. Create a pathway page where each link leads to part of the process. Look back at Figure 5-3 about buying a home for an example of this way of structuring a complex process.

Steps 5 and 6 are alternatives. You do one or the other, not both. But they aren't formatted to show that.

eHOW™

Clear Instructions on How To Do (just about) Everything

Google [   ] [Search] ○ Web ⦿ eHow.com

Home > **Home & Garden Center** > Homemaking

How to Remove Red Wine Stains From Fabric

4. Review the washing instructions on the label of the fabric. Heed any special care instructions.

5. If the fabric is machine-washable, immerse the garment in cold water and gently rub the stain out. Apply a laundry pretreatment such as a stain remover, wash in cool water and air dry.

6. If washing by hand, rub the table salt into the stain. Then pour boiling water onto it from a height of 12 to 36 inches if the stain persists and if the fabric can tolerate high heat.

Figure 9-18 When instructions include "if" statements, people have to figure out which to do. Formatting them as consecutive steps may confuse people.   www.eHow.com

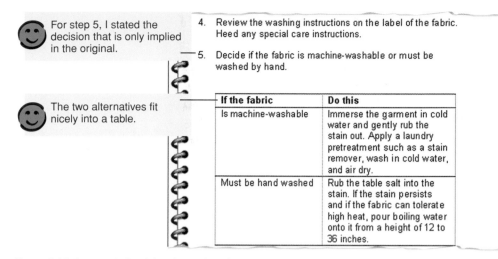

For step 5, I stated the decision that is only implied in the original.

4. Review the washing instructions on the label of the fabric. Heed any special care instructions.

5. Decide if the fabric is machine-washable or must be washed by hand.

The two alternatives fit nicely into a table.

If the fabric	Do this
Is machine-washable	Immerse the garment in cold water and gently rub the stain out. Apply a laundry pretreatment such as a stain remover, wash in cold water, and air dry.
Must be hand washed	Rub the table salt into the stain. If the stain persists and if the fabric can tolerate high heat, pour boiling water onto it from a height of 12 to 36 inches.

Figure 9-19 A suggested revision that makes the alternatives clearer.

8. Keep the sentence structure in lists parallel

People are very pattern-oriented. It's faster and easier to read a list when all the entries are in the same sentence structure.

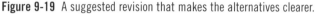

Create a blog in 3 easy steps:

1. Create an account.
2. Name your blog.
3. Choose a template.

Create a blog in 3 easy steps:

1. Create an account.
2. You must name your blog.
3. Six templates to choose from.

Did you choose the one on the left? That's the one in parallel structure. But did you first assume it would be the one on the right? If you did, that's how quickly you had built a pattern from the little tables like this in this chapter.

The other two examples you've seen in this table format both had the "good" choice on the right. I tripped you up (at least momentarily) by breaking the pattern I had created. (Sorry to do that; I did it to make a point.)

When you are writing your web content, remember that patterns help people if you set the patterns clearly and follow them well. Parallelism is an excellent pattern to create and follow.

9. Don't number list items if they are not steps and people might confuse them with steps

In a procedure, people work through the list of numbered steps in order. In other lists, you may be telling people that they have a choice among different ways of doing something. If you use numbers for both procedures and other lists, you risk confusing your site visitors. They may not realize that the second type of list is showing alternatives; they may think they have a procedure and have to do it all.

Compare two pages from the Land's End web site. Figure 9-20 is about returning items if you are in Hong Kong. Figure 9-21 is the comparable page for returning items within the U.S. Both use numbered lists, but the numbering has different meanings on the two pages.

Figure 9-20 A numbered list is appropriate here because the four list items are steps in a process.   www.landsend.com

It's interesting how often I see both great writing and poor writing on the same web site. Different writers? Perhaps. But then, sometimes, I see information that's great and not so great even on the same page. The same Land's End page that may cause confusion for shoppers at the top of the page (Figure 9-21) has a wonderful example of good instructions for reordering further down the page (Figure 9-22).

LANDS' END   SITE MAP | SHOPPING HELP | LIBRARY | OUR COMPANY | CONTACT US | OVERSTOCKS

1-800-963-4816
Customer Service

Shoppers may be confused by this list. It looks just like the Hong Kong page – like three steps. In fact, it is three alternative options.

SEARCH

Shopping Help

The writer might have helped shoppers more by
• saying at the top of the page that shoppers have three ways of returning items.
• using a bulleted list rather than a numbered list for the three options.

Track Your Order
Monogramming
Hemming/Cuffing
Gift Boxing
Gift Cards
Free Catalogs
Free E-mail Newsletter
Free Swatches
Specialty Shopper

Catalog Quick Order

Returning Items Within the US:

1. **Return Internet or catalog orders at a Sears store.**
   Just follow these guidelines:
   • Bring the Lands' End items you wish to return to any participating Sears store where Lands' End merchandise is sold.
   • Make sure to bring the original packing slip for the items you wish to return.
   • You will receive a return confirmation from Sears. Lands' End will then either credit your card, issue a refund check, or send you a Lands' End gift card, as you choose.

   Please Note: Sears cannot accept exchanges or returns from Lands' End stores, Amazon.com, or Lands' End Business Outfitters.

2. **Use our Easy Return label for a flat fee of $6.50.**
   Securely package your return, include the Return Form, and affix the Easy Return shipping label found on your packing slip. Pay no postage up front - a flat fee of $6.50 will be deducted from the amount of your refund. Simply give the package to your mail carrier or drop it off at any U.S. Post Office or collection box.

   Please note: Not all orders are eligible for the Easy Return label service.

   If your packing slip does not have one, use return methods 1 or 3.

3. **Send your return to us with the shipper of your choice.** Securely package your return including the Return Form, and send to:

Returns by country
From US
From Canada
From Hong Kong
From Japan
From all other countries
From Australia
From New Zealand
From Singapore

Figure 9-21 People may be confused by a numbered list when they are expecting steps but are getting alternative options. People tend to start Step 1 without reading the entire list. In this case, they may try to find a Sears store when the Easy Return method might, in fact, be easier for them.   www.landsend.com

When giving options, tell people they have a choice. Give them the choices as a bulleted list (not as a numbered list).

Want to reorder?
You have a choice:
• Send us your reorder with your return,
• Call us at **1-800-963-4816,** or
• Fax us your completed packing slip reorder section at 1-800-332-0103.

Figure 9-22 This piece from the same Land's End web page as Figure 9-21 is a good example of how to tell people about options. (One small fix: The fax number should wrap under the bullet so that the bullets stand out.)
          www.landsend.com

Contrasting lists and tables

Now that I have convinced you (I hope) of many good ways to use lists in your web content, let's turn to tables. Tables, like lists, are a great way to let go of the words that don't matter and let people grab the essential information.

 Think about the difference. What is a list? What is a table? When would you use each?

List
- Individual items, all in the same category of information.
- One column.
- If a list wraps to a second column, the second column is a continuation of the list. The columns are a formatting feature; they don't show a relationship.

Table
- More than one category of information.
- At least two columns.
- The columns show a comparison or a relationship.

10. Use tables when you have numbers to compare

Think "table" whenever you have sets of numbers that relate to each other in some way. Compare Figure 9-23, the original version of real estate sales figures from a blog, with the same information put into a table (Figure 9-24).

Breaking down the total, 2,841 sales were reported in TREB's 28 West districts and averaged $305,789; 1,211 sales were reported in the 14 Central districts and averaged $405,182; 1,536 sales were reported in the 23 North districts and averaged $372,455; and 1,799 sales were reported in TREB's 21 East districts and averaged $265,090.

 It's difficult to grab numbers from sentences – and especially difficult to do comparisons.

Figure 9-23 This blog includes useful numbers, but it should be formatted as a table.

toreal.blogs.com/Toronto/Toronto_real_estate_update

Sales in the Toronto Real Estate Board Districts

Location	Sales	Average selling price
West (28 districts)	2,841	$305,789
Central (14 districts)	1,211	$405,182
North (23 districts)	1,536	$372,455
East (21 districts)	1,799	$265,000

 When you have numbers to compare, create a table.

Figure 9-24 A suggested revision.

11. Use tables for a series of "if, then" sentences

Tables work with words, too. For example, we can replace the sentences in Figure 9-25 with the table in Figure 9-26 by turning the repeated part of the three sentences into column headings for the table.

In cases like Figure 9-26, you know you have a useful table when you can read each row of the table as an "if, then" sentence that makes sense. For example, the first row of the table in Figure 9-26 means: "If you are applying for Designated Mechanic Examiner, you are governed by the Aviation Mechanic Examiner Handbook."

The DME applicants are governed by the guidance in FAA Order 8610.4, "Aviation Mechanic Examiner Handbook."
The DPRE applicants are governed by the guidance in FAA Order8610.5, "The Parachute Rigger Examiner Handbook."
The DAR-T applicants are governed by the guidance in FAA Order 8100.8, "Designee Management Handbook."

 When you find yourself repeating words, as in this example, think "table."

Figure 9-25 Turn parallel sentences that show relationships into a table.   www.faa.gov

If you are applying for	You are governed by
Designated Mechanic Examiner (DME)	Aviation Mechanic Examiner Handbook (FAA Order 8610.4)
Designated Parachute Rigger Examiner (DPRE)	The Parachute Rigger Examiner Handbook (FAA Order 8610.5)
Designated Airworthiness Representatives Maintenance (DAR-T)	Designee Management Handbook (FAA Order 8100.8)

Each site visitor probably wants information from only one row of the table.

Figure 9-26 A suggested revision. With tables, you let go of unnecessary, repetitive words and make the key information easy to find.

12. Think about tables as answers to questions

Most, if not all, tables answer questions. You don't have to use the question as a heading or, in fact, anywhere in your table. But thinking about the question that the table is answering helps you set up the table.

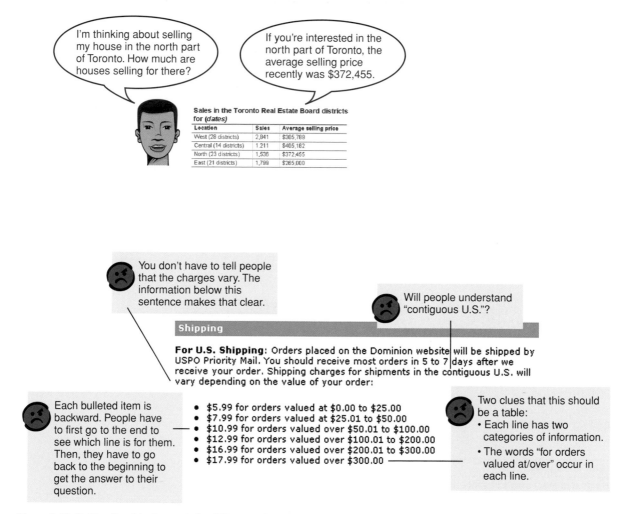

Figure 9-27 Putting the shipping costs for different order values on separate lines is good. But this should be a table, not a bulleted list. (The original screen has white text on an orange background. I changed the colors to increase legibility.)

www.dominionsaddlery.com

The information at the top is shorter and easier to grasp – and still has all the key messages.

Shipping

For U. S. Shipping:
We ship by United States Post Office Priority Mail.
Most orders will arrive in 5 to 7 days after we receive the order.

Shipping charges in the United States (except <u>Alaska and Hawaii</u>)

 The information is much easier to scan in a table than in a bulleted list.

Value of order	Shipping charges
up to $25.00	$5.99
$25.01 to $50.00	$7.99
$50.01 to $100.00	$10.99
$100.01 to $200.00	$12.99
$200.01 to $300.00	$16.99
over $300.00	$17.99

 The value of the order goes in the left column because that's what people know when they come to the table.

 The shipping charges go in the right column. People read across the row from what they know to the answer they need.

Figure 9-28 My suggested revision.

Consider the example in Figures 9-27 and 9-28. Both the original and my suggested revision use the heading **Shipping** (a noun, not a question). But, in fact, the information answers the site visitor who starts the conversation by asking, "What do you charge for shipping?" or "How much does shipping cost?" (And the question would have been fine as a heading.)

13. Think carefully about what to put in the left column of a table

If you think of your table as a series of "if, then" sentences, always put the "if" part first. Make that the left column.

Another way to say this: When a site visitor asks a question to which your first answer is "it depends," that's a clue that you need a table. What it depends on becomes the left column of the table. The answer to the question for each site visitor's situation becomes the right column.

See the related guideline about sentences (Guideline 8 in Chapter 8).

Also, look back at the very first example in this book. Figure 1-2 includes a table as the answer to "What must I submit?" With very few words, the table conveys the message: "If you are building an airport . . ." and "If you are building a heliport . . ."

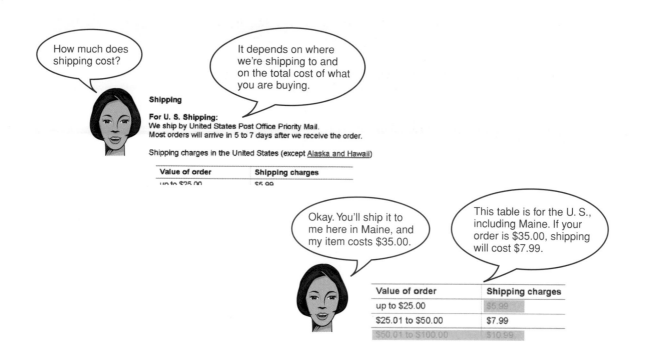

With most tables, people scan down the left column to find the situation that is relevant to them. Then, they move along that row to get the information they need.

14. Keep tables simple

Two-column tables are easiest to fit onto web pages and easiest for people to grab information from. However, sometimes you have more than two related pieces of information to give people for each row of a table – as in the three-column table about real estate earlier in this chapter.

How large can a table be before it becomes too much for users?

Thinking about table width

Let's talk about width first (number of columns). The web constrains us more than paper did.

- You can't create fold-out web pages the way you can create super-wide, fold-out, specially printed paper documents.

- One of the strongest findings of usability testing is how few web users notice a horizontal scroll bar. Anything off the right side of the screen is lost to almost all web users.

If the answer to people's question is "it depends on many things," you may not want to create a table. The table might have to be too complex for most web users or too large to fit well on a web page.

For example, the answer to "How much does a new laptop cost?" may be "It depends on how much memory you want it to have, what size monitor you want, how fast you want it to work, what weight you are willing to carry, what other features you want, and so on."

For complex situations, consider asking visitors a series of questions or giving them a form to fill out, rather than putting all the information into a table.

- You cannot assume that all your web users have large monitors with maximized windows. Even if you are giving highly technical information, consider your audiences. Are they policy makers? decision makers? managers? very busy people who find it difficult to extract information quickly from large and complicated tables?

Consider breaking up large and complicated tables into a series of smaller, more specific tables. Or layer your tables – allowing web users to drill down to more details through links in the tables.

For example, in my suggested revision to the shipping charges, I would use separate tables for shipping to different parts of the world. That would be easier for most people than a large matrix with information for different people in different columns. People have difficulty jumping over information that is not relevant to them.

Thinking about table length

Let's talk about length next (number of rows). Although most web users scroll vertically today, a long table may be more difficult to use than a long list. A table shows a relationship; people must remember the column headings for a table to understand how the pieces of information in each row relate to each other.

Again, consider breaking up very long tables into a series of smaller tables that allow you to keep the context-giving column headings close to the information.

15. Format tables on the web so that people focus on the information and not on the lines

The way your tables look can help or hinder people from getting the information that they need. Let's close this chapter with two important guidelines about formatting tables:

- Don't put thick lines between the columns or between the rows in a table.

- Don't center text in a table.

Don't put thick lines between the columns or between the rows in a table

Making each cell of a table into a box with equal weight borders all around it doesn't help your web users. People don't use tables cell by cell; they use tables to see relationships along a row. Thick lines between columns stop people from moving along the row – just the opposite of what you want people to do.

Also, heavy lines draw people's eyes. You want your site visitors to focus on the essential information in the table, not on the lines between the information.

Here are two ways to make it easy to find each row and to read across the row:

- Make the lines between columns lighter than the lines between rows.

- Eliminate lines altogether and use shading on alternate rows.

The table from the English-language visa page of the German Foreign Office (Figure 9-29) uses alternate-row shading well.

A B C D E F G H I J K L M N O P Q R S T U V W Y Z

Country	Entry visa required no/yes
Afghanistan	yes
Albania	yes
Algeria	yes
Andorra	no
Angola	yes
Antigua and Barbuda	yes
Argentina	no
Armenia	yes
Austria*	no
Australia (including the Cocos Islands, Norfolk Island, Christmas Island)**	no
Azerbaijan	yes
Bahamas	yes
Bahrain	yes
Bangladesh	yes
Barbados	yes
Belarus (see also White Russia)	yes

The shading on every other row makes the table easy to use.

Figure 9-29 Use techniques such as alternate-row shading or very light lines to help people focus on the information in tables and to help them read across the row they need.

www.auswaertiges-amt.de/www/en/willkommen/einreisebestimmungen/liste_html

Don't center text in a table

Notice how the column headings and the information in each column of the table in Figure 9-29 line up on the left of the column. That works well. Aligning text on the left makes each column easy to scan. Centering interferes with scanning in tables just as it does in other parts of your web pages.

In tables, set all column headings and columns with words flush left, ragged right. If you are giving numbers, line them up on a decimal tab.

SUMMARIZING CHAPTER 9

Here are key messages from Chapter 9:

Bulleted lists

- Use lists to make information easy to grab.

- Keep most lists short.
  - Short (5–10 items) is necessary for unfamiliar lists.
  - Long may be okay for very familiar lists.

- Format lists to make them work well.
  - Eliminate the space between the introduction and the list.
  - Put a space between long items.
  - Wrap lines under each other, not under the bullet.

- Match bullets to your site's personality.
  - Work with colleagues to establish the personality to use for bullets.
  - Don't make people wonder if the bullets have more meaning than they do.

Numbered lists

- Use numbered lists for instructions.

- Turn paragraphs into steps.

- Give even complex instructions as steps.

- Keep the sentence structure in lists parallel.

- Don't number list items if they are not steps and people might confuse them with steps.

Tables

- Use tables when you have numbers to compare.

- Use tables for a series of "if, then" sentences.

- Think about tables as answers to questions.

- Think carefully about what to put in the left column of a table.

- Keep tables simple.

- Format tables on the web so that people focus on the information and not on the lines.
  - Don't put thick lines between the columns or between the rows in a table.
  - Don't center text in a table.

Breaking Up Your Text with Headings

10

As you develop your web content, think about how to help people follow the flow of your writing or find just the section of an article that they need. One useful way is to use bold or colored headings within the article.

 Compare Figure 10-1, the iVillage page on blood pressure without any headings, with Figure 10-2, the Familydoctor.org page on the same topic with several headings. Which would you be more likely to read?

Good headings help readers in many ways

The purpose of a heading is to help communicate the content that is under the heading. Well-written headings in well-organized text help readers by

- getting them interested
- helping them get a quick overview of what is on the page
- setting the context for each section
- helping them make sense of what follows
- facilitating scanning so that they can find the section they need
- separating sections, putting a little space on the page
- making the information seem less dense and more readable

Figure 10-1 An article with no headings may seem daunting to site visitors.   www.iVillage.co.uk

Thinking about headings also helps writers

Headings form an outline of what you are going to write. Planning the headings is a way of analyzing the information you have, grouping it well, and putting it in an order that is logical for readers. (More about this follows in the first guideline.)

Figure 10-2 An article with headings encourages reading.   www.familydoctor.com

Always mark headings with the proper HTML tags, <H1>heading text</H1> for heading level 1, <H2>heading text</H2> for heading level 2, and so on. Users of screen-readers want to scan web pages just as sighted users do. They can have the screen-reader jump from heading to heading, but only if the headings are properly tagged.

Don't just slap headings into old content

Headings can be very helpful, but they can't save poorly written, poorly organized text. Going through existing content and putting in a heading every so often does not usually produce a good document. That's actually a good technique as a *first step* in revision – a way to become more familiar with the content you are working with. But it's a terrible technique if you stop there.

Whether you are writing new content or revising old content, if you find it difficult to write a heading for a section of text, it probably means that the section is not clear or covers too many points all jumbled together. Clarify the content. Break it up into smaller sections. If you find yourself writing the same heading over different sections of text, it probably means that the material is not well organized. Reorganize it to be logical for your site visitors.

Poor, arbitrary headings may hurt web users rather than help them.

Thanks to Caroline Jarrett for teaching me this technique of putting headings in old content as a *first step* in revision. Very important: This is just to get a sense of the content and to plan your revision. You will probably want to reorganize and rewrite the content with new headings in a new order.

Twelve guidelines for writing useful headings

In this chapter, we'll consider these 12 guidelines to help you help your web users with good headings:

1. Start by outlining your content with headings.
2. Ask questions as headings when people come with questions.
3. Give statement headings to convey key messages.
4. Use action phrase headings for instructions.
5. Use noun and noun phrase headings sparingly.
6. Put your site visitors' words in the headings.
7. Exploit the power of parallelism.
8. Don't dive deep; keep to no more than two levels of headings (below the page title).
9. Make the heading levels obvious.
10. Distinguish headings from text with type size and bold or color.

11. Help people jump to the topic they need with same-page links.

12. Evaluate! Read the headings to see what you have done.

1. Start by outlining your content with headings

I'm *not* talking about formal outlining with roman numerals, letters, and so on. Just put down the headings in order. If you use more than one level, indent a bit for the second level. You can then see the patterns you are creating at a glance.

(This is the same advice that I gave in Chapter 6, Checklist 6-1, where I suggested starting by putting down the questions that people would ask. Here I'm elaborating a bit to say that sometimes you'll keep those questions as your outline, and, therefore, your headings. Sometimes, you'll turn them into statements (key messages). If they are all "how do I . . . " questions, you'll turn them into action phrases. And sometimes, if you are just labeling parts, you'll use nouns. In the rest of this chapter, we'll explore when, why, and how to use each of these types of headings.)

For example, the outline for the International Aviation Art Contest web page that I constructed in Case Study 6-1 would look like Figure 10-3.

Title: International Aviation Art Contest

Outline (headings with second level indented)
Who can enter?
What is the deadline?
What prizes are there?
    State prizes
    National prizes
    International prizes
What types of poster are acceptable?
What will the judges look for?
Who must certify that the child made the poster?
Where do we send the poster?

Figure 10-3 An example of an outline for a page of web content.

2. Ask questions as headings when people come with questions

In many types of web content, questions work extremely well as headings. That's because site visitors come with questions in mind. When you write their questions as the headings in your web content, you acknowledge the conversation that they want to have with you.

As I said back in Chapter 1, I'm not suggesting that you make your entire site a huge section of frequently asked questions. That would only make it hard for people to find their specific question. I'm suggesting questions and answers (Q&A) as an appropriate writing style for many of your individual web pages, like the FamilyDoctor.org page that you just saw as Figure 10-2.

In fact, Q&A is more than a writing style; it's a fundamental viewpoint about making a web site focus on the people who are coming with questions. Of course, sometimes, you have to put a question in people's minds that they may not have thought to ask but will recognize as important when they see it on the web page.

For example, many people wonder whether pandas are really bears. Seeing the question, "Are giant pandas bears?" on the San Diego Zoo's site may draw them into finding out that pandas are, in fact, related to bears. And then they may keep reading the panda page (Figure 10-4).

Questions make very useful headings in all these different types of web content:

- articles
- explanations
- handbooks
- introductions to manuals
- policies
- press releases
- regulations
- troubleshooting information

(You can also use statements as headings in these same types of documents, as you see in the panda page in Figure 10-4. I'll talk more about statements as headings in Guideline 3 a little later in the chapter.)

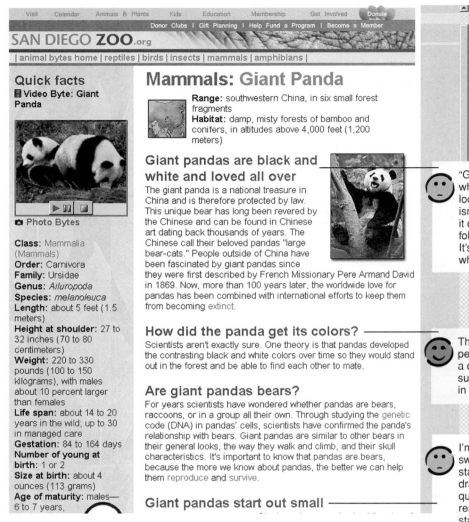

Figure 10-4 This page about pandas shows both question headings and statement (key message) headings.   www.sandiegozoo.org

Writing good questions for headings is not a trivial task. Here are four keys to writing questions that work well as headings in web content:

- Make them the questions people come with.

- Think conversation. Ask the question from the site visitors' point of view.

- Keep the questions short.

- Consider starting with a key word for fast access and accessibility.

Age of maturity: males—
6 to 7 years,
females—4 to 5
years
Conservation
status: **Endangered**
endangered

Fun facts
• They seem pretty quiet,
but giant pandas can bleat,
roar, growl, and honk.
• Giant pandas are
technically carnivores, but
they have adapted to live
mostly on bamboo. They
will eat small mammals if
they can catch them,
though!
• Like other types of bears,
giant pandas are curious
and playful, especially
when they're young. In
zoos, they like to play with
enrichment items like piles
of ice or sawdust, puzzles
made of bamboo with food
inside, and different scents
like spices.
• Giant pandas have
unusually thick and heavy
bones for their size, but
they are also very flexible
and like to do somersaults.

See them
San Diego Zoo: Giant
Panda Research Station

More
• Panda Cam
• **Read Weblogs from our
Giant Panda Team**
• **Adopt-An-Animal
Program:** giant panda
• CRES: Maternal Care
Strategies in Giant Pandas

Giant pandas start out small

Giant pandas are only about the size of
a stick of butter at birth, and they're
hairless and helpless. The panda
mother gives great care to her tiny cub,
usually cradling it in one paw and
holding it close to her chest. For
several days after birth, the mother
does not leave the den, not even to eat or drink!

Yet despite the attention they receive from their mothers, many
young pandas do not survive. Through captive propagation
programs in China and other zoos around the world, we are
learning more about the care of panda cubs and how to help them
reach adulthood.

Bamboo is food and shelter
Bamboo is the most important plant in a giant panda's life. Pandas
live in cold and rainy bamboo forests high in the mountains of
western China. They spend at least 12 hours each day eating
bamboo. Because bamboo is so low in nutrients, pandas eat as
much as 84 pounds (38 kilograms) of it each day. Pandas grasp
bamboo stalks with their five fingers and a special wristbone, then
use their teeth to peel off the tough outer layers to reveal the soft
inner tissue. Strong jaw bones and cheek muscles help pandas
crush and chew the thick stalks with their flattened back teeth.
Bamboo leaves are also on the menu, as pandas strip them off the
stalks, wad them up, and swallow them. Giant pandas have also
been known to eat grasses, bulbs, fruits, some insects, and even
rodents and carrion. At the San Diego Zoo, pandas are offered
bamboo, carrots, yams, and special leaf eater biscuits made of
grain and packed with all the vitamins and minerals pandas need.

Vocal pandas
Pandas make a bleating sound similar to the sound a lamb or a goat
kid would make. It's a friendly sound, a greeting. They don't roar,
the way you think of a brown bear roaring. But they do bleat and
honk, they sometimes huff, bark, or growl, and young cubs croak
and squeal.

Giant pandas face big problems
Today, only around 1,600 giant pandas survive on Earth. There are
several reasons why pandas are endangered:

Low reproductive rate— Pandas like to be by themselves most of
the year, and they have a very short breeding season when a male

Statements (key messages)
can work well as headings,
too.

"Vocal pandas" is not a
question or a statement. It
doesn't give us nearly as much
information as the statements
over other sections. To match
the other headings around it,
this could be "Pandas don't
roar."

The writer uses a second level
of headings sparingly. And
there's a matching heading
on the next paragraph.

Figure 10-4 *Continued*

Make them the questions
people come with

Too often I find that web writers have turned their information into questions and answers, but it's still *their* information – what they want to tell
people about themselves, not what their site visitors come to learn. The
web writers have not thought deeply enough about their audiences and
the questions those people have. They haven't organized the page by
putting the questions and answers into an order that is logical to their
web site visitors.

Case Study 10-1 shows how we can take a set of organizationally
focused questions and turn them into a set of reader-focused questions.

Case Study 10-1   Making question headings ones that site visitors would ask

If you want to complain about a bank in the United States, you might get to the web site of the U. S. Department of Treasury. They regulate *nationally chartered* U. S. banks. However, they are not the right place to go if your complaint is about a bank that is chartered by a specific state – a distinction few people have thought about.

Here's how their web page about consumer complaints and assistance started in 2006:

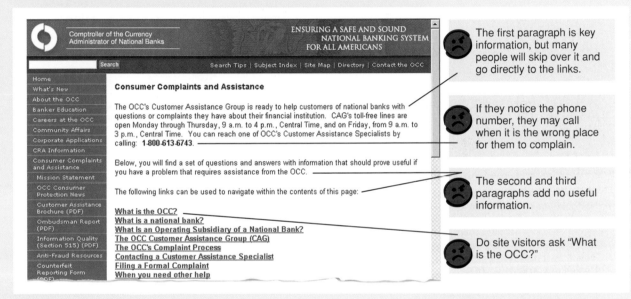

www.occ.treas.gov/customer.htm

 How well does this meet the needs of the site visitors it is for? Just think about the mental state of the person who wants to lodge a formal complaint about a bank! What adjectives come to your mind about this site visitor?

> I'm so upset and angry at what my bank did! This is intolerable! I'm going to file an offical complaint with the government!

Does this site visitor really want to know what the OCC is? The upset site visitor in the picture on the previous page might not read "What is a national bank?" because he doesn't yet know it is a question that is important for his problem.

How might the Department do a better job of getting its critical information to angry and upset people and also save themselves calls from people who should go elsewhere with their complaints? Revising the beginning and writing the question headings from the site visitors' point of view might help.

Consumer Complaints and Assistance

Related only to *national* banks and their subsidiaries
How do I know if my bank is a national bank?
Yes, it is a national bank. What do I do to complain or get help?
No, it is not a national bank. What do I do now?

Put the key message right up front in very few words.

Now the site visitor has reason to want to know about national banks.

We are the right office to talk to if you have a complaint or need help with a national bank or one of its subsidiaries.

How do I know if my bank is a national bank?
National banks usually have the words "national" or "national association" in their titles or the letters N.A. or NT&SA following their titles. About 28% of insured commercial banks in the United States are national banks.

Yes, it is a national bank. What do I do to complain or get help?
Call us at **1-800-613-6743**.
Monday through Thursday, 9 a.m. to 4 p.m. Central Time
Friday, 9 a.m. to 3 p.m. Central Time

Fragments are better than paragraphs for phone numbers and times.

A Customer Assistance Specialist from the Office of the Comptroller of the Currency can help you by answering your questions, offering guidance, and helping you to resolve complaints about national banks and their subsidiaries.

No, it is not a national bank. What do I do now?

Some people will be left with this question. Always try to answer questions people have, even if it means sending them somwhere else.

A possible revision

Think conversation. Ask the question from the site visitor's point of view

As I wrote in Chapter 8, if you use questions as headings, write as if you were recording both sides of the conversation. Use "I" for the site visitor in the question and "you" for the site visitor in the answer.

 Which version of the question about applying for food stamps in Figure 10-5 is more natural? (I copied these short pieces from two different U. S. counties' web sites.)

How can a person apply for food stamps?
You can apply ...

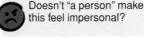 Doesn't "a person" make this feel impersonal?

How can I apply for food stamps?
You can apply ...

Write the question as if the site visitor were asking it.

Figure 10-5 Two versions of the same information.

Keep the questions short

When you use questions as headings, people often skim the question just enough to decide, "yes, that's what I want to know." After all, the real meat of the web content is the answer to the question and people are anxious to get to it.

Long questions take up precious space on the web page. Also, as headings, the questions are in bold or color, and large blocks of bold or color become difficult to read. And – despite the power of headings – some site visitors use the headings only as landing spots to see where new sections start. They don't actually read the headings.

Cut your questions down to essentials, just as you cut your content to essentials. For example, if your entire web page is on a particular topic, you don't need to repeat the topic in each question on the page. Compare Figure 10-6, which has two questions totaling 22 words as the heading, with Figure 10-7, where the heading is only 12 words long.

Figure 10-6 A very long heading may be using more words than needed to convey the message.

www.globalcrossroad.com

Figure 10-7 My suggestion for revising the heading.

If you find yourself writing a long question, ask yourself:

• Is the section of text too long? Is it really answering several questions? Should I divide it into more than one question and answer?

• Am I putting information in the question that should be in the answer?

- Am I using more words than necessary to make a connection with my site visitor?

Consider starting with a key word for fast access and accessibility

 Although questions work wonderfully well as headings for many types of web content, they have one downside. The key word in the heading is not at the beginning. If the question is short, sighted readers can see the key word quickly even if it is in the middle of the question. However, people who are listening to screen-readers may not get to the key word. They often skip rapidly from heading to heading, listening only to the first few words.

A solution that may also help sighted readers who scan rapidly is to combine a key word with the question, as in Figure 10-8.

Signature: Who must sign the application?
Deadline: When is the application due?

 Combining a key word with a question may help many site visitors.

Figure 10-8 Dual headings like these help people who are scanning rapidly with their eyes or their ears.

3. Give statement headings to convey key messages

When you write questions as headings, you play out both sides of the conversation. You put the site visitor on the page with you – the site visitor asks the question; you answer it. When you write statements as headings, you assume the site visitor has asked the question. You keep your site visitors in mind and talk directly to them, without putting them on the page with you.

Statement headings work well in the same types of documents as questions. With statement headings, you are making your key messages stand out on the page in large bold or colored type. That's what you see in Figure 10-9, a page about PayPal from eBay's web site.

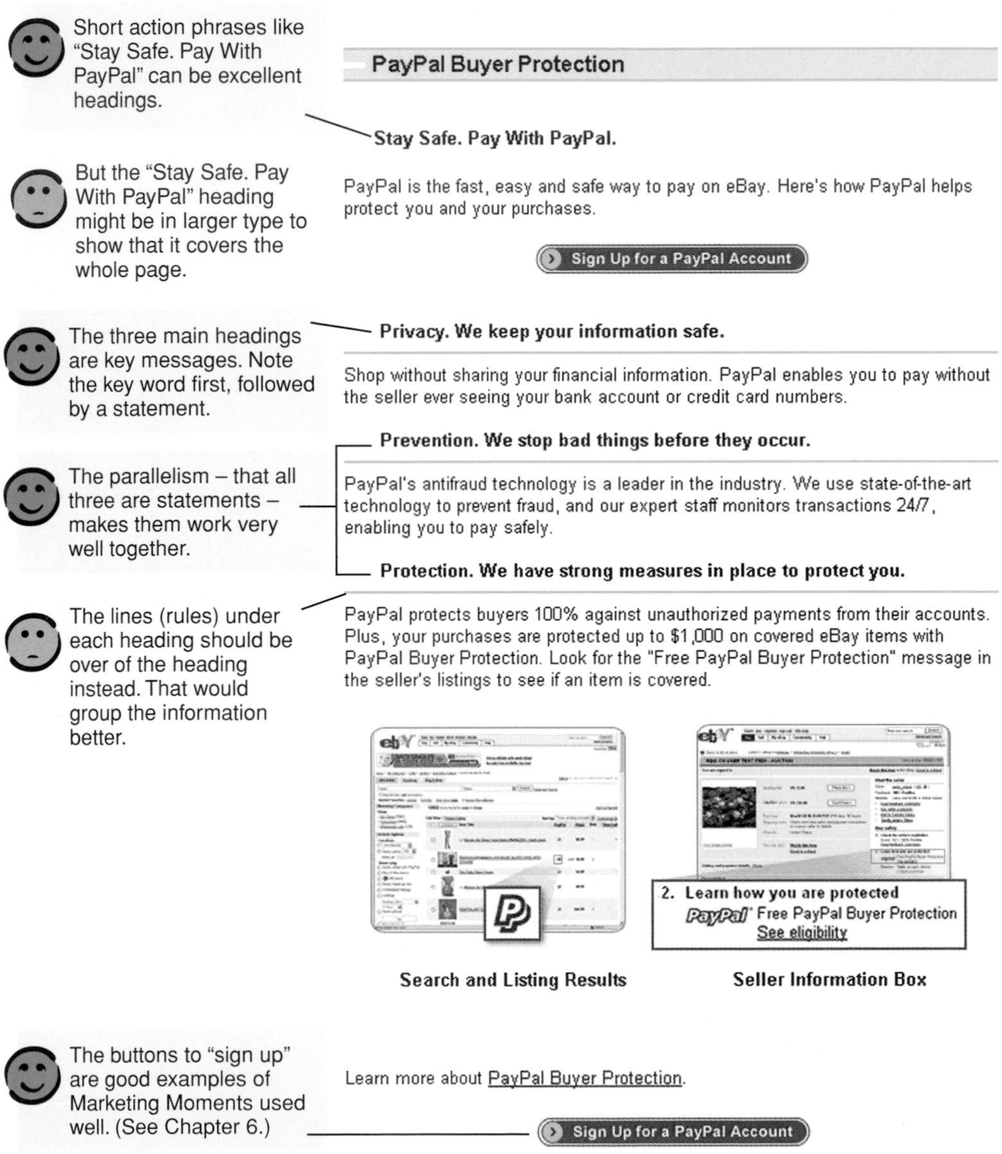
Short action phrases like "Stay Safe. Pay With PayPal" can be excellent headings.
But the "Stay Safe. Pay With PayPal" heading might be in larger type to show that it covers the whole page.
The three main headings are key messages. Note the key word first, followed by a statement.
The parallelism – that all three are statements – makes them work very well together.
The lines (rules) under each heading should be over of the heading instead. That would group the information better.
The buttons to "sign up" are good examples of Marketing Moments used well. (See Chapter 6.)
PayPal Buyer Protection
Stay Safe. Pay With PayPal.
PayPal is the fast, easy and safe way to pay on eBay. Here's how PayPal helps protect you and your purchases.
Sign Up for a PayPal Account
Privacy. We keep your information safe.
Shop without sharing your financial information. PayPal enables you to pay without the seller ever seeing your bank account or credit card numbers.
Prevention. We stop bad things before they occur.
PayPal's antifraud technology is a leader in the industry. We use state-of-the-art technology to prevent fraud, and our expert staff monitors transactions 24/7, enabling you to pay safely.
Protection. We have strong measures in place to protect you.
PayPal protects buyers 100% against unauthorized payments from their accounts. Plus, your purchases are protected up to $1,000 on covered eBay items with PayPal Buyer Protection. Look for the "Free PayPal Buyer Protection" message in the seller's listings to see if an item is covered.
2. Learn how you are protected
PayPal Free PayPal Buyer Protection
See eligibility
Search and Listing Results
Seller Information Box
Learn more about PayPal Buyer Protection.
Sign Up for a PayPal Account

Figure 10-9 Action phrases like "Stay Safe" and statements like the three main headings here work very well for some web content.
pages.ebay.com/paypal/buyer/protection.html

4. Use action phrase headings for instructions

Many of the questions that users bring to web sites are "How do I. . . ?" If you have only one such question with many other questions on a web page, it's fine to keep that as a question.

However, if you have a series of questions, all of which would start "How do I . . . ?" people may have a hard time finding the one they want.

How do I set up an account?	Setting up an account
How do I view my information?	Viewing your information
How do I change my information?	Changing your information
How do I pay online?	Paying online
How do I get help?	Getting help

 Which set of headings is easier to scan and use?

When you find yourself writing "how do I . . ." over and over, take away the repeated words and start each heading with the action word.

Action phrases make great headings in any type of instruction: manuals, procedures, or help for a web application.

Two good ways of writing action phrase headings are with gerunds (the form that ends in "-ing") or with imperatives (the "Do this . . ." form of the verb).

Instruction writers commonly use the "-ing" form when dividing web content into different tasks. An example would be the list of tasks in the right column of the table on this page. On the web, each of these headings, like "Setting up an account," would probably link to its own web page. And the specific steps on that page would probably each start with an imperative.

The imperative works very well within a web article as a heading style for tips and short paragraphs of advice. Look at the example from Celestial Seasonings in Figure 10-10.

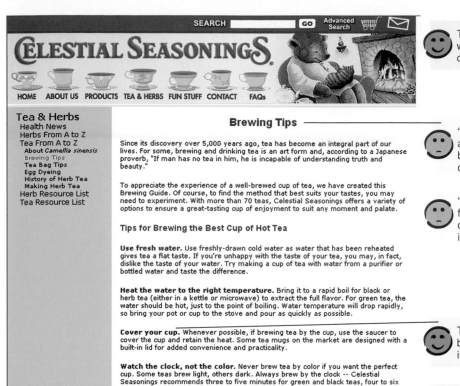

The page uses type size well to show different levels of headings.

"-ing" forms are often ambiguous. This might be better as "Brewing Tea" or "Tips for Brewing Tea."

"Brewing Tips" should be flush left, not centered, to draw people's eyes down into the text.

The tips each start with a bold heading with an imperative verb.

Just reading the bold headings gives you a good overview of what to do.

Figure 10-10 Imperative verbs, such as "use," "heat," and "cover," work well as headings for tips and instructions.

www.celestialseasonings.com

5. Use noun and noun phrase headings sparingly

I see a lot of nouns as headings. They work sometimes; but more often than not, they don't work because site visitors don't know the nouns, don't connect to the nouns, don't give the nouns the same meaning the web writer did. Nouns as headings often don't help either the writer or the site visitor understand the flow of the writing – why one section logically comes before or after another section.

Nouns label things; they aren't conversational. Unlike questions, statements, and action phrases, which provide context and some explanation, a noun has to carry all the meaning of the heading in a single word.

Occasionally, labels are all you need on a web page. For example, Figure 10-11 shows an eye-tracking picture of one person looking for tax forms

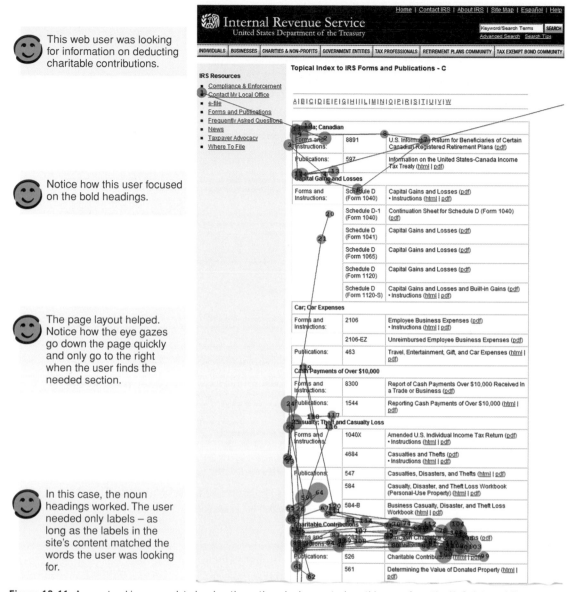

This web user was looking for information on deducting charitable contributions.

Notice how this user focused on the bold headings.

The page layout helped. Notice how the eye gazes go down the page quickly and only go to the right when the user finds the needed section.

In this case, the noun headings worked. The user needed only labels – as long as the labels in the site's content matched the words the user was looking for.

Figure 10-11 An eye-tracking gaze plot showing the path a single user took on this page from the U. S. Internal Revenue Service's web site. The page has noun headings used as topic labels. They worked in this case because the user was seeking the same words that the site uses. (Eye-tracking by Jacob Nielsen and Kara Pernice Coyne, Nielsen Norman Group. Used with permission. For more information about the study this picture comes from, see www.useit.com/eyetracking.)

and information about reporting charitable contributions. In this case, the nouns in alphabetical order worked for this web user.

Figure 10-12 is another example where labels work. It's a page from the intranet of Salesforce.com, listing the various programs that employees may use to contribute to their community. This works because the writer and other employees use the same labels for these programs. And that is much more likely inside a company than between a company and its external web visitors.

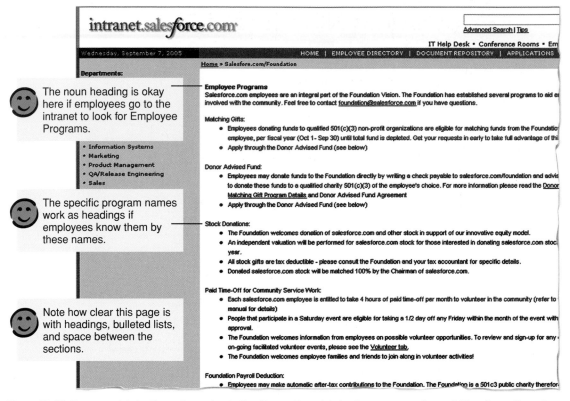

Figure 10-12 Nouns are labels. If people coming to the site use those labels, the nouns may be useful headings. (From the Salesforce.com intranet. Used with permission. Thanks to Catherine Courage and her colleagues.)

Much more often, however, nouns as labels aren't enough to meet the needs of busy people skimming and scanning for information.

Also, with nouns as headings, getting the information into logical order may be difficult. Figure 10-13 is the Tracking Your Order page from llbean.com. Notice how the noun headings *don't* help you understand what is in the paragraphs. Notice how much is stuffed under one heading that should really be in separate sections. Notice how the last paragraph belongs with information much higher on the page.

Figure 10-13 Nouns as headings can confuse people. Also, nouns as headings are harder to get into the right order than are questions, statements, or action phrases.   www.llbean.com

Figure 10-14 is a possible revision of Figure 10-13. Notice how much more informative the action headings are. Notice how thinking of individual actions means breaking up the text into smaller pieces. Notice how the order of the pieces becomes more logical when we think about these as actions.

Bringing all the headings together at the top gives people an overview and an easy way to get to one section. (See Guideline 11 later in this chapter.)

This is one of three topics that were in the long first paragraph of the original. I split the original into three separate sections.

I rewrote most of the headings as action phrases (gerunds, "-ing" forms).

I broke the pattern of "-ing" headings for the one about keeping gifts secret to get readers' attention.

I moved the section about keeping gifts secret higher on the page so that more people see and read it.

Statements probably would work as well as action phrases for the headings.

Tracking Your Order

<u>Getting email confirmation of your order</u>
<u>Getting an email when we ship your order</u>
<u>Gift order for someone on the same email? Don't let us spoil the surprise!</u>
<u>Following your order with its tracking number</u>
<u>Checking your order in Order Tracking/History</u>
<u>Changing an order or backorder</u>
<u>Checking all your orders for the past year</u>

Getting email confirmation of your order

If you gave us your email address when you placed your order, we'll send you confirmation of the order by email within two hours. This confirmation will give you

- the order number
- the total value of the merchandise

Getting an email when we ship your order

If you gave us your email address when you placed your order, we'll also send an email to tell you when we've shipped your order. (Exception: If your item ships from an off-site distribution center, you won't get this email.) We usually provide this information within two days after you placed your order.

For most orders, this email will tell you how to track your shipment.

Gift order for someone on the same email? Don't let us spoil the surprise!

The email that we have shipped your order will include information about the individual items in your order. Although the email begins with a notice that it might contain gift information, you still might want to alert the gift recipient not to open email from L.L.Bean. We don't want to spoil a surprise!

Following your order with its tracking number

You can track your shipment by using the shipper's tracking number(s) in the email we send when we ship your order.

If you deleted or did not get this email, please <u>contact us</u> and we'll be glad to give you the shipper's tracking information.

Checking your order in Order Tracking/History

You can always check the status of your order by going to <u>Order Tracking/History</u>.

Changing an order or backorder

Order: We're sorry, orders cannot be changed once they've been submitted. We process orders very quickly. Once we have started to put your order together, we can't stop the process. We apologize for any inconvenience. We hope that for most cases our faster processing time works to your advantage.

Backorder: If you have something that is on backorder and want to change that, please <u>contact us</u>.

Checking all your orders for the past year

If you set up an account at llbean.com, you can look at all the orders you've placed on the L.L.Bean web site and by phone during the past year. You can use this feature to check your current order(s), review past orders, and find items you may want to order again.

To view your order history online, <u>create an account</u>. Your complete order history will be available immediately after you've made your first llbean.com purchase.

Figure 10-14 My suggestion for reorganizing and rewriting the L.L. Bean page about tracking your order.

6. Put your site visitors' words in the headings

No matter what type of heading you write, the headings in your web content must make connections between what's in your site visitor's mind and the information you want to give. If you write the heading with words they don't know, your site visitors may not recognize that the heading is what they need.

7. Exploit the power of parallelism

In Chapter 9, you saw the power of parallelism in lists. In the same way that it works for lists, using the same sentence structure (the same pattern) for your headings helps people scan and grab information from your web pages.

Do It Yourself: Wallpaper	**Do It Yourself: Wallpaper**
Everyone loves wallpaper	Getting ready
Preparation	Preparing the walls
Removal of wallpaper	Removing old wallpaper
Straight line marking	Marking a straight line
Cutting the wallpaper	Cutting the wallpaper
Wallpaper soaking	Soaking the wallpaper
Hang the first sheet	Hanging the first sheet

 Did you find the headings on the right quicker and easier to scan and remember?

If you use questions for your level 1 headings, make all the level 1 headings questions. If you use action phrases for your level 1 headings, make them all action phrases. That is, be consistent (parallel) in the style you use within the same level of heading in the same article (or even the same type of web content).

If you choose to break the pattern, do it for a good reason. I broke my pattern on the revised L.L. Bean web page for one heading. I did it to shock readers and make that point stand out. The point about keeping your gift a secret is not a part of the flow of the process that the other headings describe. It's an "aside," so changing the heading pattern there was purposeful.

You don't have to do all the levels in the same style. In fact, it's a good idea to change the style for different levels. That's one way to help people know what level each heading is at.

8. Don't dive deep; keep to no more than two levels of headings (below the page title)

On the screen, you have less room to work with than on paper, so you can't have as deep a hierarchy of headings in a web article as you might in a typical book chapter. Web articles should be much shorter than a typical essay or book chapter. Very long articles should be broken into different sections on different web pages.

Page Title

Heading level 1

Heading level 1

Heading level 2

Heading level 2

Heading level 1

If you have a short article with short sections, a page title and then one level of headings is best. If you have a long article, you probably want a page title and then two levels of headings. Use heading level 2 for subtopics of topics.

Figure 10-2, the article on high blood pressure from FamilyDoctor.org, has a page title and one level of headings. The outline in Figure 10-3 of the web page for the International Aviation Art Contest has a page title and two levels of headings.

9. Make the heading levels obvious

Changing the way you write the different levels is one way of making it clear that you have a hierarchy of information on the page. (The outline in Figure 10-3 has questions for heading level 1 and nouns for heading level 2.)

Another way to signal heading levels is to change the format. You can show different levels of heading with type size or placement

- **Type size.** If you are using size, always make the level 1 headings bigger than the level 2 headings. People associate size with hierarchy: bigger is more important. Make the difference noticeable – at least 2 points of type size.
- **Placement.** Instead of changing size, you can indent the second-level or run it in the same line as the text (with the heading part in bold or color). The bold headings for each tip in the Celestial Seasonings example in Figure 10-10 are run-in headings.

 Make sure that the headings get larger when the rest of the text gets larger for people who change the type size. You can do that by setting headings to be a percentage of the text type, and not an absolute size.

10. Distinguish headings from text with type size and bold or color

To make all the headings (at all levels) obvious as your site visitors come to each of your web pages, use bold or color.

Whatever you choose, use it consistently, and also consider these points:

- Don't use blue for headings. Save blue for links. Many web users assume that anything in blue is a link, even if it is not underlined.
- In fact, don't use your web site's link color as a heading color. Your site visitors are likely to become confused between headings and links.
- Don't make the only difference between heading levels be bold versus color. People have a hard time figuring out whether bold is more important than color or vice versa. You *can* combine color versus bold *and* larger size versus smaller size to make the distinction between different levels.

- Avoid *italics.* They are not as effective as **bold** in indicating a heading. They don't stand out as much on the screen.

- Underline a heading only if it is a link. Most web users assume that anything that is underlined is a link.

- Avoid all capitals for all the reasons we talked about in Chapter 7.

- If you use color for your headings, make sure the color is legible against the background of your page. Also, before you select a color for headings, reread the section on color-blindness in Chapter 7.

11. Help people jump to the topic they need with same-page links

If your web page has several topics with a heading over each topic, you might make those headings into a table of contents at the top of the page. A short table of contents at the top of a web page helps people

- get a quick overview of what's on the page

- jump to a specific part of the page if they want just that part

What do you call the headings as links at the top of the page? I've heard: "anchor links," "in-page links," and "same-page links." I'm calling them "same-page links" here.

Figure 10-15 is a good example of same-page links from a U. K. group that is very concerned about making its web site easy to use. (Thanks to Tom Brinck for suggesting this example.)

Put same-page links right under the page title

Watching people in usability testing, it's striking to see how quickly they focus on the links when they come to a web page. If there's a list of same-page links near the top of the page, they are likely to just not see anything above that list of links.

Don't put off-page links where people expect same-page links

Remember that people bring expectations to your web pages. They expect that a list of links within the content area at the top of a web page will take them to information on that page. Meet that expectation.

HealthyEyes your sight is precious to us

| A A **A** | How we see | Looking after your sight | Problems & solutions | |

Text only | Accessibility   Home | Free updates | Help | Site map | Legal | Detailed search

How to get the best out of this site

⌃ Home   Site help

We've tried to make our site easy to use but if you are stuck, this section will help you.

Same-page links. Clicking on a question/link takes you down the page to where that question is a heading.

How do I get around this site?

How can I find what I need on your site?

How do I get back to your site if I leave it?

How do I change my screen resolution?

My browser is out-of-date - how can I get a new one?

Where can I learn more about using the Internet?

Bold heading. You get here by scrolling or by clicking on the first link.

How do I get around the site?

If you want to go to another area of the site, click with

Minor typo: a same-page link and the heading should match exactly. Here "this" has become "the."

Figure 10-15 Gathering up all the headings on a web page into a set of links at the top of the page helps people. They can see what's on the page and get quickly to one part of the page.

www.healthyeyes.org.uk

Don't put same-page links in the left navigation column

Just as users don't expect links at the top of the content area to go off the page, they don't expect links in the left navigation area to stay on the page. The left navigation is usually other topics that may be related, that may be in the same section of the web site, but that are not on the same web page.

I was doing a usability test of a web site as the first step to revising the site. One of the pages that participants reached had a good set of questions and answers grouped by topic. Participants liked the questions and answers but complained that they had to scroll when they would have liked to jump to the topic they needed. Several suggested "a list of the topics at the top like you see on lots of other web pages."

In fact, the list was on the page; it was in the left navigation column. But the participants' reaction was "I wouldn't look there. That's where I look when I think my answer isn't on this page." (This page is gone; the site has changed.)

Link headings as you move from paper to web

Providing same-page links is one of the easiest and most useful changes you can make if you are moving a paper document to the web. (Of course, I urge you to review the entire document, rethink it for the web, probably break it up even more than it is, and so on; but in any case, make sure that each section you make into a web page has useful headings and turn them into same-page links.)

12. Evaluate! Read the headings to see what you have done

How do you know if you've got good headings? Use this technique with both your old content before you revise and your new content when you have a draft.

1. Read just the headings on your web page – without any of the text that is under the headings.

2. Answer these questions:

- Do you understand what each heading means by itself?
- Do the headings tell a coherent story? Do they flow logically from one to the next?
- Do they successfully give you a "big picture"? Can you get the gist of all the information from the headings?
- Do they distinguish different sections? If you wanted only some of the information, is it clear where you would go for that information?

If you answer "no" to any of these questions, the headings are not working well. You may need better headings. You may need to rethink, reorganize, and rewrite the content.

SUMMARIZING CHAPTER 10

Here are key messages from Chapter 10:

- Break up your text with headings.
  - Good headings help readers in many ways.
  - Thinking about headings also helps writers.
- Don't just slap headings into old content.
- Start by outlining your content with headings.
- Ask questions as headings when people come with questions.
  - Make them the questions people come with.
  - Think conversation. Ask the question from the site visitor's point of view.
  - Keep the questions short.
  - Consider starting with a key word for fast access and accessibility.
- Give statement headings to convey key messages.
- Use action phrase headings for instructions.
- Use noun and noun phrase headings sparingly.
- Put your site visitors' words in the headings.
- Exploit the power of parallelism.
- Don't dive deep; keep to no more than two levels of headings (below the page title).
- Make the heading levels obvious.

- Distinguish headings from text with type size and bold or color.

- Help people jump to the topic they need with same-page links.
    - Put same-page links right under the page title.
    - Don't put off-page links where people expect same-page links.
    - Don't put same-page links in the left navigation column.
    - Link headings as you move from paper to web.

- Evaluate! Read the headings to see what you have done.

Legal Information Can Be Understandable, Too

Legal information abounds on the Internet – and in intranets and extranets. Many web sites need a page about privacy policies. Many include terms of use. And some sites focus on legal issues and legal documents. Letting go of the words and writing in plain language are as applicable to legal information as to other web content.

Information can be legally accurate, legally sufficient, and also clear. In fact, these attributes support each other, and many sites now strive to write their legal pages in clear, simple language.

The typical problems in legal information online can be solved without compromising the legal standing of the information. These problems include:

- text in a small, scrollable box in small type that can't be enlarged
- no printer-friendly option; printing cuts off the right side of the page
- headings that use technical computer terms, not site visitors' language
- technical language, when clearer statements are possible
- unnecessary, archaic legal language
- lots of the writing problems that we saw in Chapter 8

Ironically, some web sites have poor headings followed by good writing in their legal information while others have good headings followed by poor writing. Let's put the good headings and good writing together to have legal information that works for both your site visitors and your organization's lawyers.

Make the information legible

You may think, "no one reads the legal stuff anyway, so it doesn't matter what we do," but that violates both the spirit and the letter of the requirement that you provide information about terms of use or about privacy. Instead of burying information in a small box that people have to scroll through, give people a link to a full page where they can enlarge the type if they need to.

Make sure your legal information prints well

It surprises me that sites offer printer-friendly options for most of their information but don't do the same on the web pages with their terms of use or privacy policies. Why not? Legal information is important. People may want to print it.

Remember that you may have site visitors in many countries and that outside of the United States many people print on A4 paper, which is longer and narrower than the $8\frac{1}{2}$ by 11 inch paper that is the U. S. standard. Remember that your site must print from many different computer configurations, including old operating systems and browsers.

Use site visitors' words in your headings

Clear headings improve (and do not compromise) the legality of legal information. You can have questions or statements as headings in legal information; they are just as legal as noun-based headings.

 Compare the headings in Figure Interlude 2-1 from the International Herald Tribune and Figure Interlude 2-2 from Gap. Which set is more inviting? Which better matches what you would want to know about a company's privacy policies?

Privacy & Cookies

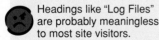 Log Files

Headings like "Log Files" are probably meaningless to most site visitors.

Cookies

Newsletters

Surveys & Contests

Figure Interlude 2-1 These headings don't connect to the questions that most people have about a company's privacy policies.   www.iht.com

What kind of information does gap.com collect?

How does gap.com use my information?

Does gap.com share my information with third parties?

How do I access my information? How do I change or delete my information?

How do I exercise my choices about receiving promotional communications?

How does gap.com protect kids' privacy?

What are cookies? How does gap.com use cookies on its site?

How do I know my order information is secure?

What about links to other websites and services?

These are likely to be the questions site visitors have about your privacy policies.

Many people won't understand "third parties." The heading might just stop after "information."

Some of these could be said more simply. "How do I exercise . . ." might be better as "How can I choose what type of emails you send me?"

Question headings are acceptable in legal information.

Figure Interlude 2-2 These headings do a much better job of getting site visitors to the information they are looking for.

www.gap.com

Avoid technical language

Technical jargon isn't needed to make information legal.

We collect information to analyze our traffic patterns.

We gather information about how visitors navigate through our web site by using clickstream data.

We collect information to understand how people use our web site.

Avoid archaic legal language

Many words and phrases that we find in legal information in English just seem to shout "This is legal stuff. You won't understand it." Phrases like "to wit," "the said example," and "heretofore" were plain language hundreds of years ago. People actually talked that way, so reading those words was easy for people – then. But language changes over time. Words come into the language. Words leave the language. Those words – and many other "legalisms" – have left our everyday language. We see them only in legal information. We don't talk that way now, so reading those words is not easy for your site visitors. Leave them out or replace them with common English words.

Figure Interlude 2-3 shows you part of a list of words to avoid from the U. S. Federal Register's *Drafting Legal Documents.*

For example, the sentence with "pursuant to" and "hereinafter" in Figure Interlude 2-4 is not necessary. Most web sites (from Italy and from other countries) don't cite the law in their privacy policies.

For more on writing legal information clearly, see www .plainlanguage.gov.

Figure Interlude 2-3 Words like the ones in this list are no longer part of our common speech. You can write clear legal information without using these words.

www.archives.gov/federal-register/write/legal-docs

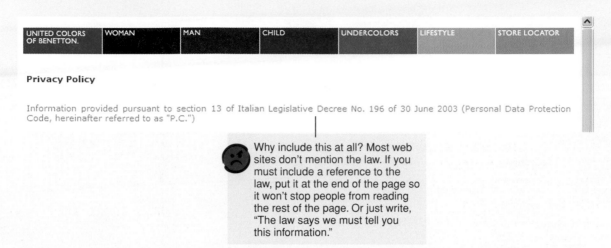

Figure Interlude 2-4 Words like "pursuant to" and "hereinafter" make legal information difficult for many people to understand.

www.benetton.com

Apply all the clear writing techniques to your legal information

You can use personal pronouns in legal information. (Consider the agreements you sign for credit cards, cell phones, cable service, insurance, and so on. Almost all of them use "we" and "you.")

 In the process of or following consultation of this web site, data pertaining to identified or identifiable persons may be processed.

 When you use this web site, we may collect data about you or people you tell us about – for example, people to whom you are sending a gift. We may use that data to . . .

You can write legal information with short, active sentences; with lists; and with tables. You can break legal information into short pieces, and each piece can still be a viable legal policy. You can give examples in legal information, as you see in the International Herald Tribune's definition of cookies (Figure Interlude 2-5).

Many site visitors do not know what a "cookie" is. A definition helps.

(A cookie is a small piece of information that our web servers send to your browser and that is stored on your computer. That small piece of information allows our computers to say, "Aha. We have seen this person before," and it also allows our computers to remember things about your past interaction with the site, like, "This person told us that they like to see the weather in Celsius, not Fahrenheit.")

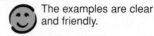
Words like "web servers" and "browser" are technical language. Many people who come through AOL, for example, don't think of it as a browser. The next sentence refers to "our computers," so the first sentence might say ". . . that our computers send to your computers . . ."

The examples are clear and friendly.

Figure Interlude 2-5 You can put examples in legal information.   www.iht.com

Case Study Interlude 2-1	Putting it all together with an example that is both legal and clear: Privacy policies

In this case study, I use all the points in the interlude to draft basic privacy policies for a web site. You may need to modify the information in these paragraphs for your web site. You may need to add other paragraphs to cover situations that are special to your site. If you do, try to write in this same style – friendly, personal, clear, and also legal. And remember to use these same principles – and all the other guidelines in this book – for terms of use and all other legal information on your web site.

Our Privacy Policy

Updated: [date]

Does [...] collect personal information about me?

What does [...] do with my personal information?

Does [...] share my information?

Does [...] store information on my computer? ("cookies")

Does [...] collect information about children under 13?

What if I have other questions?

Does [...] collect personal information about me?

If you are just browsing our web site, we do not collect any personal information about you.

We may ask you for and collect personal information, such as your name, email address, postal address, phone number, and possibly credit card information, when you

- order something on our web site, by phone, or in one of our stores
- open an account with us
- subscribe to an email newsletter
- participate in a survey, contest, or other event

If you buy from us, we may also keep records of your purchases so that you can track your orders and so that we can serve you better by tailoring information for you.

What does [...] do with my personal information?

We use personal information related to an order to process the order. We may contact you by email, phone, or postal address to confirm the order or if we have questions.

We may also use your personal information and information about your product interests to send you emails about products and promotions or to ask you questions about your preferences. If you do not want us to send you these emails, contact us.

Does [...] share my information?

We never tell anyone your email address or phone number. We may share your postal mailing information and your product interests with other carefully selected companies whose products may interest you. If you do not want us to share information about you, contact us.

Continued

Does [...] store information on my computer? ("cookies")

To recognize you as a returning customer and to show you information the way you want it, our computers put a small piece of information on your computer. This is called a "cookie."

A cookie tells us about your computer and lets our computers remember what you are currently doing or did in the past at our web site. For example, a cookie lets us track your shopping cart while you are on our web site.

A cookie does not give us any of your personal information, such as your name or email address.

Cookies also help us understand how people use our web site. They help us know which sections of the site are most popular and how people look for information on our site. We use this information to improve our web site and to serve you better.

Does [...] collect information about children under 13?

We never knowingly sell to or collect any personal information from children under 13. If you believe your child has given us personal information, please help us remove that information from our computers by contacting us.

What if I have other questions?

Please contact us. We are happy to answer your questions.

[contact Information]

Using Illustrations Effectively

11

In previous chapters, we've talked about making information visual just by arranging the text: short paragraphs, short sentences, lists, tables, headings, and a judicious use of space. Illustrations (photos, drawings, charts, graphs, maps, and so on) are also an important part of your web content.

As with all web content, in planning illustrations, you must think about your purposes, your audiences, and why people come to your site. The first questions to ask as you plan for illustrations are:

- What do I want to achieve by having an illustration here?
- What type of illustration is appropriate to achieve that purpose?

Indeed, as you go through your web content, ask yourself:

- Am I drawing a picture in my head as I read this?
- Is this difficult to explain in words?

If so, an illustration may be appropriate to explain or expand or enhance or replace your other web content.

Illustrations serve different purposes

I've been thinking about when, how, and why different types of illustrations work and don't work well on web sites. And I've come to realize that there's a continuum of types of illustrations that serve different purposes – from representational to emotional. Consider Figure 11-1.

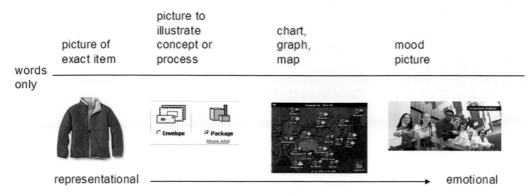

Figure 11-1 Your purpose in using a picture can range from purely representational to purely emotional (or mood setting).

Let's explore each of the four types of illustration in the continuum in more detail.

Picture of exact item

The continuum starts with purely representational pictures of the exact item. Because these pictures are so common in e-commerce sites, I'll start there and explore exact pictures in other types of web sites a few pages further on in the chapter.

If you work on an e-commerce web site, as you choose what to show in your online catalogue, think of illustrations as part of your conversation with customers. What questions do customers ask about the items? How can you best answer those questions? How can you take advantage of the web to show the answers?

Think about what aspects people want to see

For hiking boots, for example, people want to see the bottoms as well as the tops, so REI uses both static and dynamic pictures to present the parts that people want to see. (See Figures 11-2 and 11-3.)

Not every item needs a 3D video, however. Take advantage of what the web lets you do, but only when doing so adds real value for your site visitors.

In observing web users at e-commerce sites, Jared Spool found that experienced hikers rejected the offerings at a site that did not show the soles of hiking boots. Instead, they chose boots from REI because REI had pictures like the ones I'm showing here. Jared tells me (through email correspondence) that "The REI people knew to tip over the boots when shooting the pictures because the photographer used to work in the footwear department."

Figure 11-2 Think about what your customers want to see.   www.rei.com

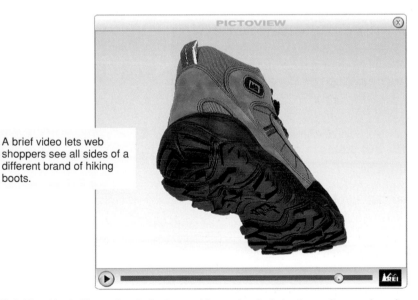

Figure 11-3 The video is like turning the boot around in your hands; but not every item needs such elaborate 3D treatment.   www.rei.com

Make sure your words match what happens

If you offer a larger picture, make sure it enlarges. If you promise other views, make sure that there really are other views. Otherwise, you are setting up expectations that you don't meet, which is likely to annoy your site visitors.

If an extra click sometimes fulfills its promise and sometimes doesn't, you are teasing your potential customers. They can't tell when they'll get what they want. Although I support the use of templates, be careful about situations in which the words in your template set up false expectations.

At GapKids.com, for example, item pages usually (perhaps always – I haven't checked every page), offer "more views." I suspect the "more views" link is part of the item page template.

Sometimes, this truly leads to other views, but sometimes it does not. Sometimes, all you get is a slightly larger version of the same view. If you want to see the back of boys' jeans, for example, you'll get that picture with some jeans but not with others.

Figure 11-4 is a girl's denim jacket with a tantalizing peek through the front of a design on the back. But "more views" disappoints; it only leads to a slightly larger view of the front and no option to see the back.

If the web writers could select among options for templates, they could provide more truthful expectations to their web shoppers. For Gapkids.com, the templates might allow writers to choose options for "See larger view," "View details," "View back" – whichever were relevant for the specific item.

Make sure the larger pictures are clear

Fuzzy enlargements, such as the one in Figure 11-5 from eBags.com, may make site visitors wonder about other aspects of your site – and your products.

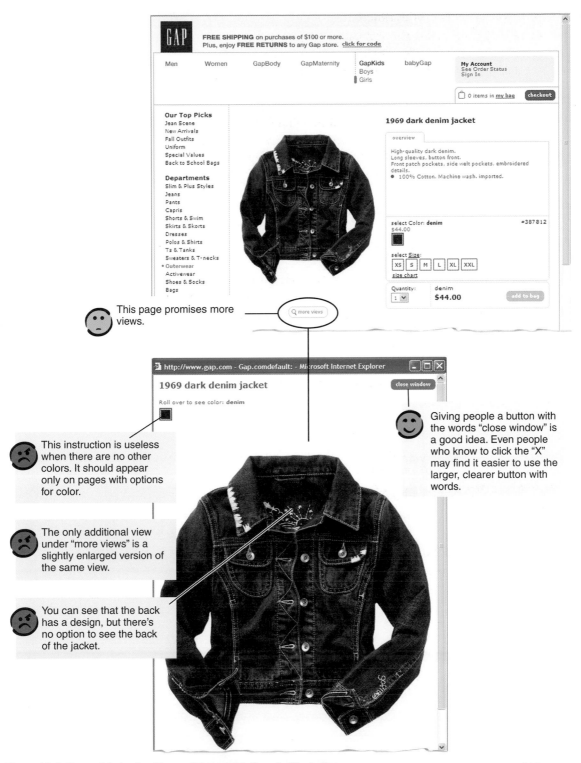

This page promises more views.

This instruction is useless when there are no other colors. It should appear only on pages with options for color.

The only additional view under "more views" is a slightly enlarged version of the same view.

You can see that the back has a design, but there's no option to see the back of the jacket.

Giving people a button with the words "close window" is a good idea. Even people who know to click the "X" may find it easier to use the larger, clearer button with words.

Figure 11-4 Be careful about setting up false expectations for illustrations.   www.gapkids.com

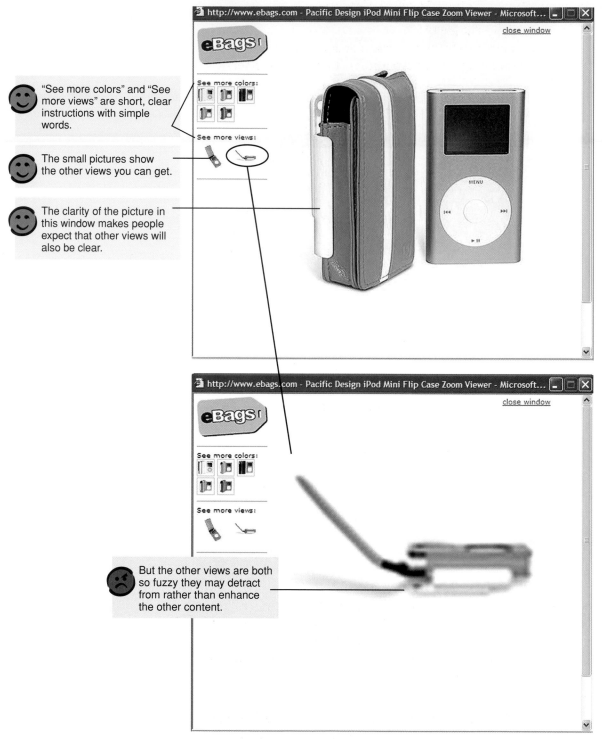

"See more colors" and "See more views" are short, clear instructions with simple words.

The small pictures show the other views you can get.

The clarity of the picture in this window makes people expect that other views will also be clear.

But the other views are both so fuzzy they may detract from rather than enhance the other content.

Figure 11-5 Make sure all your illustrations are clear.

www.eBags.com

Think about other situations in which pictures or diagrams would help people

Travel, theater, sports events, and many other situations also lend themselves to pictures or diagrams of exact items to help people serve themselves.

Think of showing, not just telling, in many situations.

Help people make connections between information on paper documents and fields on online forms

You can help people by showing them where on a card or paper document the information you want from them is located. When e-commerce sites started requiring the security code from credit cards as well as the number and expiration date, many sites included a picture of the back of the card to show people where to find the code.

The state of New Jersey sends car owners a paper document to remind them to renew their vehicle registration. The paper document includes a personal identification number (PIN) for renewing online. Many people didn't notice the PIN and, thus, couldn't do the task online. New Jersey's solution: include a picture of the paper document on the web page, indicating where to find the PIN. (See Figure 11-6.) Of course, another (or additional) solution would be to revise the paper document to make the PIN more obvious.

When the picture is a book or magazine cover or printed brochure, think about whether the link between print and web is necessary

For online booksellers, a picture of the book cover next to information about buying the book online makes sense. For journals where the

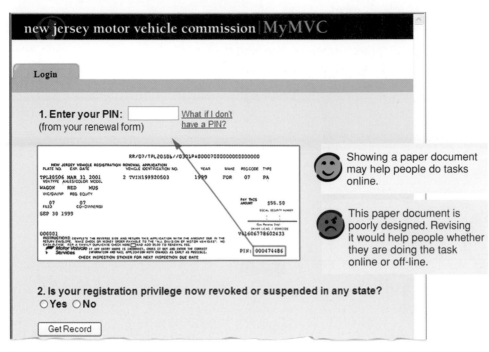

Figure 11-6 Considering questions and issues people may have in doing tasks might lead you to include pictures of paper documents for online tasks.   www.state.nj.us/mvc

publisher wants to increase subscriptions to the print version, a picture of the cover of each issue makes sense (Figure 11-7).

But as you move from paper documents to web information, ask yourself: How critical is it to maintain the connection to a print document? As I've suggested throughout this book, your web information need *not* look like the paper report or paper brochure. So, perhaps it is time to ask yourself and your colleagues whether you should continue to have a picture of a paper version with your web information.

Picture to illustrate concept or process

As we move along the continuum from purely representational to emotional (mood-setting), after pictures of the exact item, we come next to illustrations that represent not so much a specific object as a class or group of objects. The illustrations are meant to help people compare or understand quantities, dimensions, or ratios or to understand processes.

Comparing sizes

Illustrations are a great way to help people compare and choose, especially when they need to visualize dimensions or quantities.

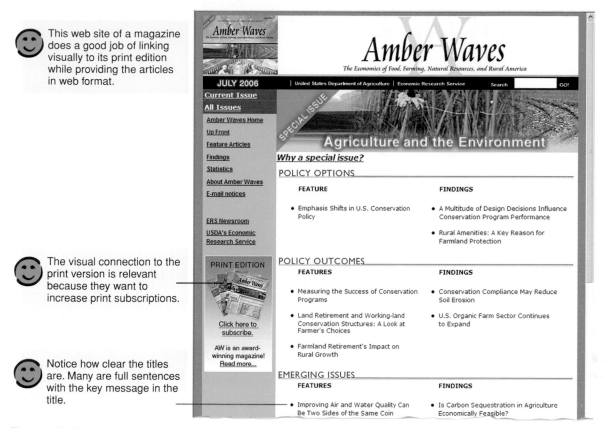

This web site of a magazine does a good job of linking visually to its print edition while providing the articles in web format.

The visual connection to the print version is relevant because they want to increase print subscriptions.

Notice how clear the titles are. Many are full sentences with the key message in the title.

Figure 11-7 Showing the cover of a book or magazine makes sense if you want people to buy the print version. Otherwise, consider *not* including pictures of print documents as you move to web-based information. www.ers.usda.gov

Have you ever gone to a web site to rent a car and been unsure of the difference between "economy" and "compact" or between "standard" and "mid-size"? Pictures can clarify distinctions like these. Compare Figures 11-8 and 11-9.

Understanding dimensions and ratios

If you are talking about objects that people recognize, a picture is often worth many words of explanation. Compare two pages from the web site of the U. S. Postal Service. The web page in Figure 11-10 is a list just in words of the types of mail that require extra postage. The web page in Figure 11-11 shows pictures of all types of envelopes. After you select the one that you are sending, the site tells you if your envelope needs extra postage.

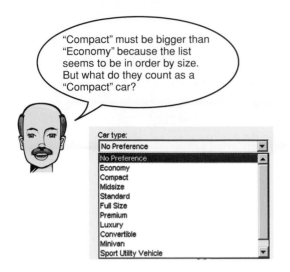

Figure 11-8 Words, such as this list of car sizes, may not be enough to help people choose.

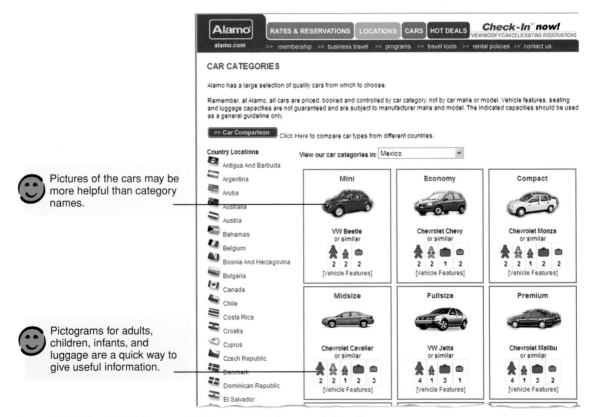

Figure 11-9 Both realistic pictures and pictograms can help convey information.   www.alamo.com

Nonmachinable Surcharge:
An additional $0.13 is required for items weighing 1 ounce or less with any of the following criteria:

A. Square letters.
B. The height exceeds 6-1/8 inches, or length exceeds 11-1/2 inches, or thickness exceeds 1/4 inch.
C. The length divided by height is less than 1.3 or more than 2.5 (length is the dimension parallel to the address).
D. It has clasps, strings, buttons, or similar closure devices.
E. It is too rigid or contains items such as pens that cause the thickness of the mailpiece to be uneven.
F. It has an address parallel to the shorter dimension of the mailpiece.

People often have difficulty visualizing dimensions and ratios.

(Back to Top ▲)

Figure 11-10 Think "pictures" for quantities, dimensions, ratios, and other numerical information.　　www.usps.com

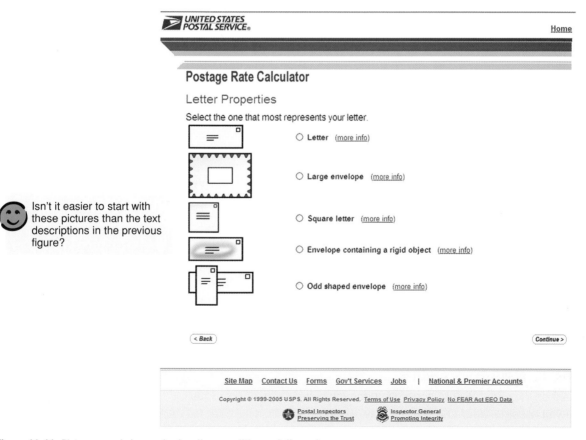

Isn't it easier to start with these pictures than the text descriptions in the previous figure?

Figure 11-11 Pictures can help people visualize quantities and dimensions.　　www.usps.com

Showing a process

Showing a process in pictures can be both eye-catching and informative. Consider the explanation in Figure 11-12, the Netflix page about "how it works."

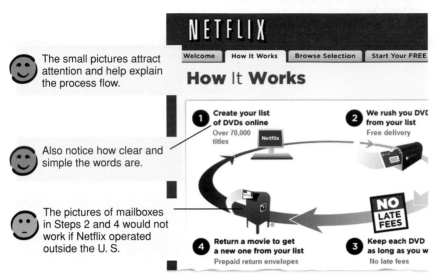

Figure 11-12 Pictures can help explain a process. They also enliven the page and attract attention. But make sure the pictures are meaningful to your audiences.

www.netflix.com

As with all web content, keep your process pictures simple. Animate the process only if that adds useful information and won't annoy people. (See more about animation, including animating processes, later in this chapter.)

Chart, graph, map

Moving further along the continuum in Figure 11-1, we come to charts, graphs, maps, and other ways of presenting data. These illustrations are not as simple to work with as the pictures in the previous two categories; they require interpretation.

Consider combining maps with lists

Maps are an excellent way to show geography, but they may not work as well as you assume. Your site visitors may

- not know the geography well enough to select appropriately
- not divide the overall map the way you do

- not recognize abbreviations you are using
- find it too difficult to click on small targets (especially true of your older web users)

Combining a map with a textual list, allowing people to choose from either, as Lonely Planet does in Figure 11-13, may be a good solution that helps people select accurately and quickly while even learning a bit of geography.

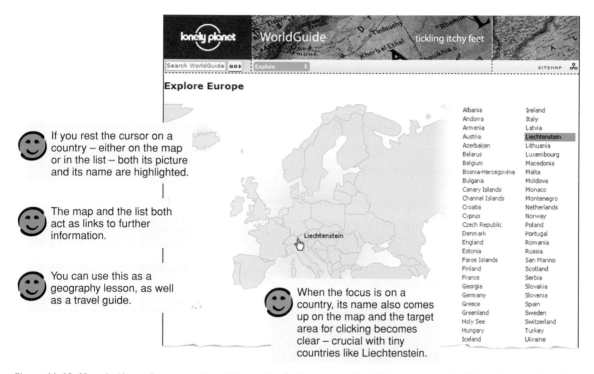

Figure 11-13 Maps by themselves may not meet the needs of all your users. Combining a map and a list may be more helpful.

www.lonelyplanet.com

A story about maps: Remember the case study about getting a copy of your birth certificate (Chapter 4, Case Study 4-1)? Everyone agrees that the paragraph of text is a very poor way of telling people what to do. When I give people the exercise of finding the best way to help people select the state where they were born, I get three solutions: the list of states (as you saw in the case study in Chapter 4), a map of the U. S., and a drop-down list. When the workshop is in Washington State, many people suggest a map. When the workshop is in Washington, D.C., very few people suggest a map. Why? Washington State is large, easy to find in a corner of the country, and very far down if you are scrolling a list of states. Washington, D.C., is a tiny speck on the map, in the middle of many very small states, and near the beginning alphabetically (as District of Columbia). Think about the people who need to choose places like Liechtenstein and Washington, D.C., when you think of asking site visitors to work with maps.

Keep it simple. Let your web users choose how much to see

Don't overload people with more information than they want or need. Instead of putting many different types of information on the same graphic, offer alternative views. Let people drill down for details. Let people choose how much to combine. Consider the way an Australian weather site gives people several choices of what to look at (Figure 11-14).

Write key message titles for charts and graphs

The rationale behind inverted pyramid writing holds for graphics as well. Busy web users want to grab key messages from the graphics just as they

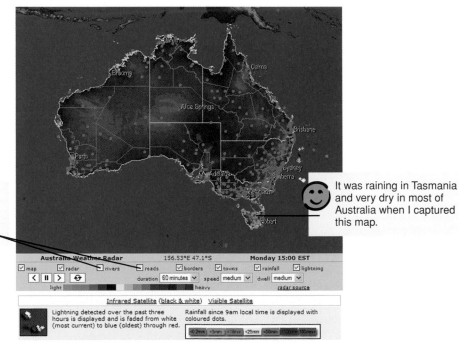

 You can keep the map simple or show many aspects, such as rivers and roads.

It was raining in Tasmania and very dry in most of Australia when I captured this map.

Figure 11-14 Pictures can send powerful messages. When possible, let your web users decide how much data to combine in one picture.   www.weatherzone.com.au

do from the text. But the traditional way of titling charts and graphs just by their subject matter ("gasoline use per month for the last 2 years") forces the web user to work at analyzing the chart and extracting the key message. Instead, you can help people take away the key message of your chart or graph by putting that message in the title ("gasoline prices have been rising steadily over the last 2 years"). The researchers at the U. S. Economic Research Service do a good job of giving illustrations key message titles, as in Figure 11-15.

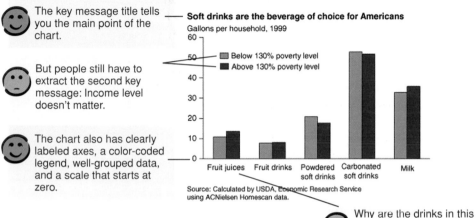

Figure 11-15 Key message titles on charts and graphs help busy web users.   www.ers.usda.gov

Follow principles of good data reporting

Accuracy is as critical in web graphics as in any other medium, and it's just as easy to mislead with statistics on the web as on paper. Don't do it. A mistake that many people make, for example, is to show only partial data, starting where the data does instead of at zero. But that magnifies and exaggerates differences in the data.

Fowler and Stanwick's *Web Application Design Handbook*, 2004, has an extensive section on designing graphics to present data.

Mood picture

And now we've reached the other end of the continuum – illustrations (almost always photos) that are primarily meant to evoke an emotional response. These photos are representational; they show real people or real objects. But their purpose is not to say "here's what the jacket that you might buy looks like" or "this is what we mean by a package compared to a letter." Their purpose is to engender good feelings about the site and the brand.

Make sure that the photos evoke the mood you want

For example, Queens University in Canada used to have a home page with a rotating set of pictures. Sometimes, it showed a picture of buildings, as in Figure 11-16. Sometimes, the picture was of students, as in Figure 11-17.

 What is your reaction to these two versions of the web page?

I've used these two versions in many workshops. When I show the page with the picture of a building, workshop participants tell me the school is "cold" and "staid" and they would not want to go there. When I show the same page with the picture of students, workshop participants tell me the school is "warm" and "welcoming" and they would want to go there. Pictures evoke emotions and moods.

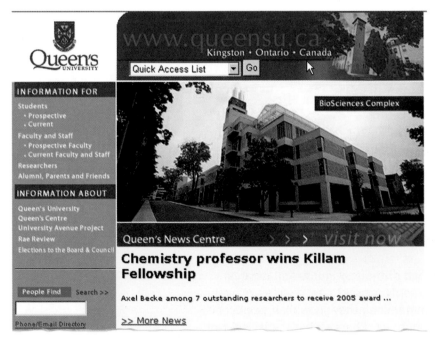

Figure 11-16 A screen from 2005.   www.queensu.ca

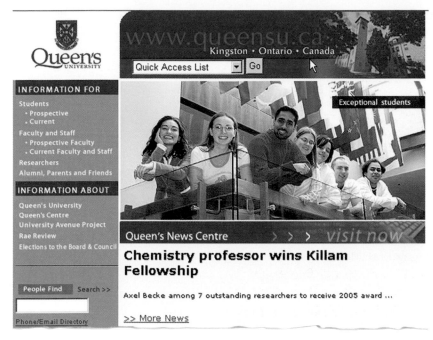

Figure 11-17 Another screen from 2005.   www.queensu.ca

That's not to say that pictures of buildings are always wrong. It's a matter of where the picture comes on the web site and who the audience is. For potential students, the building isn't meaningful. However, if you were creating a page for alumni and you knew that they were likely to have fond memories of a particular part of campus, a picture of the buildings on that part of campus might be very appropriate. It might evoke exactly the positive emotional response that you want.

Think of your global audience

As with many mood-setting photos, the picture in Figure 11-18 can be either a deeply meaningful image or just a pretty postcard – depending on your relationship to what it shows.

Figure 11-18 is from the web site of the Olympia, Washington, newspaper. Olympia is the capital of Washington State in the U. S., and the picture is of the state capitol building in its setting of evergreen trees. For local readers and former Olympians who may be reading the online version from far away, this picture probably evokes positive feelings of "home town," "my town." The picture may make some other people who come to the site realize that Olympia must be the state capital. But for others, the picture may be pretty but meaningless. Would a tag line,

Note, too, that humor is extremely difficult to manage well on the web. What is funny to one person may not be to the next. And humor is deeply cultural. What is funny in one culture is not in another. Because the web is so global, it's really hard to be universally humorous. Think carefully before using humorous graphics.

Here, as always in creating successful web content, you must think beyond yourself. The mood pictures that work for you, with your knowledge of the organization and your feelings about the organization's buildings and people might not work for people who don't know those buildings or people.

such as "The newsletter of Washington's capital city" as an addition to the name and picture make a broader audience more comfortable with and more interested in the paper's web site?

 This picture works well locally. It evokes familiarity and good feelings for people in Olympia, Washington.

But would a tag line help more people understand where Olympia is and increase interest in this web site?

Figure 11-18 The web is global. Think beyond your local audience.   www.theolympian.com

Nine general guidelines for using illustrations effectively

No matter what you are using illustrations for, keep these nine guidelines in mind:

1. Don't make people wonder what or why.
2. Choose an appropriate size.
3. Use illustrations to support, not hide, content.
4. In pictures of people, show diversity.
5. Don't make content look like ads.
6. Don't annoy people with blinking, rolling, waving, or wandering text or pictures.
7. Use animation where it helps – not just for show.
8. Don't make people wait through splash or Flash.
9. Make illustrations accessible.

1. Don't make people wonder what or why

If your site visitors have to stop to figure out what you are showing or why you are showing it, the illustration has lost its value. An illustration must make its function and meaning immediately clear – even if that meaning is just "to set the mood." The picture in Figure 11-19 is from a museum's web site. I found it so distracting – and spent so much time and effort trying to figure out what it represents – that I gave up on the museum's information without delving further into the site.

Figure 11-19 An obscure picture may be so distracting that people miss the important content on your web page.

2. Choose an appropriate size

Illustrations that are too small often violate the previous guideline. It's too hard to figure out what they are showing. Avoid using photos with a lot of detail if you are going to reduce them to serve as icons.

Make sure small pictures are clear

Look back at the small photos as bullets in the example from the U. S. National Science Foundation in Chapter 9 (Figure 9-11). The two small pictures of people are clear. You can tell what (if not who) is in each picture. But did you instantly realize that the first picture is a humming-bird? that the third is a grain held between a thumb and finger? (The second picture may be visually clear, but its relationship to the topic may be obscure unless you already know a lot about high-temperature superfluids.)

 Or consider the icons used as bullets in Figure 11-20, a page from Elvis.com, the web site celebrating the life and continuing cult of Elvis Presley. Which work well? Which cause eyestrain and make you wonder what they are trying to convey?

 And remember how many of your site visitors are likely to have vision problems. Elvis Presley was at the height of his fame in the 1950s and 1960s; his fans who were teenagers then are now in their 50s and 60s.

Some of these small pictures are easy to "get" at a glance.

But others are not.

and various menu options when visiting Graceland.

Groups

Learn about special rates and dining options for your Memphis travel group of 15 or more.

Maps & Directions

Use maps of Graceland Plaza and the Memphis area to help plan your trip.

Special Offers & Packages

Check out our special Elvis-themed packages and special offers available to you during your visiting.

Visiting Memphis

Find out what else there is to do in Memphis with links to some other great Memphis area attractions.

Hours of Operation

Read important information on Graceland's hours of operation.

Annual Events

Visit Graceland each year for Elvis's Birthday Celebration, Elvis Week, and Christmas at Graceland.

Virtual Tour

Enjoy special Graceland IPIX tours, the live GracelandCam, special images of Graceland artifacts, the photo spotlight, and more.

Special Events

Make your Elvis parties, corporate events, and other Memphis events unforgettable at one of our great event venues.

Chapel in the Woods

Walk down the aisle at Graceland's Chapel in the Woods. The chapel offers the perfect setting for your Elvis wedding.

GracelandCam™

See a live shot of the Graceland Mansion front lawn.

Figure 11-20 If you plan to reduce photos to use as icons or as bullets in front of links, keep the composition clear and simple. People may have difficulty figuring out what is foreground and what is background when the pictures are very small.

www.elvis.com

Don't use so much space for pictures that critical content gets shoved down or aside

On the other hand, don't make illustrations so large that they prevent users from finding critical content. I know I've already said this at least twice (in Chapter 3, Figure 3-12, the FedEx home page, and in Chapter 4, Figure 4-3, a Dell Computers pathway page), but it may be worth harping on because it is such a prevalent problem on the web today.

3. Use illustrations to support, not hide, content

People like pictures, but they also want to find what they need quickly. If all people see on a site is illustrations and they have to wonder where the information is, you may lose them before they get to the information. Don't play games with people who come to your site for information.

Vincent Flanders calls hiding navigation under pictures "mystery meat navigation." www.webpagesthatsuck.com.

The pictures on the home page of the University of New Mexico's Biology Department in Figure 11-21 are very nice, but where are the links to the site's information? Indeed, what information does the site have? You can't tell by glancing at the pictures – which is all the content the site gives you in its main content area.

This design just does not work; it makes people work too hard for what they need. In fact, it must not have worked for the Biology Department's site visitors because the site has changed since I captured the web page in Figure 11-21. The page is now a static set of pictures that don't change and are not clickable. But the page uses a subset of the pictures from the old page, so I wonder if people who had used the old site are even more confused now because what was clickable no longer is. In this case, a much greater change in design might have been more effective. And a page that brought the main content – the actual navigation – into the center of the home page might work best.

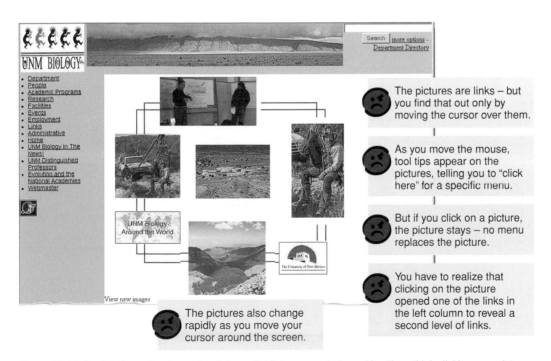

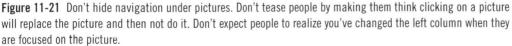

Figure 11-21 Don't hide navigation under pictures. Don't tease people by making them think clicking on a picture will replace the picture and then not do it. Don't expect people to realize you've changed the left column when they are focused on the picture.

4. In pictures of people, show diversity

People enjoy seeing people on web sites. Pictures of people help make the web seem like a personal conversation, just like the personal pronouns and questions and answers that I've been suggesting throughout the book. Pictures can suggest that your web site speaks for all the different people in your organization and that you want lots of different people to be your web users. Be aware, however, of how strongly pictures of people send messages about who you are including and excluding.

To represent your organization, show diversity, but be truthful

If your organization includes a diversity of people, show that, as Figure 11-22 from the Sacramento, California, Metro Chamber did in 2005. You'll make connections with a wide range of users and potential users of your site.

Figure 11-22 Pictures of people can make people feel included — or excluded.   www.metrochamber.org

Be careful, however. Tom Brinck shared a story with me of his experience and challenge trying to develop the visual strategy for an organization. The organization wanted to reflect diversity and wanted to recruit more minorities and women than it had. However, in usability testing, when the photos had half or more women in the group, women often laughed and said that something was wrong. They knew there weren't that many women in the organization. In an effort to show equality, the web designers had created a mismatch with current reality that seemed misleading to the very people they were trying to recruit.

To represent your site visitors, think broadly

Think cross-culturally, even within your country. Think of diversity in ethnicity, gender, and age – while, of course, being appropriate for your site. Think globally. Select photos that are appropriate for different versions of your site in different locations, while thinking about diversity for each of those locations.

Test, test, test

For all mood pictures, but especially for pictures of people, it's very difficult to predict what people's reactions will be.

 Look at the photos in Figure 11-23 from one of the institutes in the U. S. National Institutes of Health. What adjectives would you use for them? Are they appropriate to the site?

In usability testing, the pictures at this site did very well. People saw the people in the two photos as serious researchers – the mood and brand that the agency wanted to project. "Serious" seemed to work here.

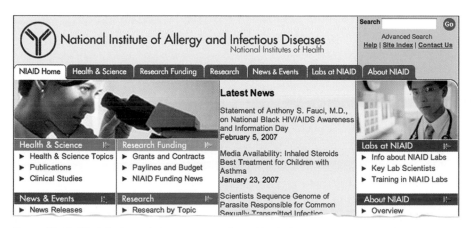

Figure 11-23 What do these photos say to *you* about this site?   www.niaid.nih.gov

However, "serious" doesn't always work. A colleague told me that his team found it impossible to include a photo with a serious expression on a health care site. With every "serious expression" picture that they tested, some people thought the person looked unhappy or even angry. The team ended up showing only smiles.

Even the grouping that you use may evoke emotions and explanations that surprise you. A site for people concerned with cancer tried a photo of a man with two children. One test participant's reaction was, "Oh, poor family. Did the Mom die?"

Putting your prototype web pages in front of people and getting their reactions is the only way to know how the pictures you picked will be perceived. You can do that in focus groups or in usability testing. Whichever method you use, don't just show the photos by themselves. Show them in the context of the web page they'll be on and the other web content they'll be with. Context matters, as you've seen in the stories I've just told.

5. Don't make content look like ads

Many web users have "ad blindness"; they ignore anything that looks like an ad. Because so many sites have ads in colorful boxes in the right column, people tend to ignore any content on the right in colorful boxes.

Although the bright colors on the right in Figure 11-24 from The Pension Service in the U. K. draw your eye, do you then ignore them and head over to the left instead? The Pension Service, in fact, has replaced this design with one that has only the invitation to enlarge the text and the link to the related but different Directgov site on the right. You saw the new design back in Chapter 5 as Figure 5-6.

6. Don't annoy people with blinking, rolling, waving, or wandering text or pictures

Movement is eye-catching. Paying attention to movement in our peripheral vision was a key survival skill when we shared space with lions on the savannah. On the web, however, movement is just plain annoying. It takes our eyes from the task we are trying to do. Don't make page elements blink or wave or roll or jump around gratuitously.

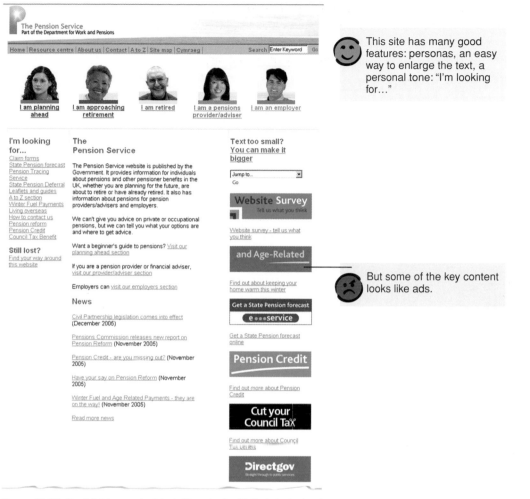

This site has many good features: personas, an easy way to enlarge the text, a personal tone: "I'm looking for…"

But some of the key content looks like ads.

Figure 11-24 Don't let key content look like ads. It will likely be ignored.   www.thepensionservice.gov.uk

Don't let text roll

Think of slow readers. Think of the older people in your audience. Think of people who need to magnify text to read it. Rolling text generally achieves the exact opposite of your purpose. It frustrates people rather than satisfying their needs.

Even scrolling ticker tape is an outdated model, not appropriate for the web. Just because people are used to it in the world outside the web, doesn't make it the best way to present that data on the web. Why not just provide a database where people can get the stock price they want without having to watch for it to come by on the screen?

Figure 11-25 Rolling text is a distraction for everyone. It's an especially poor choice on a site that serves many older users and people who speak limited English.   www.ssa.gov

Don't change content while people are on the page

The orange box in the right column of The Pension Service site from Figure 11-24 is actually a five-part sequence that keeps changing, as you can see in Figure 11-26. Why just that one? Why do that at all?

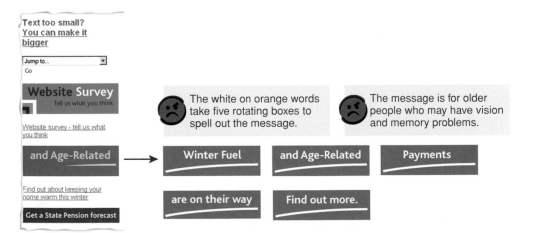

Figure 11-26 If people even realize that the box they see is only one-fifth of the message, they may have trouble putting the five parts together. Don't make your audience play games like this to understand your web content.

The movement in Figure 11-26 may keep people from finding what they need elsewhere on the page. Moreover, the page is specifically directed at older adults – who may need more time to read each part than the cycling of the pictures allows them.

Don't let animated animals, birds, butterflies, and so on, roam the page

Eye-tracking studies show that people often try desperately to move away from animation. They want to concentrate on finding and under- standing the information they came to the site to get. When a roaming animal or bird or butterfly crosses the path of what they are reading, they get distracted – and annoyed.

Weigh the trade-offs for animation carefully

Animation is so distracting that many people cannot concentrate on anything else on a page where something is animated, even if the animation doesn't intrude into the main content area. So you must ask: Is the blinking ad or other animation so important that it trumps the task the web user came to do? If you don't let people accomplish the tasks they came to the site to do, you risk losing them as future site visitors. Don't use animation to be cute. Don't use animation just to liven up the site. Remember that you market best by satisfying the need your site visitors came for, not by distracting them away from their tasks.

7. Use animation where it helps – not just for show

The only good reason to use animation is when it helps explain the content. For example, if you want to show a process, animation may be just the right tool to use. The animation supports and clarifies the content.

Learning how to tie different types of knots is clearly a candidate for animation, and the site Animated Knots by Grog uses motion and text together very well (Figure 11-27).

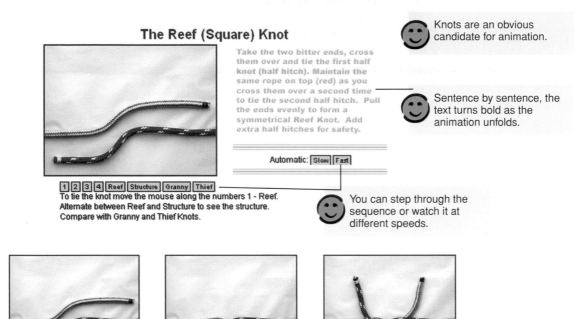

The Reef (Square) Knot

Take the two bitter ends, cross them over and tie the first half knot (half hitch). Maintain the same rope on top (red) as you cross them over a second time to tie the second half hitch. Pull the ends evenly to form a symmetrical Reef Knot. Add extra half hitches for safety.

Automatic: Slow Fast

1 2 3 4 Reef Structure Granny Thief

To tie the knot move the mouse along the numbers 1 - Reef. Alternate between Reef and Structure to see the structure. Compare with Granny and Thief Knots.

Knots are an obvious candidate for animation.

Sentence by sentence, the text turns bold as the animation unfolds.

You can step through the sequence or watch it at different speeds.

Figure 11-27 Use animation as a tool to show processes like tying knots, setting up a router, drawing, or learning to write special characters.

www.animatedknots.com

8. Don't make people wait through splash or Flash

Flash, originally from Macromedia, now comes from Adobe Software, Inc.

No splash! No Flash as prepayment for getting in!

Splash pages waste people's time

Wikipedia defines splash pages this way:

> A splash page of a web site is a sort of pre-home page front
> page, usually providing no real information besides perhaps
> a note about browser requirements and sometimes a web
> counter. Often this page is graphics-intensive and used
> only for reasons of branding; sometimes it provides a choice
> of entry points for the site proper, for instance links to
> Macromedia Flash and HTML-only versions of the site.
> The term splash screen is sometimes used interchangeably.
> (en.wikipedia.org/wiki/Comics_vocabulary)

The Wikipedia definition is in the entry for comic book. Splash pages
come from the world of comic books. But the information-rich and e-
commerce web sites that we are talking about are not comic books.

Nielsen and Loranger declare: "Splash screens must die!" (2006,
p. 111). I agree. If your web users value efficiency, why make them
click an extra time just to get into the site?

Truly unnecessary splash pages – meant to evoke a mood or set a tone –
have mostly disappeared. They've morphed in two directions – the Flash
videos that I'm going to denounce on the next few pages and the large
pictures (either static or animated) that I've already denounced several
times for pushing critical content too far down the page.

Only a few situations provide legitimate cases for a page before a site's
home page:

- Canadian government sites must start with a page giving English
  and French equal treatment. (And governments of other countries
  with multiple official languages may require similar treatment.)

- Global companies must first help site visitors find their local version
  of the company's site.

But governments and companies, today, are finding ways to help people
avoid even those splash pages. If I use an external search engine to get
to a Canadian government site, the search engine returns the correct
home page (English or French) depending on the language of my key
words. Many global companies let site visitors tell the site to remember
their location and not show them the splash page again. Think innova-
tively of how to help your site visitors get in to your content as quickly
and easily as possible – no splash, no Flash, no extra clicks.

You wear out your welcome by welcoming people too much

Making people sit through even a short movie as prepayment for using your site is not a successful marketing strategy. Don't do it.

People who come to your site want to get in to do whatever they came to do. You may be unaware of how many customers you are losing because they can't or won't get past your introductory video.

The site about free hearing testing in Figure 11-28 may be offering a great service, but finding out about it is very difficult. The site opens with an animated sequence that takes several seconds even at very high bandwidth to go from a "welcome to" message to a page of pictures that looks like a home page with options. But it's not. No matter where you click ("skip this intro," "click to enter," or on any of the pictures with captions), the site moves to its real home page. And that page is so busy that it's impossible to find anything. If you go back, thinking maybe a different click will take you to a content page on the topic of a specific picture, you have to sit through the "welcome to" movie all over again. Time and time again. Utter frustration!

People want to control their online experiences

One of the guiding principles of web design is that the site visitor must be in control of the experience. Even if you give people the option to "skip this introduction," many people get annoyed trying to find where the option is or even having to click on it.

Videos at the beginning are roadblocks for some people

It's not just the annoyance factor. If you make having Flash (or any specific technology) a requirement for entrance to your site, you are keeping some people from getting to your content. Not everyone has Flash or wants it or has time to download it at the moment when they are trying to get information from your site.

The site that shows the screen in Figure 11-29 is shutting out many potential users.

If people can get what they need at another site, they're likely to just jump to your competition. If they need the information from you, they'll have to call or write – an expensive proposition for your company and possibly an extremely frustrating experience for your customer.

The splash page builds from "WELCOME TO," adding each picture with its caption.

Eventually, it settles into this. But this is a false home page.

You can click on any picture, but you can't get directly to the topic of the picture – all links go to the same page.

All clicks lead here – the actual home page.

Too much text and no links to all the promises of the splash page.

Figure 11-28 Welcome people by giving them what they need, not by making them wait through an animated welcome message. Don't tease people with promises of links to specific content and then take them all to the same home page.

www.freehearingtest.com

Replacement content here. You need the latest Flash Player to view this site.

Download Flash Player

This is the entire home page that anyone without the latest Flash Player can see.

Figure 11-29 *It is not wise marketing to lock your front door against many of your customers.*

www.nationalmuseum.sg

A story inside a story: I always start my workshops by having people share a recent web experience with the person sitting next to them. It's an icebreaker; it gets people talking and thinking of web users; it lets us talk after the exercise about how goal- and task-oriented people are when they go to web sites. A few people share their stories with the whole group. In one workshop, a participant told this story: She had a question about her telephone service and went to the company's web site to get an answer to her question. But she could not get into the site. The first web page insisted she watch a video; her old computer couldn't show the video; she couldn't find a way around the video. But she really wanted the information. So she spent an enormous amount of time finding a phone number (with a paper phone book), calling, being passed from person to person, and became so frustrated that she decided to change her service provider. Don't put roadblocks in your site visitors' way.

9. Make illustrations accessible

For people who use screen-readers, you must annotate illustrations so that screen-readers can describe them. You do that by writing "alternative" text with the alt attribute to an image <img> tag. I'm going to call that "alt text."

Make the alt text meaningful

If the illustration is meant to convey substantive information, be sure to convey the information in the alt text, too. To write good alt text, you have to know *why* you are using the illustration. I hope that working through the continuum in this chapter has helped you think about illustrations, their uses, and their meaning.

To test whether you have a good description of each illustration, the World Wide Web Consortium accessibility guidelines suggest that you imagine reading the web page aloud over the telephone. What would you say about the image to make your listener understand it? (From www.w3.org.)

For purely decorative graphics, use empty alt text

You don't have to describe every piece of decoration on the page. In fact, hearing "decorative bullet" over and over greatly annoyed the blind web users that Mary Theofanos and I worked with. All they wanted to hear was the words after the bullet.

But if you want your site to do well on an automated test for accessibility, you must put alt text on every graphic. The solution is to use an empty alt attribute when the graphic has no content to describe: alt="".

SUMMARIZING CHAPTER 11

Here are key messages from Chapter 11:

- Illustrations serve several purposes. They can be
  - purely representational (pictures of the exact item)
  - meant to convey a concept or process
  - a chart, graph, or map
  - primarily to evoke an emotional response or to set a mood

- For pictures of exact items:
  - Think about what aspects people want to see.
  - Make sure your words match what happens.
  - Make sure the larger pictures are clear.
  - Think about other situations where pictures or diagrams would help people.
  - Help people make connections between information on paper documents and fields on online forms.
  - When the picture is a book or magazine cover or printed brochure, think about whether the link between print and web is necessary.

- Use pictures to illustrate concepts or process, to compare sizes, and to help people understand dimensions.

- For charts, graphs, and maps:
  - Consider combining maps with lists.
  - Keep it simple. Let your web users choose how much to see.
  - Write key message titles for charts and graphs.
  - Follow principles of good data reporting.

- For mood pictures:
  - Make sure that the photos evoke the mood you want.
  - Think of your global audience.

- Don't make people wonder what the picture shows or why you are showing it.

- Choose an appropriate size.
  - Make sure small pictures are clear.
  - Don't use so much space for pictures that critical content gets shoved down or aside.

- Use illustrations to support, not hide, content.

- In pictures of people, show diversity.
  - To represent your organization, show diversity, but be truthful.
  - To represent your site visitors, think broadly.
  - Test, test, test.

- Don't make content look like ads.

- Don't annoy people with blinking, rolling, waving, or wandering text or pictures.
  - Don't let text roll.
  - Don't change content while people are on the page.
  - Don't let animated animals, birds, butterflies, and so on, roam the page.
  - Weigh the trade-offs for animation carefully.

- Use animation where it helps – not just for show.

- Don't make people wait through splash or Flash.
  - Splash pages waste people's time.
  - You wear out your welcome by welcoming people too much.
  - People want to control their online experiences.
  - Videos at the beginning are roadblocks for some people.

- Make illustrations accessible.
  - Make the alt text meaningful.
  - For purely decorative graphics, use empty alt text.

Writing Meaningful Links

12

This book is about information on the web much more than it is about getting around on web sites (web navigation). But navigation is also critical.

You've seen many examples of links throughout the book, especially in Chapter 3 on home pages, in Chapter 4 on pathway pages, and in the section on same-page links in Chapter 10 on headings. And I've promised several times to cover how to write meaningful, useful links. That's what this chapter is about.

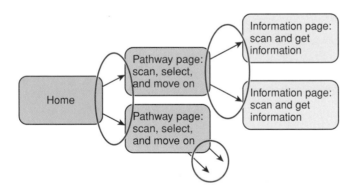

Links can be

- headlines and titles that are
  - full sentences, either statements or questions – <u>Are smaller cars as safe as large cars?</u> or <u>Chocolate – Food of the gods?</u>
  - phrases – <u>Cricket: Final hit-out for Australia before test</u>

- action phrases with verbs – <u>Contact us</u>, <u>Sign in</u>, <u>Open an account</u>
- category labels – usually single nouns or short phrases – <u>News</u>, <u>Printers</u>, <u>Citizens</u>, <u>Business</u>, <u>Ages 4–7</u>

Twelve guidelines for writing meaningful links

Use these 12 guidelines when you are writing links:

1. Don't make new program and product names into links by themselves.
2. Rethink document titles and headings that turn into links.
3. Think ahead. Match links and page titles.
4. Be as explicit as you can in the space you have – and make more space if you need it.
5. Use action phrases for action links.
6. Use single nouns sparingly; longer, more descriptive links often work better.
7. Add a short description if people need it – or rewrite the link.
8. Make the link meaningful – not <u>Click here</u>, not just <u>More</u>.
9. Coordinate when you have multiple, similar links.
10. Don't embed links if you want people to stay with your information.
11. If you use bullets with links, make them active, too.
12. Make both unvisited and visited links obvious.

1. Don't make new program and product names into links by themselves

Many organizations create new programs and new products with cute names. Once people know the name, it may make sense. It may even be memorable. But until people know what it means, it's meaningless to them.

Why should people click on a link if they don't know what to expect? Remember that your web site must serve new people not just those already in the know.

 Both The British Museum (Figure 12-1) and the Colorado Historical Society (Figure 12-2) have links to something called Compass. Would you click on it on either site? What do you expect to find? Do you expect the same type of information in both cases?

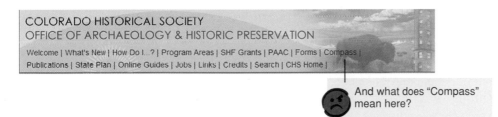

Figure 12-1 People are not likely to click on links if the words aren't meaningful to them in the context of that site. Don't use made-up program names as links.

www.thebritishmuseum.ac.uk

Figure 12-2 This screen has the same problems as the one from The British Museum – a link that uses only the program's made-up name. It doesn't explain what people will get by clicking on it.

www.coloradohistory.org

The British Museum's site called Children's COMPASS has wonderful online tours of different parts of the museum's collections and answers to many questions. It even has a facility that pronounces individual words or reads the entire text without the need for special software. But the "name as link" likely keeps all that great information hidden for many web users.

The same word, "Compass," means something totally different for the Colorado Historical Society than it does for The British Museum. In the

Colorado site, it's a database used by consultants in archeology and historical preservation. And neither site seems to be using the word in its dictionary meaning of an instrument for determining direction. But how would web users know any of this without exploring each site? And are most users curious enough to do that?

Don't start with the new name. Start with a descriptive link that is meaningful for your site visitors. If you want to use the name, introduce it in parentheses after the descriptive link or on the first content page – and show how the description and the name go together.

Acronyms often cause similar problems. Think about the broad public audience that may not know your acronyms. Even inside an organization, people typically don't know all the organization's acronyms. If some of your site visitors aren't going to recognize the acronym, spell it out, especially in links.

2. Rethink document titles and headings that turn into links

An obscure title for a report, report section, or article causes problems both on paper and on the web, but the problems are far greater on the web.

In the paper world, people have the document in hand when they see the title. They can scan or flip through the pages looking at internal headings, charts, graphs, and text to understand how the title relates to the content. On the web, people first see the title as a link – by itself – out of context (Figures 12-3 and 12-4). They have to choose to click to get more.

If the title as a link isn't meaningful, people who should click on it, may not. Result: frustrated potential readers who can't find the information they want; frustrated authors whose work doesn't get read.

Or the opposite may happen. People may click on the link expecting something totally different from what they get. In the paper world, the document is distributed only to the audiences for whom it was written. On the web, everyone may see the title. It may be on a web page they got while looking for something else. It may show up in a search.

You must think not only about the people who *should* choose the link to your information, but also those who *should not* choose it.

As a web content writer or editor, you may not control the titles of all the documents that you are turning into web pages. But take this guideline to heart and pass it on to the people who are writing those documents. You'll be helping them relate to their audiences. You'll be helping those audiences – and the document's non-audiences. You'll be saving yourself the work of having to come up with a description to clarify an obscure or misleading title.

Figure 12-3 Report titles become links on the web out of context. People don't know what they will get until they click on the link.

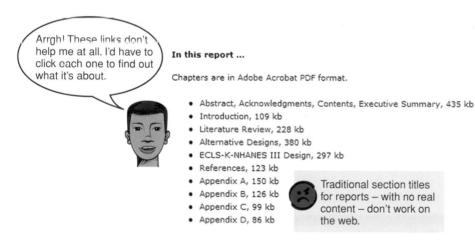

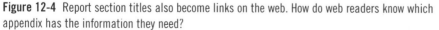

Figure 12-4 Report section titles also become links on the web. How do web readers know which appendix has the information they need?

3. Think ahead. Match links and page titles

Report titles are only one example of the way that a page title turns into a link.

As people move through web sites, the first question they ask on each new page is "Did I get where I thought I was going?" They expect the page title to match the link they clicked on. Matching links and page titles is the best way to reassure your site visitors that they are on a good pathway or have gotten to the information page they expected.

To be successful in matching links and page titles, plan them in both directions:

- As you write the page title, think of how the same words will work as the link on all the pages where the link will appear.

- As you write links, think of how the same words will work as the page title.

 Compare Figures 12-5 and 12-6. Which site makes you feel more comfortable and confident?

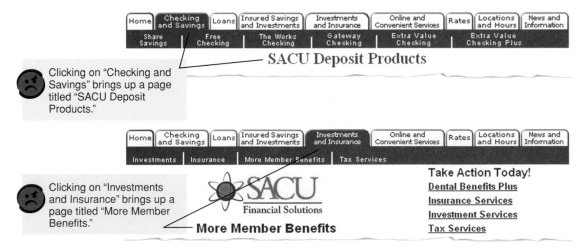

Figure 12-5 When links lead to pages with titles that do not match the links, people may be confused. They may back out thinking they got to the wrong page.   www.sacu.com

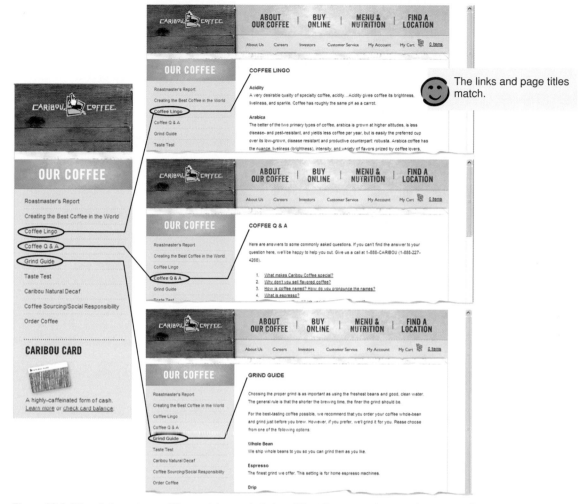

Figure 12-6 When links and page titles match, people feel confident they got to the page they expected.

www.cariboucoffee.com

This can get a bit tricky because you also have to think about consistency for both the link and the page title.

- Where will the link show up?
- What other links will go with it?
- What style are you using for all those links?
- What type of page is this title on?
- What other pages make a consistent set with this one?
- What style are you using for all those pages?

The web is in fact just that – a web – with ever-growing threads and tangles, so you may never know all the places where your page title will end up as a link. But you can strive for consistency and understanding of how your web page is linked at least in your own web site – and the larger web site it is part of if you are in a large organization.

4. Be as explicit as you can in the space you have – and make more space if you need it

When the web site of the U.S. National Center for Educational Statistics (NCES, part of the U.S. Department of Education) had a link labeled Global ED Locator, usability testing showed that some people thought it led to a directory of department employees. In fact, it leads to databases of educational institutions – colleges, universities, and libraries. Making the label more explicit made all those databases much more available to site visitors.

Figure 12-7 shows the relevant parts of the "before" and "after" versions of the NCES home page.

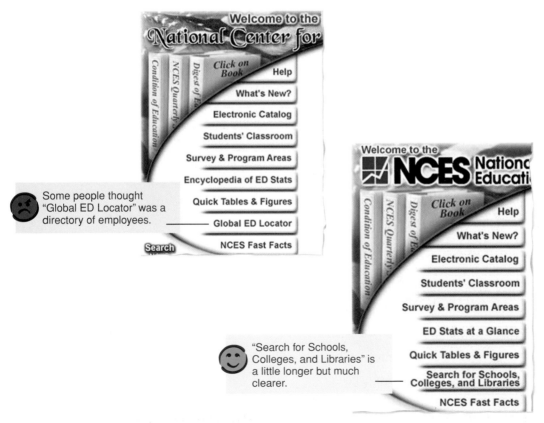

Figure 12-7 Write links in plain language with the words site visitors use.   www.nces.ed.gov

5. Use action phrases for action links

Note that not only is the new link on the NCES page in Figure 12-7 more specific, it also starts with a verb. Verbs imply "doing" and much of the web is about "doing."

In a study by Ann Chadwick-Dias and her colleagues at Fidelity Investments, web users, especially older adults, hesitated to click on links that were single nouns, like <u>Accounts</u>. When the Fidelity team changed the links to action phrases, like <u>Go to accounts</u>, web visitors of all ages were less hesitant about clicking on those links.

See Chadwick-Dias, McNulty, and Tullis, 2003.

Consider the different links from the *Chicago Sun-Times* in Figure 12-8.

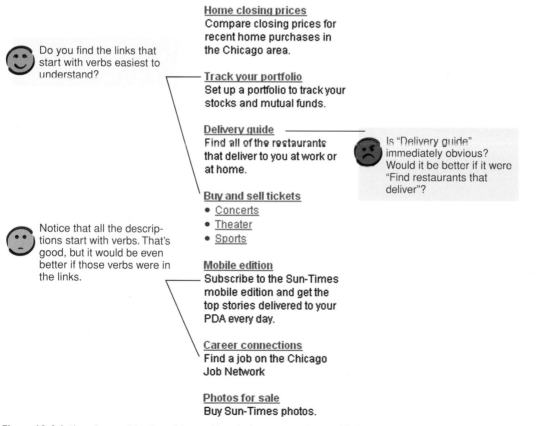

Figure 12-8 Action phrases (starting with a verb) make it easy to understand links that connect to what people come to the web to do.

www.suntimes.com

6. Use single nouns sparingly; longer, more descriptive links often work better

Single nouns or short noun phrases can work as labels and as links for general categories and overall topics, but only if your site visitors categorize information as you do, recognize the nouns you use, and give those nouns the same meaning that you do. That's why card sorting and other techniques for understanding how your site visitors would categorize and label your site's information are so critical.

In many ways, the descriptive links that lead to specific information are just like headings. All the points from Chapter 10 apply. In Figure 12-9, from CNN Money, for example, you see a set of links that works as the table of contents to a long article. In this case, the statement links (like statement headings in a table of contents) work very well.

Each of the links is a statement. They work well because they carry a lot of meaning in a familiar sentence structure.

Figure 12-9 Think of links as headings. Reread Chapter 10. Statements and questions, as well as action phrases, connect well with web users.   www.money.cnn.com

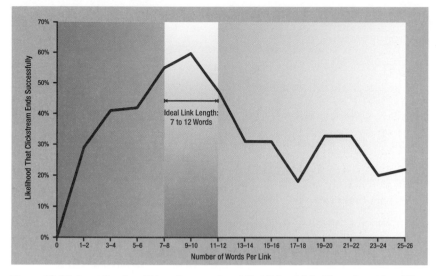

Figure 12-10 Jared Spool and his colleagues found that links of 7 to 12 words achieved the highest success in getting people to the information they were seeking. (From *Designing for the Scent Of Information,* published by User Interface Engineering, www.uie.com.)

Longer links often work even better. Jared Spool and his colleagues found that the optimal length for links is 7 to 12 words. Figure 12-10 shows the pattern they've found between link length and success web users had in finding what they are looking for.

Spool suggests that longer links are more likely to have the words your site visitors have in their minds. Longer links have better scent. (See the discussion of "scent of information" in Chapter 4.)

Longer links are also more likely to be action phrases, statements, or questions, rather than single nouns or noun phrases. They are more likely to be like the headings that people look for and relate to.

7. Add a short description if people need it – or rewrite the link

Sometimes, you can't get enough in the link itself to help people understand what they will get by clicking on it. In that case, you can add a short description with the link. Look again at the CNN Money page. Each link describing a fear has a short description explaining what the article is going to tell you is the real danger.

Also see the related discussion and examples in Chapter 4 on adding short descriptions to links.

A short description may be the only way you can help site visitors

- understand what you mean by a program with a made-up name
- clarify the meaning of an obscure report or article title
- distinguish between similar links

Better solutions, however, might be to

- not use the made-up program name by itself as the link – see Guideline 1 earlier in this chapter
- give the report or article a title that is instantly clear to your site visitors – see Guideline 2 earlier in this chapter
- think about whether similar links mean you have redundant information – see Guideline 9 later in this chapter

8. Make the link meaningful – not <u>Click here</u>, not just <u>More</u>

Another reason for making the link itself be as useful as possible – and not rely on descriptions – is that as we come to a page, we tend to focus first on headings and links. They are colorful. They stand out. They draw our eyes.

Links that just say <u>Click Here</u>, <u>Here</u>, <u>More</u>, or <u>Answer</u> give no clue about what will come up if we click on them. They don't allow us to separate one link from another. And they draw our attention away from the meaningful information.

The news section of the Toastmasters site (Figure 12-11) relies on Click here links, but if you read only the Click here links, you get very little useful information. The information is in the red headings that are not links. Compare this version to the suggested revision in Figure 12-12.

<u>Click here</u> is never necessary

Most web users today assume that something that looks like a link is a link. Years ago, <u>Click here</u> may have been a useful instruction; it's not needed any more. Don't announce links with <u>Click here</u>; just put what people will get by "clicking here" into your link format.

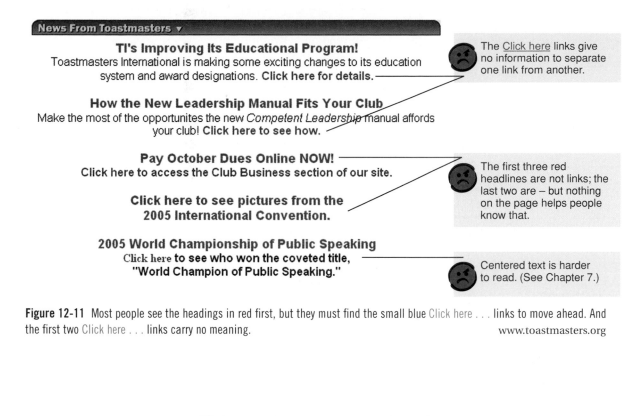

Figure 12-11 Most people see the headings in red first, but they must find the small blue Click here . . . links to move ahead. And the first two Click here . . . links carry no meaning.   www.toastmasters.org

Figure 12-12 A suggested revision.

Blind web users scan with their ears, just as sighted web users scan with their eyes. Screen-reading software helps them do this by allowing them to pull all the links on a web page into a separate list, as you can see in Figure 12-13. Can you imagine the frustration of listening when all you hear is Click here, Click here, Click here or More, More, More, More?

For more about how blind people work with web sites, see Theofanos and Redish, 2003.

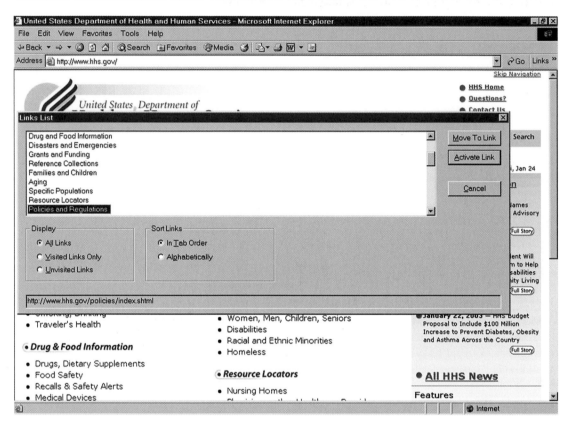

Figure 12-13 Web users who listen to the screen can ask their screen-reading software to pull all the links on a page into a list and then read only that list.

More isn't enough

 More, More, More, More is useless to a web user who is listening. (You can add words to the alt text that screen-readers use, even if you have only More showing on the screen.)

But More by itself also isn't helpful to sighted users who are quickly scanning the page. You can make links meaningful by

- adding words to specify what visitors will get "more" of

- using informative words as the link

Figure 12-14 shows how Access Washington, a portal site, explains what you will get more of in each of its sections. Figure 12-15 shows how the Exploratorium, a hands-on museum in San Francisco, highlights meaningful words in its brief descriptions, rather than relying on More.

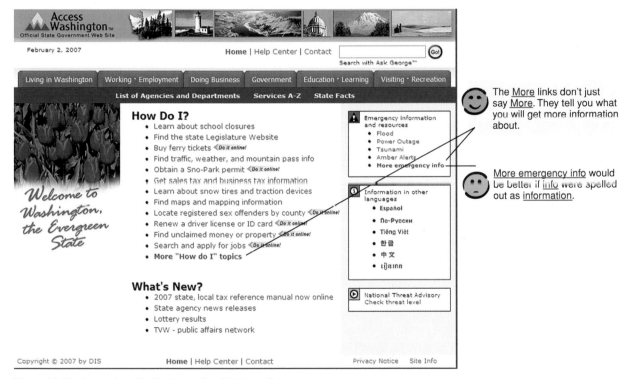

Figure 12-14   A very clear site that expands all its More links.   www.access.wa.gov

Figure 12-15 Another way to avoid More is to make meaningful words in the description into links.

www.exploratorium.org

9. Coordinate when you have multiple, similar links

This is a guideline about more than writing or rewriting links. It's a guideline about using links to understand and improve the content on your site.

Many organizations develop their web sites by allowing content owners in different departments to post information. If the same topic is covered in different departments, several explanations of the same topic may show up together as links on the web site. They may appear together on the same pathway page. They may all appear in search results.

Site visitors are likely to be confused. They would have to click on each of the links to know how the web pages are similar or different. What if the information in one contradicts the information in another?

As a first step, at least write short descriptions with the links to help people choose well. And then go beyond that. When you find that your site has several links that are hard to distinguish, don't just rewrite the links. Take the problem of similar links as the impetus to clean up the content. That probably requires collaboration – writers from different departments working together to produce consistent, coherent information for your web readers.

10. Don't embed links if you want people to stay with your information

To this point in the chapter, we've focused on links on home pages and pathway pages, where your primary goal is helping people move on.

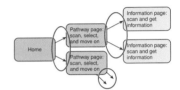

Let's turn to an issue for the information pages at the end of that pathway. As we discussed in the section on layering in Chapter 6, information pages also often include links – to more details or related information.

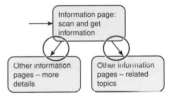

Recently, one of the hottest topics for one of my clients was this question: Is it okay to embed links in paragraphs of text or should you always put them at the end of the paragraph or even separate them from the other text entirely?

The answer, as with so many questions in creating successful web sites, is that it depends on your purposes, your web users, and why they are coming to your web site.

The point to remember is that an embedded link is always a distraction. If people choose to follow an embedded link, they leave your information in the middle of what you are saying. It's like switching conversational topics in mid-sentence.

If people are just browsing, embedding may be okay

Most Wikipedia articles are full of embedded links. The page in Figure 12-16 is just one of thousands of examples I could have selected from Wikipedia.org.

Does having many embedded links work for Wikipedia articles because people most often come to Wikipedia in browsing mode? Are they eager to see how a topic branches and connects to many other topics?

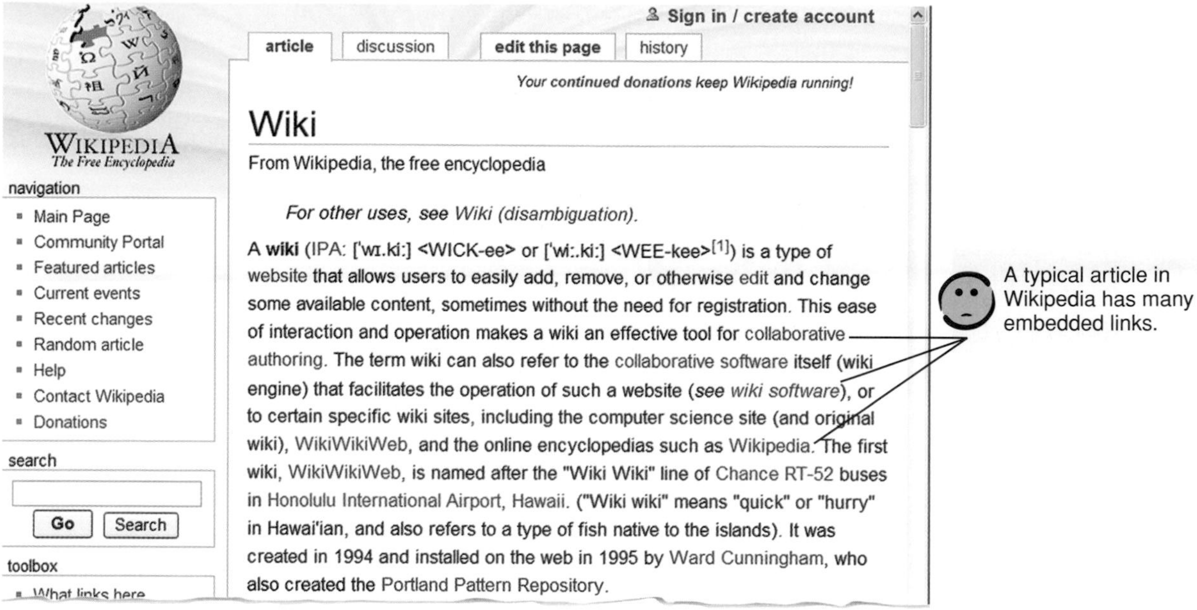

For other uses, see Wiki (disambiguation).

A **wiki** (IPA: ['wɪ.ki:] <WICK-ee> or ['wi:.ki:] <WEE-kee>[1]) is a type of website that allows users to easily add, remove, or otherwise edit and change some available content, sometimes without the need for registration. This ease of interaction and operation makes a wiki an effective tool for collaborative authoring. The term wiki can also refer to the collaborative software itself (wiki engine) that facilitates the operation of such a website (*see wiki software*), or to certain specific wiki sites, including the computer science site (and original wiki), WikiWikiWeb, and the online encyclopedias such as Wikipedia. The first wiki, WikiWikiWeb, is named after the "Wiki Wiki" line of Chance RT-52 buses in Honolulu International Airport, Hawaii. ("Wiki wiki" means "quick" or "hurry" in Hawai'ian, and also refers to a type of fish native to the islands). It was created in 1994 and installed on the web in 1995 by Ward Cunningham, who also created the Portland Pattern Repository.

A typical article in Wikipedia has many embedded links.

Figure 12-16 Embedding links in paragraphs of text may be okay in Wikipedia. People coming to this encyclopedia may be primarily browsing and, therefore, enjoy being distracted by related topics. www.wikipedia.org

But if you don't want people to wander off in the middle, put links at the end, below, or next to your main text

If you want people to read your entire sentence or paragraph or article, don't invite them to leave by embedding links in the middle of what you are writing. Otherwise you are muddling up two tasks for your site visitors: reading and moving on.

The chances of people coming back once they've been enticed away by a link are low. So put links where you are ready for people to take up your invitation to change what they are focused on. For example, compare Figures 12-17 and 12-18. Figure 12-17 is part of a page that I extracted from the section on spas at About.com. For Figure 12-18, I've moved the links to follow each small section of text.

Embedded definition links that open a small window and don't change the entire screen are okay. They clarify the ongoing conversation; they don't change the topic. (Look back at Figure 6-12 in Chapter 6.)

Different Types of Spas

Some people get confused about what a spa really is. That's because, back in the sixties, a spa was basically a "fat farm" where people went to lose weight. Today there are several different types of spas.

The most common is the day spa. This is for people who want to drop in for one or two treatments, or perhaps even indulge in a half-day, with lunch. Spa treatments are not cheap, so make sure you choose the right day spa for you. And when the day arrives, here's how to make the most of your trip to the day spa.

Other first-time spa-goers have their first spa experience on vacation, at a resort/hotel spa. Resort and hotel spas come in a wide range of sizes and style from small private inns like The Harbour Inn in St. Michaels, Maryland, to the lavish, sprawling resort spas in Hawaii.

People who are interested in weight loss or jump-starting a health lifestyle often choose destination spas that offer an all-encompassing spa experience. Examples are Lake Austin Spa Resort or Canyon Ranch.

Figure 12-17 A page with many embedded links.   www.about.com

Different Types of Spas

Some people get confused about what a spa really is. That's because, back in the sixties, a spa was basically a "fat farm" where people went to lose weight. Today there are several different types of spas.

Day spas

The most common is the day spa. This is for people who want to drop in for one or two treatments, or perhaps even indulge in a half-day, with lunch.

> More about day spas
>
> Spa treatments are not cheap
>
> Make sure to choose the right spa for you
>
> When the day arrives, make the most of your trip to the day spa

Spas at resorts

Other first-time spa-goers have their first spa experience on vacation, at a resort/hotel spa. Resort/hotel spas come in a wide range of sizes and style from small private inns to lavish, sprawling resort spas.

> More about resort and hotel spas
>
> The Harbour Inn (St. Michaels, Maryland; a small private inn with spa)
>
> Lavish, sprawling resort spas in Hawaii

Destination spas

People who are interested in weight loss or jump-starting a health lifestyle often choose destination spas that offer an all-encompassing spa experience.

> More about destination spas
>
> Lake Austin Spa Resort (an example of a destination spa)
>
> Canyon Ranch (another example of a destination spa)

Figure 12-18 The same information with the links not embedded.

11. If you use bullets with links, make them active, too

Let's end the chapter with two short sections on formatting.

In usability test after usability test, I've watched frustrated web users try to click on bullets rather than on the words next to the bullet. Whenever you use bullets next to links, make the bullets clickable, too.

12. Make both unvisited and visited links obvious

One of the basic principles of human behavior is that it is easier for people to work by recognition than by recall. Products should "afford themselves" – make it obvious how to use them – rather than require people to remember what to do.

Humans have limited short-term memory capacity, and in working on the web, your site visitors want to concentrate on their goals, not on memorizing links. Don't make using your site more difficult by burdening people's memory when you can help them by making links obvious and by indicating which links have been visited and which have not.

Use your unvisited link color only for links

Don't use the same color for links and non-links. (Look again at the example from Toastmasters in Figure 12-11, where some of the red headlines are active links and some are not.) That teases your users, who don't want to be teased.

People don't want to have to rely on mousing around the page to figure out what is and is not a link.

Show visited links by changing the color

Nielsen and Loranger (2006, p. 60) list "Links that don't change color when visited" as the first of eight original usability problems that continue to be serious web design flaws. They give it three skulls (the most serious condemnation, "still a high-impact usability problem").

According to Nielsen and Loranger, 74 percent of web sites do change the link color for visited links, so people expect to be able to see at a glance which links they've already been to. When links don't change color, people have to *remember* where they've been – and they often can't remember. So they revisit the same link again (and often again), wasting time and effort. Or they skip the right link, thinking they've already tried that one.

Of course, the problem is made worse by links that aren't clear and obvious. So writing your links to help people choose appropriately in the first place is critical. Even if your links are clear, help people understand what they have done and haven't done on your web site by showing where they've been, that is, by changing color for visited links.

SUMMARIZING CHAPTER 12

Here are key messages from Chapter 12:

- Don't make new program and product names into links by themselves.

- Rethink document titles and headings that turn into links.

- Think ahead. Match links and page titles.

- Be as explicit as you can in the space you have – and make more space if you need it.

- Use action phrases for action links.

- Use single nouns sparingly as links; longer, more descriptive links often work better.

- Add a short description if people need it – or rewrite the link.

- Make the link meaningful – not Click here, not just More.
  - Click here is never necessary.
  - More isn't enough.

- Coordinate when you have multiple, similar links.

- Don't embed links if you want people to stay with your information.
  - If people are just browsing, embedding may be okay.
  - But if you don't want people to wander off in the middle, put links at the end, below, or next to your main text.

- If you use bullets with links, make them active, too.

- Make both unvisited and visited links obvious.
  - Use your unvisited link color only for links.
  - Show visited links by changing the color.

Getting from Draft to Final Web Pages

13

Your job as a web content writer isn't over when you've first created the content. Whether you are a blogger, a solo author on your own web site, or part of a larger organization, you will have better and clearer content if you include editing, revising, and proofreading in your writing process. If you have colleagues and stakeholders, you may also need to give your drafts to them and then negotiate with them about what to say and how to say it.

Your attitude about reviewing and revising can go a long way to making it a smooth and productive process. Make it fun. Make it a learning experience. As Tom Brinck told me to tell you when he reviewed the first draft of this chapter:

> You should delight in feedback and getting your content just right. You should enjoy the surprises and discovery when people come from a different perspective and want something you totally didn't expect. If you're brewing in resentment over having to suppress your supposedly good ideas, you're going to die young of stomach ulcers. Take the opposite perspective: Share your ideas and love what you learn, not as your ideas are "shot down," but as your ideas compete in an ecology of good ideas and improve as a result.

To help you get easily and successfully from first draft to final web pages, this chapter has six sections with lots of guidelines and tips:

- Think of writing as revising drafts
- Review and edit your own work

- Ask colleagues and others to read and comment
- Put your ego in the drawer – cheerfully
- Work with a writing specialist or editor
- Make reviews work for you and your web site visitors

Think of writing as revising drafts

 Do you ever get writer's block? Find it hard to sit down to write? Procrastinate as long as possible?

Some people find it hard to start writing because they think that whatever they put down has to be perfect on the first try. Not so!

Your first draft should not be your final draft. A good way to get over writer's block is to remember that you can fix it later. Perfection is never achievable, but you'll get closer to it with each revision. (And you must at some point stop revising and meet the deadline to publish!)

When you look at a book like this one, you see only the final result. You don't see the many, many drafts it went through. If you watched me for half an hour, you would see lots of backspacing; deleting; cutting, adding, and moving of text; rewriting; starting over; staring into space; trying something and rejecting it; and so on. Writing is actually a very messy activity.

Successful writers read their own work. They read it many times. They read it, revise it, read it again, revise it again, and so on. Successful writers share their work in draft, try their writing out with relevant audiences, and revise based on what they learn from their early readers.

Review and edit your own work

You should be your own first editor. (But not your last editor. See the tips later in this chapter on getting help from others.)

Read what you wrote

If you've ever been embarrassed by an email you sent without reading what you wrote, you know how little things slip by. Your fingers may not have typed what you thought they did. You may have left out a word – or put in an extra one. You may have thought you were making sense and, then, on reading it, wonder what you meant.

Read while you are writing. Read when you've finished a section. Read when you've finished the draft. Ask yourself:

- Does it actually say what I meant it to say?
- Is it as clear and concise as I can say it?
- Would someone else take the same meaning from it that I do?
- How does it fit with whatever it has to fit with? my other writing? other content on the web site?
- Are the sentences grammatical? Are the words spelled correctly?

Check your links

If you include links in your content, click on each one to be sure it goes where you think it is going.

Check your facts

Make sure what you say is accurate. Think about where your facts came from and how reliable those sources are. How do you know the web sites you used or the books or journals are credible?

For example, Wikipedia is a great community resource – but anyone can edit it, so the facts may not be right. Search engines may find the most frequently visited sites, but that doesn't guarantee the credibility of the information on those sites. Just because you read the same information over and over on different sites does not necessarily mean it is true. The sites could all be copying each other or the same original site.

When considering the credibility of what you read on a web site, ask questions like these:

- Is an author listed?
- What can you learn about that author?
- Is it a government site from a reliable government agency?
- If it is a commercial site, are they marketing a product and slanting information for their marketing?
- If it is a non-profit organization's site, are they non-partisan and non-partial, or are they pushing an agenda?
- Do the facts make a consistent whole, or does information in one place contradict information in another place?
- Does the web page have a date so that you can tell when the information was written?

And remember that you can check facts off the computer, too. Find a person who knows and check the facts with that person. Check in books and paper journals – but remember that just because it's in print (paper or web), doesn't make it true. Books – even textbooks – sometimes copy errors from each other.

Put your web draft away; don't post it yet

Many good recipes require rest time for the food. So does good writing. When you have finished a draft and your immediate revisions, put it away. Save it and close the file.

Even for a blog, you can usually wait a bit and reread your entry before you post it. I know some bloggers who write at lunchtime and then post in the evening. Blogging software lets you put your post into draft mode before you publish it.

If you aren't blogging or writing an emergency news item, you should be able to put your draft away for a day or two.

Why let the writing rest?

When you are too close to what you have written, you are likely to miss the problems in it.

- You don't notice flaws in the logic or gaps in the information. You know what you want to say, so you don't see where your readers may not follow your points.

- You don't notice typos. You read the words you intended to write instead of the ones that are there. Or you skip over words that shouldn't be there.

You can, of course, fix and repost after publishing. The web has the tremendous advantage over paper that you can do a next edition immediately. However, that may annoy readers. For example, most blog software reposts articles to the RSS feed every time the article is edited. It can be really irritating to get the same article several times with just minor fixes each time. Your readers will wish you had read it carefully and fixed it before posting it in the first place.

Read this sentence:

Read it again carefully. Do you see the problem? Did you see it when you first read the sentence?

What can you do when reading it after it has rested?

When you open the file after a few hours or a few days, you'll read it with fresh eyes. Ask yourself:

- Is this really what I want to say?
- Can I say it more clearly? more concisely?
- Do I need to add anything to make it clearer?
- What can I cut?
- Does it have the right tone?
- Are there headings? enough headings? in the right places? in the right words?
- Does it have extra words, missing words, typos?

Read it out loud

Reading web content out loud may seem like a strange thing to do, but good writing has good rhythm. Good writing actually sounds good when it's spoken. So reading what you've written out loud is a good way to find out if your sentences and paragraphs are short enough and if your words are clear enough. If you hesitate, stumble, or have to take too many breaths in one sentence, rewrite!

Use dictionaries, handbooks, and a style guide

Don't mislead, misinform, or annoy your readers by misspelling words or using words incorrectly. Lots of help is available – online or on your bookshelf. Use it.

Keep a dictionary (or dictionary site) handy

Check not only for spelling but to be sure you are using words correctly.

Get a grammar handbook if you aren't comfortable with grammar

If you aren't comfortable as a writer and wish you knew more about making sure you are writing grammatically correct sentences, go to your nearest bookstore and buy yourself a handbook of grammar. You can get

For a book about punctuation that is fun to read, get *Eats, Shoots & Leaves,* by Lynne Truss.

Note that the author is British. Some of the rules she gives are not the same as U. S. standards.

used ones inexpensively, and grammar rules change slowly. Pick one where the presentation appeals to you. They say pretty much the same thing – at least for each variety of English (U. S., Canadian, British, etc.).

Don't overuse a thesaurus – stay with a consistent set of words

A thesaurus (a compilation of synonyms) may be useful if you are looking for just the right word to express a thought. But for business, technical, scientific, or legal writing, do not use a thesaurus to find several ways of saying the same thing. Once you call a "widget" a "widget," don't change part way through to "gadget." You'll confuse your readers. You'll make it harder to translate your content. And if you are writing a legal document, a judge may assume you are talking about two different things.

Also, make sure that you fully understand the meaning of the words you choose. Even if a thesaurus lists two words as synonyms, you often can't just substitute one for the other. Check words that are new to you in a dictionary. Play it safe; use the short, simple plain English words you know.

If your organization has a style guide, use it

A style guide can tell you whether your organization writes "email" or "e-mail," "data base" or "database." Remember that site visitors are likely to see your content and content written by others in the organization in the same visit to your web site.

See the Interlude immediately after this chapter on *Creating an Organic Style Guide.*

Run the spell checker but don't rely on it

You know that the spell checker on your computer is only checking each word against its internal dictionaries.

Read this sentence out loud:

Eye kin knot sea ewe bee four to daze meeting.

Spell checkers would say it is fine, but, of course, it isn't.

- If the word is in the dictionary, the spell checker will accept it, regardless of whether it's the right word in the right place. (If you've ever typed "now" when you meant "not" or "our" when you meant "out," you know what I mean.)

- If the word is not in the dictionary, the spell checker will reject it, even if it's the right word in the right place. (On my own computer, of course, I've added my name to the dictionary; but if you try it on yours, the spell checker will probably want to turn Redish into "reddish" or "radish.")

Blindly accepting the spell checker's suggestions can be very embarrassing. Even if you agree with the spell checker that you spelled a word wrong, don't just click on the spell checker's first suggestion. Look at all the suggestions carefully to find the one you meant to write.

It can be equally embarrassing to assume that the spell checker caught all the errors in your web writing. A good hint is to know your own typical typing problems. What do you typically misspell? What typically happens when you are typing quickly? I'm a fast typist, and I often end up with "the" when I meant to type "they" or "them." The spell checker doesn't catch those errors, so I have to be particularly diligent in looking for them. The spell checker doesn't catch punctuation errors, so if you sometimes put an apostrophe in a plural where it doesn't belong, you have to watch out for those stray apostrophes in your own writing.

(Similarly, you can run the grammar checker – but don't rely on it. Use it to show you when you've written a passive sentence or an overly long sentence. But don't blindly follow its advice. It can't read your meaning, and its algorithms too often lead to erroneous reports.)

Ask colleagues and others to read and comment

Your goal is to communicate. Start by sharing with a few others to be sure you are communicating well.

Ask a few people what your key message is

Find a few people who are part of the audience you want to reach. This may be your spouse, partner, roommate, children, mother-in-law, neighbor, friend who knows a lot about the topic, friend who knows very little about the topic . . .

Ask them to read your web content and tell you what they think your key message is. Don't just ask for their reaction. Ask them what they think you are saying.

Have someone else read it out loud to you

Ask at least one or two people to read it out loud. Where they hesitate, stumble, or reread: rewrite!

When you have people read your draft out loud and tell you what they think you've said, you are doing a type of usability edit. For more on that and other types of usability testing, see www.usability.gov and this book's web site at www.redish.net/writingfortheweb.

Share partial drafts

If you are writing a lot of web content, don't wait until you have it all ready. Share one article or part of an article to see if you are on the right track with level of detail, tone, organization, writing style, and so on. That could save you lots of time and grief. The earlier you learn what to change, the less effort it takes to make the changes.

Get feedback online

In addition to traditional ways of sharing drafts (for example, emailing the draft or a link to the draft to people or distributing the draft to an internal group through your content management system), consider how the Internet can help you get feedback on your content. You can have contact us options, email to the webmaster, private feedback to the author, reviews, public comments that are really an open conversation among your readers, and so on. These may be moderated or not; threaded and searchable or not; expecting an answer back or not.

You probably think of these as post-publication feedback; and, indeed, some of these feedback mechanisms become available only after your web content has been posted. But think of how to use them or variations of them for pre-publication feedback as well.

Depending on how much you want to limit (or not) the audience for your drafts, you might set up

- a group blog or a Yahoo! or other group for sharing drafts among a given set of people

- a small Wiki for a group of people who edit each other's writing

- a site on which to pre-publish drafts and invite comments

    - Many groups put out pre-prints of their articles for discussion before the articles appear in formal journals. And pre-prints have been joined by e-prints that include papers that never become formally published. Check out arxiv.org.

    - The future of the web is likely to be even more interactive and conversational than it currently is. I see the web not only as a conversation between you and your site visitors (the theme of this book), but as a much larger conversation among many people. In the future, we may see much more public sharing of drafts both of web content and of material that will eventually appear in print, like book chapters.

Pay attention to the feedback

Take advantage of all the feedback you get, both before and after you publish. I'm focusing in this chapter on feedback *before* you publish your web content. But what you learn about your content, your style, your level of detail, and so on, *after* you publish can help you do a better job of the next web content you write.

Work with colleagues to get a uniform style and tone

Many writers are part of an organization where the web site represents the organization and not the individual writers. If you are in that situation, you have to make sure that you – and all your fellow writers in the organization – are writing the same way. Readers should not be able to tell who wrote what on the web site.

Put your ego in the drawer – cheerfully

Did you bristle at that last paragraph where I said that readers should not be able to tell who wrote what on the web site? If you are writing poetry, or fiction, or your own blog, your voice as author is a large part of what you are projecting through your web site or your blog. That's fine. But if you are writing in an organizational setting, it's not about you as author. It's about communicating clearly so that the people who come to the web site can find what they need and understand what they find.

Of course, you should take pride in your work. That pride can be in working as a team with colleagues to have a web site that has a consistent writing style, a consistent tone, a consistent vocabulary, and a consistent message.

Don't get into arguments about what "I" like or what another "I" likes. Put your "I" away. Make everyone else put their "I" away. Get out your personas (see Chapter 2). Talk about the conversation that your site visitors come to have with you and what information, style, tone, and vocabulary will work best as your (collective) conversational response.

Also put your ego in the drawer when you get reviews and feedback. Listen with an open mind. Don't get defensive about your writing. That doesn't mean you have to take every suggestion a reader or editor or reviewer gives you. It just means you have to consider it carefully. (More on this in the section later in this chapter on working with reviewers.)

Work with a writing specialist or editor

In addition to your own reading, reviewing, editing, proofreading – and trying out your writing with colleagues and your audience – you may also benefit from working with a writing specialist or an editor.

Editors do many tasks, from coordinating projects to checking facts to getting manuscripts ready for publication (in print or online). Rather than focus on those aspects of an editor's job, however, I want to talk about two specific ways in which writing specialists and editors can help you as a writer:

- focusing on the big picture with you
- copy editing for you

You may want different people as your "big picture" editor and as your copy editor. Although some people can do both well, the two tasks require different skills. Certainly, the two types of edit require separate passes through the material.

Have someone focus on the big picture with you

The big picture editor focuses on audience, appropriateness of the content, overall organization, and coherence throughout the writing. A big picture editor should start by asking:

Professional writers always have editors to help them.

- What are you trying to achieve?
- Who are your audiences?
- How will those people use what you are writing? What are they coming to your web site to do? What are their scenarios?

With the answers to those questions, the big picture editor should read and comment on how well you have

- made your key messages obvious
- organized your messages for the audiences
- shown your organization through the headings
- written sentences that will make sense to your audiences and are easy to read
- chosen words that your readers are likely to understand

A big picture editor should be able to help you improve all those aspects of your writing. In fact, a big picture editor should be working with you from the beginning of your project and you should be sharing outlines and drafts throughout the project.

Have someone copy edit for you

Copy editing, on the other hand, is looking at the "little picture" – the nitty-gritty details of grammar, spelling, and punctuation. The best copy editors are very detail-oriented. They read the words and sentences very carefully.

Great copy editors are good spellers. They know the conventions of grammar and punctuation. If they are part of an organization, they are familiar with the organization's style.

Copy editors can save you lots of embarrassment and greatly improve your work. They may catch the typos that you just haven't seen no matter how many times you have read what you wrote. They check consistency of style. They make sure that a sentence with a plural subject has a plural verb. They may suggest changing a long run-on sentence into two shorter, clearer sentences.

If you can possibly get the time of both a big picture editor and a copy editor, you will find both very helpful. Learn from them. Consider it mentoring, not just a chore to be passed off to someone else.

An editor should work *with* you. Editing should not be something that is "thrown over the wall" and then "thrown back again." Especially in web writing, you and the editors must agree on what conventions you are following and which, if any, you are purposefully *not* following. You and the editors have to be in agreement on whether fragments are okay, on whether you can start a sentence with "But . . ." and end a sentence with a preposition, on whether questions make great headings, and so on.

All the hints in the next section about working well with reviewers apply to working well with editors, too.

Make reviews work for you and your web site visitors

In organizations, putting together a successful web site requires team-work. And some members of that team may be reviewers of your web content. Your web content may have to go through review with

- managers, who are accountable for the content
- policy analysts, who make sure the messages are in line with the organization's policies
- lawyers, who make sure the messages won't get the organization into legal trouble
- technical staff, who check accuracy
- editorial staff, who check consistency with style
- publication staff, who check consistency with formatting and templates

Of course, not all content goes through all those reviews. And you may, yourself, fill one of the positions in that list.

How can you make working with reviewers (and reviewees) be a positive experience rather than a nerve-wracking and frustrating one? Let's talk about reviewing in three stages:

- setting up good reviews
- getting useful information from reviewers
- making good use of reviews

Setting up good reviews

Good reviews start at the beginning of a web writing project – not at the end. When you know you have an assignment to write web content, find out who will be reviewing what you write.

Meet with the reviewers when you start the project

Discuss and agree on

- roles and responsibilities
- the schedule for drafts
- your plans for the content

Practice the doctrine of no surprise

The surest way to get a negative reaction is to shock your reviewers by showing them something that they do not expect and to which they can exclaim, "That's not the way we write here!" Never shock your reviewers. Always work with them *before* you deliver a draft so that they know what to expect. Deal with any concerns they have about overall style or content issues *before* you give them material to review.

Doctrine of no surprise: Work with reviewers *before* giving them a draft so that they know what to expect.

Help your reviewers understand good web writing

In discussing your plans for the content, work with the reviewers so that they understand

- your purposes in writing the part of the web you are working on
- the site visitors you are writing to and their relevant characteristics
- the scenarios you expect your site visitors to have related to your content

If your reviewers are not familiar with personas and scenarios, this might be a great time to introduce the concepts and to introduce your specific personas and their scenarios.

If your reviewers are likely to expect a different writing style than you plan to use, work with them so that they realize the importance of an audience-focused, key-message-first, simple-language style. Show them samples of good writing on similar topics from other web sites. If examples from this book will help you and your reviewers, use a few (with credit, please). Create a "before" and "after" for even a small piece of your web content to show reviewers what you will be doing. Get them to express their concerns so that you can discuss those concerns and allay their fears.

Getting useful information from reviewers

Stay in touch with your reviewers, without overdoing it.

Tell reviewers when the schedule changes

Schedules change. If a change affects when you will get material to your reviewers, let them know. Negotiate with them on new dates. Don't just assume they can accommodate every slip in the schedule.

Give reviewers a "heads up" a few days in advance

Everyone on your web team is overly busy, including your reviewers. Remind them when you are about to send a draft.

Make your expectations clear

It's frustrating to expect a technical review and then get your copy back with nothing more than a few commas changed – incorrectly. You can improve your chances of getting what you need if you make your expectations clear.

Deliver your drafts for review with individual cover emails. Tell each reviewer

- what stage the draft is at
- what specific help you need from that reviewer
- when you must have the review back
- to call or write you if they have questions or need to renegotiate dates

And remind reviewers politely that you expect them to comment and suggest, not to rewrite. Writing the content is your job.

If you have specific needs, let reviewers know

In your cover email, you may be reminding each reviewer of that reviewer's role. In addition, you may have specific questions for different reviewers within your material. Develop a way of asking that makes it obvious you have a question and who the question is for. I often use square brackets, [ ], put the reviewer's name in bold, and use a bright color so that it stands out on the screen, as in this example:

> [**Jim:** Please tell me who is responsible for approving travel requests. I want to turn the passive sentence in the original into an active sentence here. Please fill in the blank for me at the beginning of my sentence. Thanks.]

Making good use of reviews

When you get reviews back, read them carefully and with an open mind.

Don't let your ego get in the way

Reading reviews is another good time to put your ego in the drawer – cheerfully. Don't get defensive about your writing. Be open to reviewers' comments. You don't have to agree with all of them. You may not have to – or be able to – make all the changes every reviewer wants. But you must read and consider them all.

Don't automatically accept changes

If you are not sure that a change a reviewer recommends is correct, find out more. Do the research to find out what is correct.

Reviewers may give you conflicting suggestions. If their facts differ, you need to find out which facts are correct. If their conflicts are about style, work to resolve the differences – or to convince them of the style you are using.

If you think a reviewer's change is not in the best interests of your web users or will hurt rather than improve your writing, think about why the reviewer made the suggestion. Don't just dismiss the comment. Think carefully before deciding what to do. For different reviews and different relationships between you and specific reviewers, what you do may be any of the next four suggestions.

Rewrite to avoid misunderstandings

If a reviewer misunderstood something you wrote, you may not have stated it as clearly as you could. Try again. And, then, if possible, run that piece by the reviewer again.

Persuade, if you can

If the reviews that trouble you are based on different perceptions of purpose, audience, scenarios, or appropriate style, you may need to evangelize clear writing. Within the constraints of your corporate culture, push for clear web writing even for legal and technical information. Your web users need you to do this for them. I hope the examples and the rationales in this book not only persuade and mentor you but also prove useful to you in persuading and mentoring others.

Negotiate, if necessary

The teamwork that successful web sites require often involves compromises and negotiations. Don't make reviews confrontational situations. Work with reviewers to put accurate, reliable, and clear information on your web site. Remember that even legal information can be legally accurate, legally sufficient, and also clear and easy to understand.

See the Interlude titled Legal Information Can Be Understandable, Too.

Let reviewers know what you did and did not do

Communicate! Communicate! Communicate! Reviewers who feel that you ignored their comments in one round of review are less likely to give your materials a thorough review in the next round. Keep a summary of the changes you made and did not make, especially for technical, legal, and policy reviewers. If you have several rounds of review, include the summary from the previous round with each new round.

SUMMARIZING CHAPTER 13

Here are key messages from Chapter 13:

- Think of writing as revising drafts.
- Review and edit your own work.

- – Read what you wrote.
- – Put it away; don't post it yet.
- – Read it out loud.
- – Use dictionaries, handbooks, and a style guide.
- – Run the spell checker but don't rely on it.

- Review and edit with colleagues and others.
  - – Ask a few people what your key message is.
  - – Have someone else read it out loud to you.
  - – Share partial drafts.
  - – Get feedback online.
  - – Work with colleagues to get a uniform style and tone.

- Put your ego in the drawer – cheerfully.

- Work with a writing specialist or editor.
  - – Have someone focus on the big picture with you.
  - – Have someone copy edit for you.

- Make reviews work for you and your web site visitors.
  - – Set up good reviews.
    - – Meet with reviewers when you start the project.
    - – Practice the doctrine of no surprise.
    - – Help your reviewers understand good web writing.
  - – Get useful information from reviewers.
    - – Tell reviewers when the schedule changes.
    - – Give reviewers a "heads up" a few days in advance.
    - – Make your expectations clear.
    - – If you have specific needs, let reviewers know.
  - – Make good use of reviews.
    - – Don't let your ego get in the way.
    - – Don't automatically accept changes.
    - – Rewrite to avoid misunderstandings.
    - – Persuade, if you can.
    - – Negotiate, if necessary.
    - – Let reviewers know what you did and did not do.

As you create your web content, you and your colleagues may have questions about grammar, spelling, punctuation, and writing style.

Organic = start small and let it grow as issues and questions arise.

Use a style guide to keep the site consistent

At any given time, some aspects of every language are in transition. For example, many words come into English with a hyphen, like "e-mail," and over time lose the hyphen. But different people and different organizations are at different places in the transition. Some still use the hyphen; others don't. To have a consistent web site, you have to decide where your site is in that transition.

Remember that we discussed web sites' personalities in Chapter 3. Organizations, like their web sites, have personalities and corporate cultures. (And that's true for all types of organizations and communities, not only for businesses. Government agencies, universities, non-profits, listservs, other online communities all have their own cultures.) Language is an important aspect of any culture: how formal or colloquial the language should be ("cannot" or "can't"?); what is acceptable usage ("each person . . . they"?); how words are used ("website" or "web site"?).

A style guide can help authors and editors keep a web site consistent. In fact, even if you are the only author (doing a blog, perhaps), a short "cheat sheet" style guide may be useful. I've created one for this book, so I don't have to look back at other chapters to remind myself that, for this book, at least, it's "web site" and "web" and "Internet."

A style guide can also help by reminding authors and editors of points of grammar, spelling, and usage that are not in transition but that many people aren't sure about, such as, "affect" versus "effect," "that" versus "which," or "its" versus "it's." Figures Interlude 3-1 and Interlude 3-2 show you the beginning of the table of contents and one entry from the style guide for a web site.

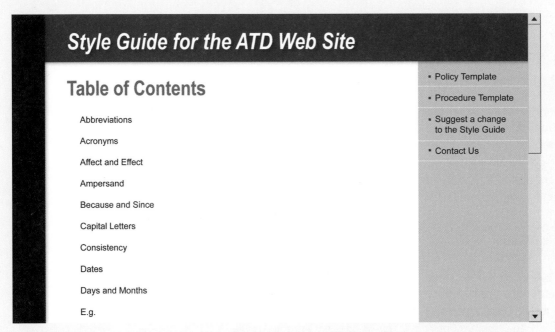

Figure Interlude 3-1 Part of the table of contents of a style guide for web writers. (ATD is a made-up name, but the screen is based on a real example that I developed with a client's web team.)

Style Guide for the ATD Web Site

Affect and Effect

What is the difference?

Most of the time, "affect" is a verb and "effect" is a noun.

> **Examples of "affect" and "effect"**
>
> This policy affects only new customers.
>
> This policy takes effect on January 1.
>
> The effect of this change will be to reduce the time it takes to prepare web pages.
>
> *Note: You can often write a better, shorter sentence without "effect."*
>
> **Possible revisions of the examples, without "effect"**
>
> This policy starts on January 1.
>
> This change will reduce the time it takes to prepare web pages.

- Policy Template
- Procedure Template
- Suggest a change to the Style Guide
- Contact Us

Figure Interlude 3-2 One entry from the style guide.

Don't reinvent

If you work in a large organization, first find out if other style guides already exist. If there is a corporate style guide, consider how applicable it is to your web site. Don't just ignore it. Work with whoever owns it to turn it into the organic, online style guide you need.

Don't repeat the entire universe in your style guide. Many excellent general style guides exist for writing grammatical English. Pick one and have all the web writers agree to use it.

Focus instead on what the web writers aren't sure about or what they argue about.

Appoint an owner

As with any web content, a style guide needs an "owner." Someone must be responsible and accountable for writing and maintaining it. The owner might convene a committee that represents different groups within the organization so that there is communication both ways between authors/editors and the style guide owner.

Make it easy to create, to find, and to use

Here are several tips for creating a usable and useful style guide:

- Put it online in an easily accessible place.
- Start small. Don't try to write it all before you get it out there.
- Make it organic – let it grow from authors' and editors' needs.
- Use the database model that we discussed in Chapter 5. Make each topic its own small index card. Don't write a book!
- Make it easy to find topics – both by searching and by browsing.
- Write it clearly, using all the guidelines for clear web writing.
- Do usability testing to make sure that authors and editors can find and use it.
- Have an easy-to-use feedback mechanism that allows and encourages people to ask more questions and suggest new topics.

Bibliography

Accessibility: www.w3.org/wai; for links to information on accessibility for specific countries: www.w3.org/wai/policy/.

Barnum, C. M., 2002, *Usability Testing and Research,* New York: Longmans.

Blicq, R. A., and Moretto, L. A., 2001, *Writing Reports to Get Results: Quick, Effective Results Using the Pyramid Method,* 3rd edition, New York: Wiley–IEEE Press.

Boiko, B., 2004, *Content Management Bible,* New York: John Wiley & Sons.

Brinck, T., Gergle, D., and Wood, S., 2002, *Usability for the Web,* San Francisco: Morgan Kaufmann.

Carroll, J. M., 1990, *The Nurnberg Funnel: Designing Minimalist Instruction for Practical Computer Skill,* Cambridge, MA: MIT Press.

Chadwick-Dias, A., McNulty, M., and Tullis, T., 2003, Web usability and age: How design changes can improve performance, *ACM Conference on Universal Usability,* November, 30–37.

Clark, H. H., and Haviland, S., 1975, Comprehension and the given-new contract. In Freedle, R. (Ed.), *Discourse Production and Comprehension,* Hillsdale, NJ: Erlbaum, 1–40.

Coney, M., and Steehouder, M., 2000, Role playing on the web: Guidelines for designing and evaluating personas online, *Technical Communication,* 47 (3), August, 327–340. (Available at www.ingentaconnect.com/content/stc/tc.)

Cooper, A., 2004, *The Inmates Are Running the Asylum: Why High Tech Products Drive Us Crazy and How to Restore the Sanity,* 2nd edition, Indianapolis: Sams.

Courage, C., and Baxter, K., 2004, *Understanding Your Users,* San Francisco: Morgan Kaufmann.

Darwin Information Typing Architecture (DITA): www-128.ibm.com/developerworks/xml/library/x-dita1; also http://dita.xml.org/.

Dillman, D. A., 2007, *Mail and Internet Surveys: The Tailored Design Method—2007 Update with New Internet, Visual, and Mixed-Mode Guide,* Hoboken, NJ: John Wiley & Sons.

Dixon, P., 1987, The processing of organizational and component step information in written directions, *Journal of Memory and Language,* 26, 24–35.

Dumas, J. S., and Redish, J. C., 1999, *A Practical Guide to Usability Testing,* revised edition, Bristol, England: Intellect.

Flanders, V., Mystery Meat Navigation, www.webpagesthatsuck.com/mysterymeatnavigation.html.

Flower, L., Hayes, J. R., and Swarts, H., 1983, Revising function documents: The scenario principle. In Anderson, P., Brockmann, J., and Miller, C. (Eds.), *New Essays in Technical and Scientific Communication: Research, Theory, and Practice,* Farmingdale, NY: Baywood, 41–58.

Fowler, S., and Stanwick, V., 2004, *Web Application Design Handbook,* San Francisco: Morgan Kaufmann.

Hackos, J. T., 2004, *Content Management for Dynamic Web Delivery,* New York: John Wiley & Sons.

Hackos, J. T., and Redish, J. C., 1998, *User and Task Analysis for Interface Design,* New York: John Wiley & Sons.

Holtzblatt, K., Wendell, J., and Wood, S., 2004, *Rapid Contextual Design,* San Francisco: Morgan Kaufmann.

Jarrett, C., 2000, Designing usable forms: The three-layer model of the form, www.formsthatwork.com/ftp/DesigningUsableForms.pdf.

Jarrett, C., and Minott, C., 2004, Making a better web form, *Proceedings of the Usability Professionals' Association Annual Conference,* available at www.editingthatworks.com/ making%20a%20better%20web%20form.pdf.

Johnson, J., 2003, *Web Bloopers: 60 Common Web Mistakes and How to Avoid Them,* San Francisco: Morgan Kaufmann.

Krug, S., 2005, *Don't Make Me Think! A Common Sense Approach to Web Usability,* 2nd edition, Indianapolis: New Riders.

Larson, K., 2004, The Science of Word Recognition, www.microsoft.com/typography/ctfonts/WordRecognition.aspx.

Morkes, J., and Nielsen, J., 1998, Applying writing guidelines to web pages, www.useit.com/papers/webwriting/rewriting.html.

Nielsen, J., 2006, F-Shaped Pattern for Reading Web Content, www.useit.com/alertbox/reading_pattern.html.

Nielsen, J., 2000, *Designing Web Usability: The Practice of Simplicity,* Indianapolis: New Riders.

Nielsen, J., 1996, Inverted Pyramids in Cyberspace, www.useit.com/alertbox/9606.html.

Nielsen, J., and Loranger, H., 2006, *Prioritizing Web Usability,* Indianapolis: New Riders.

Nielsen, J., and Tahir, M., 2001, *Homepage Usability: 50 Websites Deconstructed,* Indianapolis: New Riders.

Older adults as web users: www.aarp.org/olderwiserwired.

Pirolli, P. L., 2003, Exploring and finding information. In Carroll, J. (Ed.), *HCI Models, Theories, and Frameworks, First Edition: Toward a Multidisciplinary Science,* San Francisco: Morgan Kaufmann, 157–192.

Pruitt, J., and Adlin, T., 2006, *The Persona Lifecycle: Keeping People in Mind Throughout Product Design,* San Francisco: Morgan Kaufmann.

Quesenbery, W., 2006, Storytelling and narrative. In Pruitt, J. and Adlin, T., *The Persona Lifecycle: Keeping People in Mind Throughout Product Design,* San Francisco: Morgan Kaufmann, 520–555.

Redish, J. C., 2005, Media of the future: Web? Paper? *Intercom,* 52 (1), January, 20–25.

Redish, J. C., 2004, Writing for the web: Letting go of the words, *Intercom,* 51 (6), June, 4–10.

Rosenfeld, L., and Morville, P., 2006, *Information Architecture for the World Wide Web: Designing Large-Scale Web Sites,* 3rd edition, Sebastopol, CA: O'Reilly.

Rubin, J., 1994, *Handbook of Usability Testing,* New York: John Wiley & Sons.

Rockley, A., 2002, *Managing Enterprise Content: A Unified Content Strategy,* Indianapolis: New Riders.

Scanlan, C., 2003, Writing from the top down: Pros and cons of the inverted pyramid, www.poynter.org/dg.lts/id.52/aid.38693/column.htm.

Society for Technical Communication Usability and User Experience Community: www.stcsig.org/usability. (Has a great bibliography, lists of resources, and templates for usability activities.)

Spool, J., Perfetti, C., and Brittan, D., 2004, *Designing for the Scent of Information,* North Andover, MA: User Interface Engineering.

Spool, J., 2005, Galleries: The Hardest Working Page on Your Site, www.uie.com/articles/galleries/.

Stone, D., Jarrett, C., Woodroffe, M., and Minocha, S., 2005, *User Interface Design and Evaluation,* San Francisco: Morgan Kaufmann.

Theofanos, M. F., Mulligan, C. P., and Redish, J. C., 2004, Redesigning the portal of the Department of Health and Human Services, *User Experience* (magazine of the Usability Professionals' Association), 3 (6), Spring, 4–7.

Theofanos, M. F., and Redish, J. C., 2003, Guidelines for accessible and usable web sites: Observing users who work with screen readers, *Interactions,* X (6), November–December, 38–51. (This paper is also available at www.redish.net/content/papers.html.)

Theofanos, M. F., and Redish, J. C., 2005, Helping low-vision and other users with web sites that meet their needs: Is one site for all feasible? *Technical Communication,* 52 (1), February, 9–20. (Available at www.ingentaconnect.com/content/stc/tc.)

Truss, L., 2004, *Eats, Shoots & Leaves: The Zero-Tolerance Approach to Punctuation,* New York: Gotham.

U. S. Department of Health and Human Services, 2006, *Research-Based Web Design & Usability Guidelines,* 2nd edition, Washington, DC: Department of Health & Human Services. (Available online at www.usability.gov.)

Usability: www.usability.gov; also www.stcsig.org/usability/; www.upassoc.org/usability_resources/.

Usability Professionals' Association: www.upassoc.org.

Subject Index

Index of Web Sites Shown as Examples

About the Author

Janice (Ginny) Redish is president of Redish & Associates, Inc. As a specialist in plain language and usability, Ginny helps government agencies and private companies create successful web sites.

Ginny works closely with her clients to review their current web sites, understand their web users and their users' scenarios, conduct usability studies, analyze their current content, and revise the content to meet both the organization's goals and their web users' needs.

Ginny is sought after as a speaker and workshop leader. She is a dynamic instructor who has trained hundreds of writers and subject matter specialists in the U. S., Canada, Europe, and India in writing for the web and other topics.

Her earlier books include two classics on usability techniques:

- *A Practical Guide to Usability Testing* (with Joseph Dumas, Intellect Ltd., first edition, 1993; revised edition, 1999)
- *User and Task Analysis for Interface Design* (with JoAnn Hackos, John Wiley & Sons, 1998)

In addition, Ginny serves on the editorial board of three journals and has published numerous papers and book chapters on various aspects of usability, task analysis, accessibility, document design, plain language, and writing for the web. She is the author of several articles on www.usability.gov, including the article on writing for the web.

Ginny's work has brought her many awards, including the Rigo Award (ACM SIGDOC, 1995), the Alfred N. Goldsmith Award (IEEE PCS, 2001), the status of Fellow of the Society for Technical Communication, and the President's Award from both the Society for Technical Communication and the Usability Professionals' Association.

Ginny is a graduate of Bryn Mawr College and holds a Ph.D. in Linguistics from Harvard University.

Ginny's web site: www.redish.net

Web site for the book (with more articles and ways for you to ask questions and join the discussion): www.redish.net/writingfortheweb